KEITH FLOYD was a highly acclaimed and influential chef whose groundbreaking television series not only changed the way cookery programmes were made, but introduced a nation to the joys of food. He made more than twenty series and authored over twenty-five books. In later years he lived quietly in France. He died on 14 September 2009.

'Keith Floyd is a gastronomic icon. He inspired a nation to fall in love with food, cooking and with Floyd himself'

Marco Pierre White

'If someone was to be given the mission to be the first ever chef to go to the moon it would have to be Keith Floyd, because there's no place left on earth from where we have not already enjoyed and loved watching him cook'

Jean-Christophe Novelli

'Floyd's autobiography lurches, like its subject, from hilarity to madness and gives fascinating insights into fame and its dangers . . . Best enjoyed with a large glass of wine!'

Good Book Guide

D1322414

Stirred But Not Shaken

The Autobiography

KEITH FLOYD

With James Steen

PAN BOOKS

First published 2009 by Sidgwick & Jackson

First published in paperback in 2010 by Pan Books
an imprint of Pan Macmillan, a division of Macmillan Publishers Limited
Pan Macmillan, 20 New Wharf Road, London N1 9RR
Basingstoke and Oxford
Associated companies throughout the world
www.panmacmillan.com

ISBN 978-0-330-51158-2

The acknowledgements on page x constitute an extension of this copyright page.

3 5 7 9 8 6 4 2

A CIP catalogue record for this book is available
from the British Library.

Typeset by Ellipsis Books Limited, Glasgow
Printed and bound by CPI Group (UK) Ltd, Croydon, CR0 4YY

This book is for some very special people: my children, Patrick and Poppy Floyd, as well as (in alphabetical order) Giles Benson, Alisdair Cuddon, Ian and Janice Fairservice, Tony Finn, Peter Gardiner, Dr Ernest Guillem, Brenda and Edward Harding, Paul Hickling, Widge Hunt, Rita Jelinski, Hugh McHardy, David and Celia Martin, Jean-Christophe Novelli, Connor O'Leary and Danny Ryan (Phuket), Bill Padley, Carol Payne, Heide Roache, James and Iwona Whitaker and Peter and Trish Winterbottom. It is also for Nathalie and Cyril in Montfrin and for the staff of University Hospital, Staffordshire.

All of the above have helped to save my life – and my sanity – sometimes over many years. Thank you.

Also for Clive North on camera and Andy MacCormack assistant camera, Tim White on sound, Steve Williams on lights, David 'can I have one of your sandwiches?' Pritchard director, and Frances Proudfoot-Wallis on G&T but only after 7pm. Jonathan Lloyd, thank you for being one of the nice guys in the world of agents, and for the introduction to Sidgwick & Jackson. Giles Sequiera read the manuscript and gave judicius advice. He deserves a drink, but ends up with a thank you here.

And here is a list of the not very special people who have been a hindrance and a pain in my life. The shits who have stitched me up are ... oh, hang on, the lawyer says I can't name them. But they know who they are, and so do I.

EXTRACT FROM 'KEITH FLOYD BLUES'

By Bill Padley

I woke up this morning
Ol' Floyd is back in town
I was getting drunk by lunchtime
Unconscious by sundown

He's a wizard in the kitchen
And a wizard in the bar
He can make a bottle disappear
Just like a superstar

I've got the Keith Floyd Blues
My liver just ain't working anymore
It's gonna take a hundred doctors
To get me back the way I was before . . .

ACKNOWLEDGEMENTS

The process of writing this book has been cathartic, thera-peutic and at times bloody difficult. In fact, some days it was like having the flesh ripped from my bones.

Our memory banks contain vaults that are locked and on occasion it takes time to break into them; time to think back and reflect.

Why is a great question to ask others, but often it is not one you want to ask yourself. This book has been one big Why. Frequently, there are moments when the answer is, 'I haven't got a clue. That's just me.'

There are those I am determined to acknowledge for assisting in the creation of *Stirred But Not Shaken*. If 'thank you' is tossed like a coin to a beggar it means nothing, but here I say thank you to all of those who have helped and I say it with utmost sincerity.

I am indebted to Celia. She has been patient and kind and she has supported this project from the start. She has typed, she has jogged my memory and she has been there. Every author needs a Celia but there is only one Celia, and I feel incredibly privileged that she is with me.

I am extremely grateful to the wise people who work for Sidgwick & Jackson. They include Stuart Wilson, Mark

Handsley and Duncan Calow. Gentlemen, I raise a glass to you.

In particular, I want to acknowledge the invaluable contribution of my editor, Ingrid Connell. My thanks to Ingrid are threefold: first, for having confidence in this book; second, for retaining confidence; third, for steering it, for providing words of supreme wisdom and for making it happen.

I thank *Which?,* the publishers of *The Good Food Guide*, for allowing the reproduction of extracts from the *Guide*. And thank you Marco Pierre White, Jamie Oliver and Jean-Christophe Novelli.

I also thank James Whitaker for writing the foreword and for encouraging me to do my one-man theatre show *Floyd Uncorked*.

Then there is 'the ghost', James Steen. In France and Spain we have been together, working, eating and drinking. Only now does he tell me his own secret: the first cookery book he ever owned was written by a bloke called Keith Floyd!

James has worked with extreme sympathy and understanding of the catastrophic life that I have led and has shown tenderness and patience throughout.

Picture Acknowledgements

All photographs are from the author's personal collection apart from the following: Page 4, top © David Pritchard, bottom © Scope Features.

Every effort has been made to contact copyright holders of photographs reproduced in this book. If any have been inadvertently overlooked the publishers will be pleased to make restitution at the earliest opportunity.

FOREWORD

By James Whitaker

Keith was tricky. Never with me but he was as far as many are concerned.

I knew Floydy for around twenty years and we hit it off from the beginning. But I know that he was not an easy person with whom to have a continuing relationship. Four ex-wives will testify to this.

But ... if you were a rugby lover like me, a man who enjoyed his food — as long as you didn't start talking about pretentious nosh – and preferably not female, you would have got on fine.

In fact I loved the man.

Did he drink too much? Was he irrational and unpredictable? Did he smoke like a chimney? Did he live way beyond his means? The answer to all four questions is a resounding Yes.

But he was such a generous person (sadly sometimes with other people's money), was so animated with the aspects of life that interested him and such a brilliant cook that I found it all too easy to forgive him when he did something quite appalling.

Despite all his illnesses – heart problems, high blood pressure, worrying signs of cancer and an inability to enjoy food in later days – he was a fascinating man and a cook who could see off any other chef I have ever come across and I include the likes of Marco, Gordon and Jean-Christophe.

Astonishingly, when you consider how much alcohol he could, and did, consume when he was not fighting life-threatening illnesses, I never saw Floyd out of his mind, incapable of expressing himself in an interesting, fluent manner. What a player!

Goodness knows why we always got on and never had a cross word in the twenty years I knew this genius.

I can be dogmatic, never owed a penny to anybody in my life (except for a mortgage) and, worst of all, am a f*****g journo.

Despite being a reporter and proud of this in his youngest days, Floydy clashed with scribblers repeatedly over the years including the likes of Lynn Barber and A. A. Gill and, in my opinion, with good reason.

Keith seemed to invoke jealousy in others although, interestingly, not with fellow cooks, all of whom respected him for what he achieved over more than forty years of cooking.

Floyd was the original TV cook superstar and even today can be seen several times a week on the satellite channels preparing wonderful dishes from around the world. India, Thailand, Italy, the UK, Spain and from his beloved France.

He didn't do this from the comfort of cosy studios where the lighting is sublime, the sound under control, and the cooker in perfect working order. No, he cooked on the edge of a beach with a charcoal barbecue, or in the middle of a bustling market in central Italy. If somebody came up to talk to him in the middle of what he was doing, with the cameras rolling, he did not get stroppy and temperamental. He bantered back.

At the same time he'd famously take a swig from his

favourite glass of red wine and say 'cheers' to the camera and, thus, the audience of millions who would watch him. In fact, vino was not his favourite tipple. He'd get rid of the tinto when he could and take a glass of whisky, in preference, any time.

Floyd was an artist and, as such, typically among such people, seemed incapable of abiding by the rules of mere mortals. There's a long history of arty people being unable to look after their finances, stay married to the same woman for long, behave in an always acceptable manner.

I saw this side of Keith, never suffered from it.

I have met his last three wives and know his most recent one, Tess, quite well. Although all of them began with good vibes none of these marriages could be considered a triumph, which is so sad.

He reached a time of his life when he could have done with peace both from without and within. Despite the love and loyalty of many people this did not appear to be being achieved.

He had children – I've met both Poppy and Patrick – but Keith didn't see much of them although he talked with some pride of them both. Again, a shame. I suppose Floydy's ideal pals, with whom he could spend hours, were rugby-loving (in fact, preferably, rugby-playing) chaps who enjoyed a drink or eight, and didn't worry about the banalities of ordinary life.

Keith was a generous and perfect host when he had sufficient money in his pocket which, sadly, wasn't often in later days. He always supported with solid cash Kinsale Rugby Club and Esher Rugby Football Club (helping the juniors, financially, to go on tour and then lavishly entertaining them) while, at home, he gave perfect lunches. Ludicrously, when I first met Keith, somebody told me that he didn't cook at all 'these days'; that somebody cooked 'for him'.

What a travesty. Floydy cooked sublimely. He was a perfectionist and every morsel was mouth-watering. Tragically, in the last year of his life Keith could hardly bring himself to eat any of his own nosh. He had no appetite which is why he began to look so thin and somewhat older than he really was.

Another of his generous gestures came a couple of years ago when my wife and I were dining with two friends in Manilva, Southern Spain, at the Roman Oasis restaurant owned by his generous friend Paul Hickling, who truly looked after Keith in recent years.

As we were shown to our table the waiter said that Keith Floyd had arranged a present for us to celebrate my wife's birthday. The next thing we knew, a bottle of Dom Perignon appeared ... moments later a large pot of caviar, Beluga of course. Quite unnecessary (Keith didn't have money then either) but we enjoyed every mouthful.

Floydy was a performer of the highest calibre. No matter what he had been doing all afternoon he would get up on a stage in the evening and put on a performance that would stun and delight. With a smart suit and a nifty bow-tie he would look good too, however rough he might have felt inside. Like a true professional he could turn it on for the audience or the camera at the click of a finger.

Equally, this autobiography will rivet you. Keith was a great storyteller. Lucid and amusing even when he'd had far too much to drink and smoke.

I guarantee you will spend a long time smiling even though, at times, you will feel like crying for him.

ONE

The anteroom was brilliantly lit by cut-glass chandeliers that hung from the high ceiling. Stewards in their white mess jackets, with golden epaulettes and long black aprons, were shuffling with trays of drinks.

The members had come from all over the country to be at the annual games night of the Alexis Soyer Appreciation Society, though this grand title was merely a euphemism for the excuse to have the mother of all piss-ups.

They held elegant cigarette holders, smoked fine cheroots and wore moleskin waistcoats. Despite their posturing and this crescendo of back-slapping and bullshit conversation – such deep subjects as the runners and riders at Haydock Park, the inevitable outcome of the Ashes, boasts of sexual conquests and stories of huge wins at the roulette table – there was not a gourmet among them. They were gourmands, guided by insatiable stomachs rather than the rules of the so-called art of fine dining. They strutted in their well-cut suits inherited from their fathers and grandfathers, with their hand-made, high-polished but down-at-heel boots and shoes.

It was like some weird Orwellian farcical nightmare of pigs about to root gluttonously around the trough.

But before dinner there were games. The dining room was

oval and in the centre was a boxing ring; the first event of the evening would be the traditional ten-round bare-knuckle boxing match, the victor's reward a suspension of the club's subscription fees, a crate of port and a dozen jeroboams of Taittinger Comtes de Champagne. Money, unlikely cheques and scrawled IOUs were passed among the assembled crowd as they placed their bets on what was usually a very brutal fight.

The master of ceremonies called the house to order, the members took their seats, and the fighters were pompously and ceremoniously announced. There was a stirring burst of the huntsman's gallop from the minstrels' mezzanine gallery and the battle commenced amid cheers, boos, cries of, 'I say, well done ... harder, boy, harder ... keep your left up, no, keep your left up ... oh my God, the boy's a girl.'

In the excitement, I drank whisky after whisky. Some members I hadn't seen in many years and I couldn't remember their names or their faces.

The crazy evening continued. The boxing ring splattered with blood, vomit, piss and water was quickly cleared and a regiment of waiters fluently assembled the enormous polished dining table, which was swiftly adorned with fine silver plate, shimmering claret goblets and solid silver trophies.

Soup was served, the oysters were gulped, whole lamb was carved with dexterity by an ancient maître d'hôtel who surely had been Dr Jekyll. Sweetmeats and trifles came and went. Château d'Yquem evaporated like an oasis in the desert. The port spun in ever-decreasing circles and the cigar smoke billowed purple waves, clouds above our heads as the evening slipped away and glided down the teak passageway to my bedroom, where I twisted and turned uncomfortably on this hard mattress.

I tried to reach the bedside table for a glass of water but with the tubes from my nose and electrodes on my chest and the ventilator choking my breathing I could not move. Feebly, I pressed a red button, expecting one of the stewards to arrive.

I was sweating. I was frightened.

No steward arrived. Just a man in a white jacket with a stethoscope and a briefcase, from which he took a syringe and injected my arm.

Some hours, or maybe days, later morning came, along with the cool, clean-shaven posse of doctors and specialists who grouped themsleves around my bed, talking about me while they pressed their cool fingers over my stomach.

They talked jocularly and loudly with one another about this 'remarkable recovery' that had occurred.

I said to them, 'How did you enjoy the dinner and the boxing?' Silence. I said, 'Well, surely you were there. It was a great night. I mean, there was the betting, there was the port, there was the whole baron of lamb, and then there was dawn. How do you manage to have such a place in what appears to me to be a hospital?' It was a hospital.

'Mr Floyd, you have been hallucinating. The medication we had to give you to keep you alive together with the effects of – how can we say it? – an overindulgence in alcohol . . . The night nurses recorded your cries and your conversations with yourself.

'You were suffering a nasty case of delirium tremens,' continued the doctor. 'DTs, Mr Floyd. We have played our part. Now it is for you to play yours. Drink again as you have before and you will die.'

It was not until weeks later, still in the early months of 2008, that I discovered that for two or three days and nights my twenty-five-year-old daughter Poppy, who had flown from her home in France, and my forty-year-old son Patrick, who had taken the bus from his home in Bristol, had been with me in that hospital in Staffordshire. They had sat beside me holding my hands and willing me to pull through.

I was completely unaware of my children's presence but without them I would not be here to tell you this story you are about to read, this story about a cook who became what to my mind is glibly and spuriously called a *celebrity* (I prefer the term *curiosity*). A cook who was shaken from the roots of his passion for food and stirred into the mythical and meaningless world of showbiz.

But I am here to tell you that, despite all that I hope you will now learn about Keith Floyd, you will see that although he was stirred he is no longer shaken. I'm still standing.

Let's go back ten years, shall we? Or was it fifteen? I'm damned if I can remember. Though does it matter?

I was sipping a shot of iced vodka and sucking caviar and soured cream off the little blinis in the front end of a 747 on a Qantas flight from Heathrow to Sydney. The chief purser showed me a copy of the *Sunday Mirror*, which contained a damning and embarrassing two-page article on my so-called riotous alcohol-driven sex life as described by an ex-girlfriend.

He said, 'Just to tell you, Mr Floyd, I have suppressed all the copies of the *Sunday Mirror* on the plane so you can walk freely without people staring at you.' That's what I call service.

Even in the comfort of first class it's hard to while away the time. I have difficulty in sleeping on planes. Invariably I don't like the movies that are on offer, I exhaust books and magazines all too quickly and sometimes I just slip into an introspective, reflective mood. I think thoughts like, who am I? What am I? What would my father think of me flying first class to Australia when his own sister took a £10 passage for a new life in the 1950s? He'd be amazed.

As I sipped and as I sucked, I reflected on my three failed marriages and my friends who had managed to stay married.

What is it about me that I always appear to have set one foot out of line, even if I haven't? And at the risk of being accused of protesting too much, I don't think I have been a bad husband, though we'd all say that, wouldn't we?

And I thought of friends of mine, no names, no particular pack drill, but a mate of mine – who shall remain anonymous – married to an absolutely magnificent woman. He didn't come home until four in the morning. When his wife asked where he'd been, he said, 'Oh, I was having a drink with Floyd.' He wasn't.

So I have got a kind of reputation. Many of my friends' wives mistrusted me. As a restaurateur it is the nature of my business to be outgoing, courteous, flattering or indeed even flirting with lady customers, or spending time, sipping port, with their husbands. It's just what you do. It doesn't mean that you are chatting up people all the time.

I was thinking about old friends Mark and Joy and David and Celia. Now, neither Mark nor David were what you could call saints, being good old drinking boys. But they managed to maintain their marriages perfectly well.

I suppose I was envious of David. He had this wonderful, slightly dotty but vivacious wife called Celia. I had known her for as many years as I'd known David. I said to myself, why couldn't I have a wife like Celia? Why couldn't I have someone like her and not get into trouble with my relationships?

And I couldn't find an answer. Perhaps I had spent too much time in my jobs, being a chef, being a restaurateur, being on television.

I felt that you had to earn enough money to build a barricade and then some more, to build a shelter inside that barricade and to be able to bring home a rabbit to feed the family . . . that's what I thought was important. And I would do whatever it took to try to create that situation.

Some people might have thought I was neglecting them. But from my perspective, it was the reverse. My working so hard was an expression of my love for them.

Anyway, soon I'd be in Sydney. And there's a great city. I was looking forward to the trip, so enough of the self-pity.

TWO

It was my first trip to Australia and promised to be quite an easy gig for extremely good money.

All I had to do was stand in front of a camera, which I'd been doing for about fifteen years, and praise a brand of ready meals that was being produced by Continental Foods. In return for a few days' 'work' I'd collect £110,000.

Actually, that's not quite accurate. Yes, I would collect £110,000 and return to Britain with it, but at that point I'd be handing a sizeable chunk of it to my agent.

My agent was a man called John Miles, whose client base included every single well-known British disc jockey, and me. We'd been together since the mid-eighties, when fame came knocking and the phone started ringing off the hook.

Invariably, it was not my phone but a phone somewhere at BBC Plymouth and messages were sometimes, I would later discover, not passed on to me or were passed on to me when I happened to meet so-and-so several months later in the bar. Then the message was relayed as a by-the-way, while ordering a couple of pints of Bass and a packet of cheese and onion crisps.

They were inconsequential messages from publishers like, 'We really want Keith to write a cookery book, money no object.

Can you get him to call us ASAP?' Or they were unimportant, minor requests for me to do this or that, again 'money no object . . . but he must call pronto or we'll find someone else'.

So I set myself the task of finding an agent, but it turned out to be one of Herculean proportions. I approached the top roster of established agents, accomplished and reputable men and women who, I hoped, might find it within themselves to represent me in return for a considerable slice of my earnings.

They all turned me down flat. They said, 'But you are not a footballer.' And they said, 'But you are not an actor.' No one wanted to touch me. They all agreed, 'Cooks don't have agents.'

Cooks don't have agents. How strange, how extraordinarily peculiar does that sound in today's world? The television chef of the twenty-first century cannot move without being surrounded by a phalanx of agents, minders, PR people, and assistants who will answer the phones, write down the messages and pass them on with the respective degree of urgency.

Having received one refusal after another I was coming round to the realization that I would have to learn to exist without anyone being able to get hold of me. Then I thought of John. Like me, he was based in Bristol, but, unlike me, he had a West Country brogue that was creamy and soft on the ear. I asked him if he'd take me on, but had to warn him I was at that time in debt, and facing the possibility of bankruptcy. We got together over a drink one night and he said, 'Keith, old boy, it will be a challenge but my wife thinks I should represent you!' As I was digesting his words and reaching out to shake his hand, John added, 'I charge 20 percent'.

I said, 'Yes.' And I didn't think much of it. At the time I was penniless so I did the maths and concluded, if John gets

20 per cent of a hundred quid, what does it matter to me, a bloke who is broke?

I am convinced that John believed I was a disc jockey. I mean, he *knew* I was a chef and a restaurateur, but sometimes if I was doing a cookery demonstration he would make a comment about how I should turn up not with magnificent ingredients and a selection of recently sharpened knives, but with a box of records. 'Just put them on and play them.'

Something strange had happened in John's head, and Keith Floyd was playing gigs just like Dave Lee Travis, Steve Wright, Simon Bates and Tony Blackburn . . . I am sure that John reckoned that a couple of hundred food lovers paying to get into the church hall to witness me at the stove and hear me share some culinary knowledge would, in fact, prefer to see me spinning discs, and blasting out Chuck Berry and the Rolling Stones.

Anyhow, that was John and as Qantas crossed the world I allowed the hostess to top up my champagne flute, so that I could toast my memories of the days when I reckoned if John gets 20 per cent of a hundred quid, what does it matter to me, a bloke who is broke? Now I was about to earn him £22,000.

A chauffeur met me at the airport and took me by limousine to the Sebel Townhouse Hotel, which is not there any more but throughout its thirty-year existence was a ludicrously luxurious shelter for the likes of Frank Sinatra, Liberace and Bette Davis. It was a rock 'n' roll type of place, used by Led Zeppelin and Bob Dylan and if I had heroes, which I don't, then Dylan would be one of them.

It is also said to be the city's first major hotel to accept credit cards, possibly because on departure guests were presented with such suitably large bills that payment otherwise would have required the traveller to carry trunkloads of cash.

But I did not need to worry about bills. I did not need to concern myself with credit cards or cash, because the tab for the gig – to use John's favourite word – was being picked up first by the advertising agency and ultimately by the client, Continental Foods.

As I strolled into the hotel lobby and headed to reception, I was greeted by a large board upon which sat a brass plaque, into which these words were engraved: 'The Sebel Townhouse welcomes'. Beneath the plaque was a list of names of guests who were due to arrive or had recently checked in. The impressive names included Warren Mitchell, Robert Sangster, Miles Davis, Barry Sheen, Ian Botham, Elton John (who, incidentally, held his wedding reception to Renate Blauel at the Sebel) and so on and so forth. There, at the top of the list, was 'Keith Floyd'.

I didn't get it. I stood in amazement for a moment, a sort of head-scratching, dreamy moment, wondering why my name was even on the board, let alone at the top. Meanwhile, staff were fawning and being incredibly polite to me, treating me like I was the Shah of Persia.

I didn't stand for long, however, because I was suffering from a bad foot and was exhausted by jet lag. So I thought I'd get a comfortable seat in the little horseshoe-shaped bar, cosy and intimate, and perk myself up with a large whisky, water no ice. I managed to find a hiding place: at that point in my life I didn't want to be seen drinking too early; these days I wouldn't give a hoot and I might have a pastis in a moment.

A man, short, bald and moustached, entered the room. I knew him to be Alf Garnett, the bigoted, loud-mouth, racist, homophobic, working-class aitch-dropping character from

Till Death Us Do Part, the television series which during the sixties had kept me and millions of others entertained – and millions of others outraged by the controversial dialogue. But they still watched it, didn't they?

Although I was doing my best not to be spotted, I stood out like a lone man in a bar, possibly because I was a lone man in a bar. And as I sensed Alf Garnett noticing me with one hand clasped around my glass and the other massaging my sore foot, my mind was numbed by the anxiety of what I should call him were he to speak to me.

A succession of questions charged through my brain: God, what do I do? What's his name? It's not Alf? Or is it? No, of course not, but is he 'sir'? Shall I call him 'sir'?

He did indeed speak to me, and when he did I discovered that I had the misconceptions of many other television viewers. I presumed that he would talk like Alf, the bigoted, loud-mouthed, racist, homophobic, working-class aitch-dropper. I had no idea that in real life, as they say, he spoke like a titled lord.

'Floyd,' he said in the well-enunciated boom of the Shakespearean actor that he is, and as if were long-lost friends. 'How many times have you stayed at this hotel?'

My turn to talk and I opted for 'sir'. I said, 'Erm, well, sir, it's my first visit.'

He waved a hand towards reception, where the board announced today's influx of well-known guests, and simultaneously delivered another boom: 'I've been coming here for fourteen years. I'm having the billing changed.' We had a chat, long enough for me to remember his name was Warren Mitchell, and he told me how he was in Sydney to play Alf Garnett by day and appear in a Chekhov play by night. He is a man of immense knowledge and intellectual resource.

We actually got on very well and, like me, he was a rugby fan. He told me a lovely story of a time when he and Richard Burton were in Dublin and trying to get tickets for Ireland versus Wales. In order to acquire the tickets to the match they had to spend ages in a hat shop, trying on hats and buying hats: they didn't want the hats but the bloke who ran the shop had black market tickets and the only way to the tickets was to feign interest in the hats. Warren Mitchell is a man who gets things done.

I went up to my room, snoozed happily, and when I next set (aching) foot in the lobby I glanced at the welcome board and noticed that I had been demoted to second place. Warren's name was perched proudly at the top of the list.

What followed was a week of standing in front of a camera.

I'd made many commercials for TV, radio and print. Quite a lot of them were really good and some even won industry awards. One of the best was for the Irish Tourist Board. The copywriter wrote: 'Walk down any street in Ireland and you'll pass a brilliant pub . . .' Then there was a shot of me walking down the street towards the camera, passing a pub, and saying, 'That's a stupid idea,' about turn, and into the bar.

Another great one: we were filming some incredible old monuments, lighthouses, various kinds of architectural wrecks on the west coast in Tralee. The scriptwriter, copywriter, call them what you will, had written something like: 'Look at these fantastic old wrecks – just another part of Ireland's appeal.' The joke was, when I said old wrecks, the camera focused on me.

Strange people called up John Miles. One wanted me to make a TV commercial for crunched-up cereal. Instead of using breadcrumbs, people would dip their fish into this mix. I asked, 'Why?'

They said, 'We've overproduced.' And despite the many hundreds of thousands of pounds they offered me – and with the agreement of my agent – I turned it down.

As I did when a Japanese corporation asked me to endorse a product called Prawnies.

Now, I've got nothing against the Japanese although I did find it funny one day in Bangkok airport when the tour leader of a crocodile of camera-clicking tourists (you knew he was the leader because he held high above his head a vibrantly coloured umbrella) saw me smoking in one of the booths on one of the walkways. The tour leader pulled down his umbrella, pushed open the heavy glass door, asked me for a light and drew deeply on an American cigarette. Leaderless, the crocodile continued on.

Anyhow, I like saki. I drink a lot of it. I like Japanese food and I can cook it. Or, you should say, I can cut it, because so much of it is raw.

I once stayed in a hotel in London at the same time as the newly married – I don't know what he's called – Emperor or Crown Prince of Japan and his spouse. I think they needed several rooms just for the trunks and several trunks to put all the security guards in to sleep at night.

But I wasn't going to endorse Prawnies, which are like those dreadful crabsticks that are endemic in supermarkets and pubs all over Britain.

The corporation was going to take this product, which, by the way, was made from seaweed and had nothing at all to do with fish, and punch it out in the shape of a shrimp. I have my principles, and even for the vast sums they offered me I would not compromise them . . . but today, Thursday, 9 July 2009, as I sit under the midday Spanish sun, barely able to walk, waiting for my best friend, Doctor Ernest, to remove the titanium clips from my stomach so that I can take up the prescribed chemotherapy course . . . Now, I wish to fuck I had taken their money.

So I was in Sydney, hoping to get some sun, but mostly standing in front of a camera and praising a brand of ready meals. The ad guys were there, lots of them, and they all clutched clipboards.

I did the first take, delivering my lines about these wonderful ready meals and how they were made with delicious pasta. Someone shouted, 'Cut!' Behind the cameras I could see clipboards flapping. The ad guys seemed jittery. Something was not quite right.

A man with a clipboard emerged from the darkness, stepped from behind the cameras, and crossed the invisible line between me, the performer, and them, 'the creatives'.

He said, 'Floydy. Can you say par-ster rather than pasta?'

I said, 'Sorry?'

He repeated, 'Would you mind, Floydy, saying par-ster rather than pasta?'

'No', I said, 'I will not say parster – it is pasta.'

'Yeah, but in Australia we call it parster.'

I said, 'Did you ever think of getting an Australian to do the commercial? You've flown me halfway across the world, you've been brilliant to me, but I ain't saying parster.'

Funny really, I can remember the time when pasta was virtually unheard of in Britain, but Bristol, the city in which I lived and worked, had a rash of trattorias with singing Italian waiters in their blue-and-white-hooped sailor tops. They sang 'O sole mio' and wielded a pepper mill that was so huge they probably thought it was an extension of their manhood. It was overt sexual innuendo.

As an aside, I remember going for dinner at a trattoria in Bristol, which was a great city for trattorias, and on this particular night I discovered spaghetti. They served spaghetti Bolognese, a dish which is on every menu of every trattoria in Britain, but doesn't exist in the same form in Italy. To the British, as well as the Americans, it is a dish of minced beef and onion cooked in tomato sauce and then dolloped over the long pasta.

But in the Italian city of Bologna, the home of Bolognese, the sauce is actually tomato with meatballs, perhaps veal or veal and beef mixed together. The Bolognese people would get their protein from the rice or pasta, and the number of meatballs per serving depended on the financial circumstances of the household.

When I discovered spaghetti it was a type of pasta that came in two forms. The first was immersed in tomato sauce and packaged in a yellow-wrapped tin, courtesy of Heinz 57 varieties. But if you were really smart, you bought the dry pasta which came in dark blue sugar paper, a little sticker on the front.

My friend Bob Baker and I were wondering why we didn't try to make our own spaghetti Bolognese. So we popped in to Mr Dodoesky's Polish delicatessen and bought the dried stuff, in the sugar paper tube. That bit was easy. The next bit was difficult. How would we turn this new (to us) but strange ingredient into soft tubes on a plate? Should we soak it in the bath overnight? Should we break it up? No, because it's not broken up when it arrives on the plate. Follow the instructions on the packet, you say. There were no cooking instructions on the packet.

Eventually I found out that if you boiled water and slowly

pushed the spaghetti into the liquid then the pasta would soften and curl into the pan and eventually it would cook.

What a discovery! Bob and I consider ourselves quite clever, but establishing how to cook dried pasta was to us a mind-shaking gastronomic event.

John Miles flew into Sydney, partly to see me but at the same time meeting people to fix deals for his DJs. We got to the final day of the shoot in Sydney and the ad guys said, 'Thanks a lot, Floydy.'

They handed me an envelope.

In the envelope was a banker's draft to the value of £110,000. The good thing about drafts is that they are not like a cheque; they don't bounce; they can't bounce. The bad thing is that if they are lost or stolen they can be cashed by the thief or finder. Effectively, I had just been presented with £110,000 in cash.

Let's cut to me in a bar or two, a few hours after being handed the draft. I was celebrating, and celebrating with the envelope and the 110 grand in my jacket pocket (which anyone stupid could have told me is stupid).

I'm not sure how the evening ended, or for that matter how the next morning began. But at some point I awoke in my hotel suite, glorious sun shining through the windows and bringing me back to life with its warmth.

I reached for my jacket so that I could kiss good morning to the banker's draft. Empty pocket. The envelope and draft had gone. I searched the suite – closets, cupboards, bathroom cabinets, minibar, every square inch scoured and examined – but nope, the draft was missing.

I smoked a cigarette. Then another.

Then I got dressed and took the lift down to the lobby, past Warren Mitchell's top billing on the welcome board, and asked to see the general manager. 'I have lost an envelope that contains £110,000,' I began, and I could see from the look of anxiety on his face that I was bringing him more grief than the combined demands of Led Zep, Bette Davis and Liberace.

Not wanting the police to be called to his hotel, the manager summoned his staff and then mounted his own search that would turn out to be exhausting and laborious. He despatched his minions to all corners, nooks and crannies of the hotel. 'Check the laundry and laundry chute,' he said, and then with a cursory glance at me looking jaded, he shouted at the backs of his staff, 'and don't forget the bars.'

The search went on for the whole day, but to no avail. The following morning it had still not been discovered. My money was gone, and it was not as if I could phone the ad guys to ask for another banker's draft. By now they would be on another shoot and clutching brand new clipboards, ordering directors to reshoot and telling performers how to pronounce 'chicken' or 'rice' or 'zarzuela'.

While I reflected on my stupidity, carelessness and foolishness something bizarre happened.

A man in a suit came into the hotel, passed the board that welcomed Warren Mitchell first, and went up to reception, asking to see the general manager. When the manager appeared, the man in the suit handed him *my* envelope with *my* banker's draft inside it.

'We've been searching high and low for this,' said the general manager. 'Where did you find it?'

'I didn't find it. Keith Floyd gave it to me.'

'Gave it to you?' said the manager, puzzled and probably more than a little irritated by the amount of time and effort his staff had invested in the search for the draft.

In fact, it was a case of an inspector calls.

The man in the suit turned out to be an inspector for the good people of the Australian Inland Revenue, and then he explained how he'd come by my draft . . . A couple of nights earlier, he and his colleagues had attended a banquet at the hotel, a banquet for the Inland Revenue. (Yes, I know, odd, isn't it? The Inland Revenue don't hold banquets in Britain, but then again, the blokes at Britain's Inland Revenue don't pronounce pasta 'parster'.)

There were some 200 guests at the event and during the feast, the inspector said, someone had spotted me in the hotel. 'We asked Floydy to join us for a drink,' he continued, 'and he came and sat at our table. We had a bit to drink and it was all good fun.'

Yes, nodded the general manager, all very interesting, but how had the inspector acquired the envelope that contained the draft?

'Oh,' said the inspector. 'At the end of the night, I asked for Floydy's autograph. I had a pen but no paper. Floydy reached inside his jacket looking for something to write on, and then he said, "Don't worry. I've got some paper." He was holding the envelope.

'Look,' added the inspector pointing at the paper in his hand, 'He signed his autograph, "best dishes, Keith Floyd". Then he gave the envelope to me. Then he said goodnight and went to bed.'

Many people spend their lives trying to avoid handing a

single penny to the Inland Revenue. I was in the peculiar position of being able to give them – albeit, unwittingly – 110 grand, and then have it handed back to me.

On the return flight to London I was looking forward to a good meal first-class style, followed by a snooze. The crew began to serve the food, and I eyed up the smoked salmon and fillets of beef that were being presented to the other passengers, Kylie Minogue included.

Yet while everyone else got their food I was given nothing. I was being missed out for some reason. Then the chief stewardess, who was a large extrovert Australian, placed a dish in front of me, saying, 'There you go.' I looked down at the plate. Upon it was a ready meal; a product of Continental Foods, which I had just been advertising. It was pasta. Or was it parster?

I stared in disbelief and didn't feel like eating it. After a couple of minutes the stewardess and her colleagues erupted into howls of laughter. 'Only kidding,' she said, before whisking away the ready meal. Then she returned with the proper meal, the smoked salmon and fillet of beef that Kylie and Co. were enjoying.

The stewardess boomed for all to hear, 'Floydy, what have parsley and pubic hair got in common?'

The question certainly made a change from, 'Would you like a pillow?' or 'More coffee, sir?' I thought for a moment.

'I'm terribly sorry,' I said, 'but I don't know.'

'They both get stuck in your teeth.'

I've got one: what do air stewardesses and chapter openings have in common? Both can bring you back down to earth.

THREE

My father killed himself, I'm sure of it. By that I mean he stopped taking the medication.

It was 1984, and I had just made the pilot programme for *Floyd on Fish*, which I'll come to a little later in this book. At the time my dad, Sidney, was not a well man. He was suffering from emphysema, an illness caused by his years of chain-smoking. Most days of his life he had worked his way through a hundred cigarettes.

So the pilot programme was done but had yet to be broadcast. It was still being edited and polished, but I wanted my dad to see the rough cut. Sadly, he seemed to be too ill and I told myself that he would have to wait for the finished version, which he could watch at home when it was screened.

I had recently married my second wife, Julie, and the mother of my daughter Poppy, and did not know that fame was just around the corner. Who does?

I spent long days and nights in my restaurant, Floyd's, in Chandos Road, Bristol. It was a busy place and I was the chef, the boss, the restaurateur. At two in the morning, when maybe I should have been at home being a father, I was usually at the restaurant, by the kitchen's back door, putting out the bins.

And I was at the restaurant the night my mother phoned. She said, 'I can't wake Dad up.'

I had a restaurant full of people . . . I couldn't just leave. Of course, I could have done. I just thought that I couldn't.

Don't ever go into the restaurant business. It kills marriages, it kills relationships, and it kills life. It kills everything.

Eventually I managed to get over to my parents' house. My mother was distraught and frail and wrinkled, and yet with the seeds of her geraniums already on the windowsill to propagate before the forthcoming spring. Mum greeted me with the words, 'Can you go and see if you can wake him up?'

She went into the front room and closed the door, and I was left standing alone at the bottom of the stairs.

Clumping my feet up and down heavily, I marched on the spot. To my mother's ears, it would have sounded as if I was walking up the stairs.

I left a pause, a silence of a minute or so, so that she might assume I was pulling back the sheets from my father's face to check if he was still breathing. And then I marched again on the spot, banging down my feet at the bottom of the staircase – supposedly the sound of my walking back down the stairs.

Then I walked into the front room and said to my mother, 'Our dear dad is dead.' And I hugged her and repeated, 'Our dear dad is dead.'

It is to my eternal shame that I pretended . . . pretended to walk up the stairs, pretended to check my father, and pretended to walk back down the stairs. I couldn't see the man that I loved and respected so enormously lying there a victim of his patience, of his kindness, of his tolerance.

As I said, I'm sure he killed himself. I am convinced he

stopped taking his medication because he considered himself to be a burden on my mother. He was living in an oxygen mask, sitting in his little garden.

Up to the start of spring he would hang grease balls from the trees in the garden, a tasty treat for birds to eat during the winter. And he would sit in his garden, staring at the grease balls, exasperated and unable to breathe properly. Like father like son: I also have grease balls hanging on the trees for the birds to eat.

His legacy was characteristically thoughtful and kind. It was a booklet he had written for my mother.

It began, 'Dear Winnie', and what followed was a sort of catalogue of what she might need to know about their house: 'The outside tap for watering in the garden is to the right-hand side of the door . . . The Prudence insurance man comes on Thursdays . . . The fuses are in the box beneath the staircase.'

He detailed every facet and function of the running of their little ex-council house so that my widowed mother would have this booklet to help her through the remaining years of her own life. It was by no means a patronizing gesture on my father's part. He had provided her with a survival manual, which I think is pretty impressive.

He was a private person with dignity, and he would rarely talk about the Second World War, what he had seen during his days as a soldier, what effect it had upon his mind. People didn't.

Our relationship was at its best when I was an adult and he was an elderly man. I was a restaurateur by then and used to take him for lunch in places like Harvey's in Bristol.

Harvey's was the apex of fine dining for the bloated, pompous and self-assured businessmen, or even indeed the city's founding fathers. It would seem old-fashioned today, but when Dad and I went to Harvey's it was trendy. In fact, it had been designed by a young Terence Conran: dividing walls were built from wine bottles and looked outstanding.

If at Harvey's they offered Dover sole à la meunière, thus it was. I should remind you that, like all simple things, this simple dish of that fine firm-fleshed fish fried in butter needs much love and attention when being cooked. The black skin of the sole is ripped off the fish's back and with a pair of scissors you trim around the outside to remove the now protruding bones.

You dry it, you pat it and you dust it lightly with flour. You fry it gently for a minute or two on both sides with a little olive oil. Then you take it from the pan, rest it on kitchen roll and clean off any little bits of burnt flour. In a fresh new pan, you melt a generous chunk of butter and continue frying on both sides. If you fried it in butter from the beginning the butter would burn, but by first cooking in oil you have eliminated that possibility.

The fish at Harvey's was served with the foaming golden butter poured over it, and with half a lemon neatly wrapped in fine, white muslin so that the pips would not squeeze from the fruit on to your plate. A pot of genuine tartare sauce was the accompaniment, with its correctly home-made mayonnaise base, capers and gherkins, both finely chopped.

Dad and I got together over these occasional lunches, sometimes in the luxury of Harvey's, sometimes over a pint of cider, a wedge of authentic Cheddar cheese and a hunk of bread in Clifton's legendary Coronation Tap, which served only Taunton cider. And these lunches – these moments at the table together – strengthened our relationship, made it more intimate.

We were in Harvey's one day, sipping our Chablis premier cru and lifting the firm fresh morsels of flesh from the sole à la meunière, when from his wallet – soft brown, smooth and aged – Dad removed a small, not very clear, black-and-white photograph.

The picture showed him dressed in a sari and standing beside a bare-breasted Sinhalese woman. He revealed to me that during the war, when he was based in Ceylon (now Sri Lanka), this woman had been his mistress and companion.

He felt it was time for me to know. And in his shy and modest way he explained that in wartime he needed the comfort provided by that irreconcilable affair. It didn't diminish his respect or his love for my mother, he said, and I knew that to be true.

The fact is, Dad was quite a good storyteller and although I don't recall everything he said during that particular Bristol lunchtime, I was reminded of a short story written by Nicholas Monsarrat. It is one of several in a book he called *HMS Marlborough Will Enter Harbour* (a horrifying tale of a captain's battle to bring his shattered destroyer back to harbour after being attacked by U-boats on an Atlantic convoy duty).

The short story that probably had the most pathos, and was the most moving, centred on a war-shocked, shattered sea captain on a rare forty-eight-hour leave in London. Befuddled and sodden by whisky, and after cocktails in the blacked-out Dorchester, the captain found his way to some piano bar in Soho, where he met his female date, took her back to the hotel, made love, and then slumped into a tortured alcoholic coma.

He awoke in a panic before dawn knowing he had to return to his ship and thought the least he could do without waking the woman by his side was to leave a £5 note on the pillow.

A generous price for a prostitute in 1943. The chilling denouement of the story was that the woman was not a hooker. She was his wife. The wretched effects of battle had combined with alcohol-induced delirium to mess up the captain's mind.

As my dad would say so many times, 'All is fair in love and war.'

Long before I was born my father had been a lay preacher and was a good man, so what did I make of him when he showed me the photograph that was an exposure of his adultery? There in black and white, as they say. Did it change my opinion of him?

Absolutely not at all. I didn't understand what the significance of it might have been. Have you had an experience of war? Although I was in the army, I did not see action.

I only have experience of the war second-hand through literature – Wilfred Owen, Robert Graves, Siegfried Sassoon, of Simon Raven and Evelyn Waugh, and *All Quiet on the Western Front*. War is something most of us have been spared from. Why should I judge my father for an infidelity that took place when he believed perhaps that his days – or even his hours – were numbered?

I've lost all the skills my father taught me. I could wind copper wire around a cotton reel and make a generator. I could build a crystal radio. I could solder things. On my first motor car, a 1935 Austin 7, I could grind the valves, replace the kingpins. I could do all that because of my father, who taught me and encouraged me to use my hands.

Now I feel as if I know nothing. I sometimes wonder if it would have been better if I could have stayed with my old dad, and now I could spend my days tinkering with my car.

*

Dad was an extraordinarily mild man who, like other extraordinarily mild men, rarely lost his temper. When pushed to the limit he'd say 'damn' or 'blast'. You knew when he was in a particularly filthy mood because that's when he'd couple both expletives: 'Damn and blast. I've had enough.' (Though not too loud.)

I don't know a lot about him. In his younger days, he appears to have been a very bright young man who came from a working-class background in the Solihull district of Birmingham.

He had an Irish mother whose maiden name was Kate O'Reilly. I never met his father, but Dad had a brother Tom who worked for Land Rover in Birmingham. Uncle Tom was an alcoholic and possibly a homosexual, but this was in the fifties, when you couldn't be one. He was a wonderful uncle to me.

My dad had always been a keen cyclist and as a teenager he would spend weekends bicycling from the Midlands to wherever his rapidly peddling feet would take him.

One weekend he cycled from Birmingham to the West Country, to Taunton, to Barnstaple, and stopped for a breather at Wiveliscombe, or Wivey, as it is known by its couple of thousand inhabitants. I think it's categorized as a small town, but to me it is merely a village. Here in Wivey, he bumped into a seventeen-year-old girl called Winifred Ruth Lorraine Margetts.

He was so drawn to this young lady that he set his heart on marrying her. Before making her his wife, of course, he had to go through a period of courtship as was still the norm in the thirties.

The courting days involved my father making frequent but exhausting cycling expeditions from Birmingham to Somerset in order to walk out with her. Then he'd be on his bike again, heading back to Birmingham, where he could recover before making the next trek to the West Country. Clearly, travel was in the Floyd blood.

I have been told that Wiveliscombe derives its name from a time when most of the men of the parish had no wives, hence *wife-less-combe*. (Quite how the population grew, don't ask.) But times change and this is where my father found the woman who would become his wife.

As a teenager, Dad managed to get himself into a college where he studied something like a degree in electro-engineering but, like every other person of the time, his life – his future – was dramatically changed for him by the outbreak of the Second World War. He joined the Signals Regiment and was posted, as I have said, to what was then called Ceylon.

I haven't talked about my dad much before, and it's been very nice to talk about him today.

When I came along on 28 December 1943, we lived in Southampton, though I didn't see anything of my father because, of course, he was away fighting the war. And I cannot remember a single thing of my childhood until my dad returned to be with us in Southampton.

My earliest recollection of life features my father and it is this: Christmas morning and Father Christmas has brought me a train set, and not just any train set but a good Hornby 0-gauge clockwork set. The problem is, it is circular, barely more than a foot or two in diameter, with a point, and two pieces of extension line. Alas, no buffer. I say to my dad, 'Father Christmas is stupid. He didn't bring a buffer. How's this train going to work? It'll run off onto the carpet.'

After the war Dad couldn't continue his studies so I think he became a tailor or something of that sort, but whatever the case he didn't make his electro-engineering dreams come true.

He had a job with the Electricity Board, in the days when every home had an electricity meter fitted with Bakelite framed doors and inside a machine that whirred around. My father's task was to repair such machines. Then he worked for the Fawley oil refinery on Southampton Water and he was back on his bike, cycling off with his lunchbox.

I also remember in Southampton, maybe in 1947, that my dad made me a garage and a showroom, and the garage doors, made from the front covers of electricity meters, opened to reveal Dinky toys inside. That's how capable he was.

He was exceptionally good with his hands. If a clock didn't work he would make it work. If a tree was damaged in a storm he would restore it. If a path needed to be laid he could do it.

He didn't – wouldn't – accept that problems didn't have a logical solution. It might take him one hour or ten, but he always believed that something wrong or broken could be put right. He wouldn't say, 'It's broken. That's it. Can't fix it.' Dad didn't do 'It's broken' or 'It's no good.' He'd sit and think, given time and patience I can fix that. And he was incredibly patient.

Yet in my childhood and teens my father wasn't a strong presence in my life. It is more as if he was there, secretly doing everything: going to work, bringing back the money and not making a big deal about it.

He was meticulous about finances, though not mean. He carefully kept a book of financial expenditure and earnings, something along the lines of Dickens's Mister Micawber: 'Annual income twenty pounds, annual expenditure nineteen pounds nineteen and six, result happiness. Annual income twenty pounds, annual expenditure twenty pounds ought and six, result misery.'

At bedtimes Dad would read to me, my favourite being Robert Louis Stevenson's *Treasure Island*. A man of profound religious conviction, Dad didn't impose his religion on anybody, which shows thoughtfulness.

He was such a nice man, such a modest man, that my mother sometimes became frustrated with him. She felt he wasn't aggressive enough, wasn't ambitious enough. He would just carefully keep the accounts of the house.

Then there was my sister, Brenda, four years my senior, and that four-year gap was considerably significant in the standing of our relationship. I suppose what I am trying to say is that she was immensely superior and bossy.

Brenda took on quite a religious fervour for a while and I didn't like her at all. She used to do wicked things like make me polish her shoes. When we had to do the washing-up after Sunday lunch, I would dry the plates, which she would then dip back into the washing up water. This meant, of course, that I had to dry each plate twice.

Brenda was also very bright and was always, as far as I could tell, hysterical about her hair and about her clothes.

Our happiest times together were when we had what we called midnight feasts, taking place probably in the early evening. Brenda had a penchant for getting tomatoes and parsley from the garden, and we'd eat them with slices of cheese.

And Brenda was there when I cooked for the first time. For one of these feasts I picked runner beans from the garden. I put them into boiling water. No, not ambitious. A knob of butter and a handful of grated cheese were placed on top of the hot beans to melt and delight our young taste buds.

FOUR

When I was about eight years old the family uprooted. We moved from Southampton to Wiveliscombe, where my mother was raised, where my mother and father conducted their courtship, and where my mother's parents lived. I was sent to Wiveliscombe Primary School.

I don't think the move ever pleased my father. My grandparents had said, 'There's a place near us that you can have for five shillings' rent a week.' And it turned out to be a cottage that was right next door to my grandparents. Now he was neighbour to his in-laws, and I think that my father felt as if he had lost his independence.

I lived on the landing; didn't have a bedroom. There was a curtain at the top of the stairs, and when it was pulled back, there was my bed.

My memories of life in Wivey are happy, and many of them are food-related. Dad provided and Mum created; quite an interesting thing. He was in charge of preparing the garden. Mum was in charge of growing it.

This was in the days when sugar came in packets of sugar paper, actually folded and wrapped by the man who then weighed it on a red scale and poured the granules into the bag and folded it over. And that man happened to be my uncle in the County Stores in Wivey.

We bought the groceries once a week, Tuesday I think. These included half a pound of butter which was supposed to last until next Tuesday. However, my mother spread the butter thick. She didn't give a hoot about making it last but was more concerned about giving pleasure. When the butter was gone there was lard or dripping. In cash-strapped times, we'd have a breakfast of Shredded Wheat with hot water and a scraping of margarine on top of the cereal.

Sunday was always an explosive day. After Sunday school and church choir in the morning, I'd return home knowing that when it came to lunch, my mother would push the boat out. She'd cook the best joint of beef or pork or lamb, or one of the chickens which we kept. I know what a headless chicken is because my grandfather used to limp down the back yard, get a chicken and cut off its head.

We'd eat pease pudding and boiled ham with parsley sauce and butter beans. Or we'd have rabbit stew. No, it didn't have wine in it but it was a bloody good rabbit stew nevertheless. Sunday lunch was always a wonderful meal prepared in community with my grandparents who lived next door, and various other relatives and friends, probably about fourteen of us.

Then we'd go for a walk, picking watercress from the crystal stream for the watercress sandwiches that my mother would later serve as part of Sunday afternoon tea.

Monday: washing day. This was done in a big copper tub, out in the back yard; it was fired up by a gas ring and set to boil. Sheets and pillowcases were put into the boiling water, along with suet puddings tightly wrapped in muslin.

The evening meal was shepherd's pie (made from the

remaining lamb of Sunday's joint) or minced beef (made from the beef joint if we'd had beef on Sunday), served with potatoes. Sure, it was leftovers but it was still damned tasty. Dad would return home from work at six o'clock, and evening meals were timed to coincide with his arrival.

Tuesday: my mother made a soup from the same joint that had provided lunch on Sunday and dinner on Monday.

Wednesday: perhaps we'd have tripe and white onion sauce.

Thursday: the day for faggots – made from the lights, liver and heart of the pig, all of it minced, wrapped in cawl and then braised in water with sage and onion – and served with peas. My mother did not often use Oxo cubes. Instead, she made sauces and juices from the meats she had roasted. The gravy for the duck came from roasting the giblets and the feet, and the gravy for the lamb came from the bones of the lamb.

But she made an exception when it came to those faggots. Just as I love Heinz tomato soup at certain times, I think there is a place for Oxo cubes and it's when they are crumbled and used to enrich the stock that accompanied the faggots. It's OK. In fact, it was perfect. Albert Roux, Raymond Blanc and Gordon Ramsay, don't tell me any different.

Fried liver with burnt onions was another Thursday favourite. It was joined on the plate by crisp, streaky bacon with a heavy rind. The rind that we didn't chew was then nailed on to a tree in the garden for the birds to dine upon.

Friday: the fish man came in his van, so a lot of fish was bought and we'd have cod or halibut for dinner. The fish was dipped in beer batter, deep fried and served with chips – hand-made chips.

Saturday: fish again. Or we might have a feast of boiled pigs' trotters, cooked with vinegar, salt and pepper.

My mother's Friday fish purchase often included salt cod, known in France as *morue* and highly esteemed. The fish is salted and dried to preserve it. On Saturday night the salt fish, looking like a dreadful dried piece of stuff that you could have soled your shoes with, was put into water to soak. On Sunday mornings it was removed from the water and then poached in milk for breakfast. Salty and fishy, it's fantastic.

Which takes us back to Sunday lunch, and if we'd had lamb or beef last week, today we might dine on a pig's head – complete with tongue and brains – which only cost a shilling, compared to a joint of pork, which cost a million pounds, or so it seemed.

My grandfather was a great character and often around. He was a cobbler, making and repairing shoes and boots; some might say an ironic career as he only had one foot.

He had lost a leg in the First World War, during the Battle of the Somme, and it had been replaced by a tin leg. Around his waist he had a huge red buckle, attached to which was a strap that held the false limb in place.

I would sit on my grandfather's workbench marvelling at the way he would take a nail from his mouth and quickly bang it into the soul of a boot; a mechanical and relaxed movement. When my son Patrick came along a couple of decades later, he used to sit on the worktop next to the stove watching me chop onions.

If my grandfather was at our home on Sundays then he would carve the joint. On weekdays, he would return from his workshop and join us for lunch, which was served on a varnished table that could be extended and was covered by a white tablecloth. We had the sort of salt cellars that looked like they could be used under piano feet.

My mother served food as my grandfather stomped over to

the wireless – the radio – and tuned it in. 'This is the BBC Home Service,' a posh voice would say. 'Here is the news.' We'd listen to what was happening in the war in Korea . . . and at that point there was silence, respectively observed in the fearsome presence of my grandfather, who was really quite a nice chap and kept dropping his cigarette ash all over his legs, much to the irritation of Ruth, my grandmother.

She was a slight, bespectacled woman with self-permed hair and something of an aquiline nose, and as she walked, or busied herself about the kitchen, she would nod her head as if she were a pecking chicken. My grandmother was sharp and missed nothing. She wore a floral housecoat over her skirt and blouse. She would hastily take off the housecoat when the door of the shop opened, the bell ringing to announce the arrival of a customer.

Speaking of my grandmother, she features prominently in my early memories of punishment, and injustice. My friends and I used to go scrumping for apples and plums, which wasn't a crime, and I was also quite interested in archaeology so divided my time between the two activities.

For instance, I'd go to Castle Rock, climb into the caves and cut out quartz. One day, the others were pinching apples and plums while I dug up the nearby earth and found what I considered to be ancient relics. I saw a piece of broken pottery and then scrabbled some more and found the equivalent of about £20 in shillings and half-crown pieces. The money had been buried, though why I do not know.

I shared the loot among my friends and returned home, content at feeling rich. 'Where did you get this?' asked my grandmother. She assumed I had stolen it. 'I didn't steal it. I found it.' But she wouldn't listen, or maybe she didn't want to listen. Her punishment was twofold. First, she kept half of the money. Second, she told my mother that I must have stolen the money. I am sure my grandmother betrayed me because she was greedy. She wanted the cash.

This stirs memories of another incident, and this time I was genuinely guilty. I was in a shop and stole a Dinky toy, which is what kids do.

At home there was a tribunal, with me the accused, and Dad concluding, 'Now you go out to the garden and take one of the bamboo canes from the tripod of runner beans. Then bring it back here.' Duly, I obeyed. I was both victim and executioner. In other words, I had to go and select the cane that was going to whip my arse for stealing a Dinky toy.

Mum was very strict. She was generous and extremely kind but also very strict. In the morning she would scream from the bottom of the stairs, 'Keith, get up. Time for school.' I might as well confess (if that is the right word) that I am an insomniac, and I wonder if it stems from childhood. I'm always worried about tomorrow and I have terrible nightmares, more of which later.

But if my mother instilled insomnia within me, then I also inherited her generous streak.

The pictures took place at Wivey on Friday nights in the town hall and Mum was working at a cloth factory, Fox's West of England Cloth. Her walk home took her from the factory, past the potato fields, in which as a twelve-year-old boy I would toil for hours behind the harvest tractor, filling sacks with new spuds, then up past the brewery and then up Golden Hill and into Silver Street. But I would ambush her halfway along the route, as she trudged past the potato field. I'd leap out and say, 'Mum, it's Friday night. Can I have a shilling to go the pictures, please?'

She always gave me a shilling but often she couldn't afford it.

A shilling was a shilling; a lot of money. Then off I'd go, to see *Rock Around the Clock*, or *Blackboard Jungle*, or maybe (and here we get a little serious) *Henry V* or *Richard III*.

And in that same town hall, at the age of about ten, I think I was a cub, rubbing sticks together to make fire, and being watched over by Akela, who was an old, bearded wizard. He smelt of urine and dampness, and always had a smouldering log fire in his dwelling. I got all my badges for drawing and for fishing and woodcraft. Not witchcraft.

And again in this same town hall, I played Mowgli in *Jungle Book*. My mother ripped up some sheets, providing me with the Mowgli loincloth. My father painted my face, arms and legs with cocoa to give me the jungle boy's dark skin. My grandfather handed me one of his cobbler's knives to complete the look. And I stood on the boards of the stage of the town hall, in front of an audience and said, 'I am Mowgli.'

I find it interesting that what my family lacked in finances, they made up for with ingenuity – to mix cocoa with water to paint me brown, and rip up a sheet and tie-dye it.

In 1953, when I was nearly ten, there was a huge fête in the village recreation ground to celebrate the Queen's coronation. Villagers competed in a tug of war; there was dancing and biting apples from a barrel. And there was a fancy dress competition, which Brenda and I entered.

Brenda was Elizabeth I in a satin dress and a bodice. I was Sir Walter Raleigh, with a golden-quilted padded waistcoat with steel stair rods built into it, created by my father, who had heated the metal over the fire in order to bend it. I wore a felt hat which my parents had steamed and reshaped, and I carried a rapier, the handle of which was a darning mushroom (a mushroom-shaped object that Mum would put it into the elbow of a sleeve or into the foot of a sock to hold it in place while stitching).

Along with forty other children, Brenda and I paraded in front of the adults. There were the boys' prizes and the girls' prizes; first, second and third. Brenda and I both won first prizes. After a consultation among the committee members, it was considered incorrect that two children from the same family should come first.

So Brenda won and I didn't. And as we're being honest throughout, I may as well say that to this day I am still burdened by a wicked sense of injustice, which is silly, isn't it?

As Brenda was exceptionally bright, she obtained a scholarship to Bishop Fox's school, in Taunton. To earn a bit of pocket money, she took a variety of part-time jobs, working as a chambermaid at the White Hart Hotel in the village, as well as cleaning and waitressing.

She was cunning, too. My parents gave her a bicycle but then she claimed it had been stolen. It hadn't. In fact she was keeping it in a friend's garden and collecting the school bus money from my parents. She'd leave home, the money jangling in her pocket, and then pop round to her friend's house, get on her bike and cycle to school.

Brenda was forever falling in love with boys who were deemed 'unsuitable' by my parents. She went to the monthly hops, as dances were called, at the cider factory in Wivey and my father would arrive to pick her up at the agreed time of ten. He'd be at the door, saying, 'You come out.' And she'd be in her fifties clothes, bopping away and resenting being dragged home at ten when the others were allowed to stay until eleven.

When I was in my teens, Brenda instructed me to climb on to my Vespa scooter and whizz off to deliver a note to her fiancé, Edward. I expect the letter said something like, 'Do you love me or not?' He must have said yes, because they got married.

Edward was a very brash salesman who worked for Green Shield stamps and I didn't like him at all. He was far too flashy and, in my view, he used to humiliate my father. He'd say, 'I've earned this much this week . . . Look at my bonus,' and all the rest of it. I didn't have much in common with Brenda and Edward at all.

Anyhow, many, many years have passed and things change dramatically. People's experiences influence them and I think I could say that although it was late in life before we sort of got it together, we did get it together.

You couldn't have a more caring and a more loving sister than Brenda. She is absolutely wonderful to me, doesn't get in my face, and would do anything to help and support me. Edward, whom I couldn't stand for years, has turned out to be a really good, first-class person. What's more, he looked after my mother when she was ill and I was abroad.

Brenda did a series of extraordinary things. Quite late in life she went to university and at one point she worked for a large construction company that planned to build a bypass in Devon. There was a huge controversy about the intended bypass because the local people didn't want the landscape obliterated.

Meanwhile, as I was considered a local celebrity I was asked to put my weight – insubstantial – behind a campaign to oppose the road. I did so.

Brenda and I found ourselves in the bizarre situation where sister was building it and brother was fighting against it. At that time, my relationship with Brenda was pretty non-existent and we never discussed the bypass face to face. It was only a decade or so later that we were able to sit and talk about it, and laugh about it.

FIVE

It was bucketing down in Montfrin today.

Montfrin is a small town in Provence that sits between Avignon and Nîmes, and is an hour's drive from the French south coast and the sea. Like Wivey, it has the village feel about it and I am drawn to such places.

For much of the year Montfrin is baked by Mediterranean sun, which can be dodged by wandering the narrow, cool, cobbled streets, which are dark and shaded by tall medieval houses.

And the Café du Commerce, in the town's little square, is the hub and has a shaded terrace, where the locals natter while drinking rosé, pastis with its pungent whiff of aniseed, whisky or even coffee, and watch the comings and goings; a boy leaves the *boulangerie* clutching half a dozen baguettes and accidentally drops the load on the road as he cycles up the hill; a stream of men and women pop into the *tabac* to blow a few euros on cigarettes and a few more on Lotto, the national lottery; a distinctive large, bearded man drives slowly past the café in his black Rolls-Royce, returning to his chateau at the top of the hill, where the yield of his olive trees provides him with an award-winning oil.

Not much happens in Montfrin, apart from Life.

That is, not much except the flood of 2002, during which

the population decreased by one when an elderly man drowned, and the residents – many of whom saw their possessions swept away in the waters – were united, were brought together, by the need for food . . . the need to survive.

And not much happens except for the dramatic arrest of a drugs cartel a few years before the flood, said to have been the biggest ever cocaine bust in France. The images of cows floating down streets and gun-wielding police performing dawn raids might be considered off-putting for prospective housebuyers.

But I love this place. Montfrin, as far as I am concerned, is dead ordinary. It hasn't got any antique shops. It hasn't got any painters pretending to be famous. It hasn't got geraniums hanging from window boxes.

In 2000 I bought a house here, with the ambition to make it my permanent base, and the ambition has since been achieved. Then I was married to my fourth wife, Tess; now she is my ex-wife.

Nevertheless, I am here in Montfrin today, thinking back to my childhood in Wivey and to my mother. She was an amazingly intuitive cook but she felt ashamed of her cooking.

Mum firmly believed that because she wasn't using the most expensive ingredients then she was not giving the best to her family. She was totally unaware that, in fact, she was cooking the equivalent of classic French country dishes: tasty, wholesome, nutritious food. The pigs' trotters or the snails from the privet fence, or tripe, or salt cod: she thought all these foods were inferior and she was ridden with guilt because she couldn't afford anything else.

In France, Italy and the Mediterranean these dishes are considered to be the height of gastronomy and husbandry.

Mum didn't know this though. She did not know how good she was. So there was my father who, despite overseeing the household accounts, was not mean, and my mother, who was extravagant but thought she was mean. And work that one out.

Alas, I didn't inherit my mother's ability to bake. Now, give me any kind of fire, whether it's a dried Indian cowpat, which is like a piece of dried turf in Ireland, or give me some vine roots, or charcoal or gas flame and I am pretty sure I can cook anything, anywhere. But I do not have the fingers that go with pastry, bread and cakes. You either have, or you have not.

It is, incidentally, an accepted fact that the route to becoming a brilliant cook is either through the patisserie side of things or through the charcuterie side. Two examples are those culinary giants, brothers Albert and Michel Roux. Michel, who earned Michelin stars at the Waterside Inn by the Thames in Bray, became an apprentice baker in France at fourteen years old. Albert, who earned Michelin stars at Le Gavroche, became an apprentice sausage maker. Michel went the pastry way, Albert the meat way.

When I met Gordon Ramsay for the first time he was Marco Pierre White's pastry chef and he was very good at pastry. I'm not and I find that a problem at all times. I love eating desserts but I can't create them.

Nevertheless, my mother could cook and she was the one who gave me a passion for food and cooking. So I have my mother to thank, as well as Mother Nature because, you see, my childhood was spent outdoors, deep within the countryside, gathering things to eat.

I remember foraging for mushrooms in the misty September mornings and picking blackberries in the sweltering days of

August. I remember collecting elderberries for my father to make his dreadful elderberry wine.

There were the frozen Sundays in November, when I picked the frosted Brussels sprouts from the garden, and the mornings when I lifted the potatoes before peeling them for Sunday lunch.

I gathered chestnuts and beech nuts under foot, and cob nuts from the hedgerows. And I remember fishing, still a favourite pastime of mine, and catching trout – though my friends and I didn't even know it was trout. I'd spend time with my mother in the kitchen, maybe licking out the bowl for the Christmas puddings, which she made in September.

You cannot lead a childhood like that and not consider yourself blessed.

But then life changed. It has a habit of doing so.

Brenda, who was considered the brains of the family, had previously passed her eleven plus (and has since acquired degrees in lots of things), but I was seen as a different story.

In short, my parents were convinced that I was thick and were afraid I wouldn't pass the eleven plus. So they sent me to Wellington School to sit the common entrance examination. If I passed I would be assured of an 'assisted' place: my parents would receive a grant but still have to contribute to the fees – a modest sum perhaps for many people, though not for them.

I passed! But then I thought, why are my parents doing this to me? Why do they think I am thick?

This was bizarre. There I was, the raw ten-year-old Somerset kid from the village suddenly cast into a public school, where the other boys had fathers who were MPs, accountants, barristers and airline pilots. I was very much the outsider.

The other boys at Wellington wore smart uniforms, while my clothes were made by my mother. As well as looking after the family, she worked hard on the looms in that mill, making cloth. She was able to buy cloth at a discount because it was slightly flawed, thus providing her with the material that would become my uniform.

My fellow pupils wore black toe-capped Oxford brogues while I had Tuf shoes, the Doc Martens of the day. Although ugly, Tufs were revolutionary and popular because they had an all-in-one sole and heel moulding, which meant they infrequently required repair – not good for my grandfather's business.

I was embarrassed not to have the manners, the wherewithal and the skills of my peers. The Floyds had nothing but the families of these boys owned large houses and expensive cars; one lad was from Persia and particularly interesting because his dad drove a Cadillac.

Were the other lads sensitive to me? They got sensitive quite quickly because of my fists. There was the risk of bullying, intimidation or mockery because I was clearly from a different background and if the other boys attempted to tease or intimidate me I wouldn't take it. I'd just whack them. Maybe it was here that I first realized the rights of equality. I dislike prejudice.

Later, as an adult, I hit a few people though I don't go around picking fights. In fact, I am more the peacemaker and if I see a squabble I am inclined to try to calm everybody down.

I loved long-distance running, though not in this instance because I was influenced by *The Loneliness of the Long-Distance Runner*. But I was greatly affected by the northern writers like Sillitoe and Keith Waterhouse. I sometimes wondered if I was Billy Liar, trapped in a small town dreaming of escape. And *Saturday Night and Sunday Morning*, although it took place in the north, quite clearly reflected to some degree the lifestyle of my fabulous Uncle Ken (who you will meet later). Anyway, I looked forward to winter because it meant rugby, a sport at which I excelled. I played flanker, small but fast and hard, and there's one word that doesn't ordinarily enter my vocabulary. It's *fear*. I have no fear. I could tackle the biggest boy and didn't care if I broke my nose. In fact, I did break my nose. And it was through my sporting abilities that I got on to terms with being at a public school.

We played away at Millfield and beat them, which was fantastic because Millfield prides itself on having produced the best athletes and sportsmen, and generally the best people in the world.

Good food was the reward for playing. I remember when we played at Blundell's School, in Tiverton, and after the match we were treated to a spectacular tea of rich fruit cake, brown bread and honey, jam and scones, as well as Shipham's potted meat and potted crab.

I also loved school dinners at Wellington. We had boiled ham with parsley sauce and butter beans, and beef stew and dumplings. It was substantial, plain, unsophisticated food cooked by quite terrifying, busty middle-aged women, and I thought it was brilliant.

Academically, I was, curiously, very good at English. I won the essay competition at the age of twelve, when I wrote a story that began, 'Where the balls of sweat dripped off the tethered horses like droplets of mercury and splattered into the ochre, midday sand . . .'

When I'd finished reading my words to the class, the master said, 'You've just taken that off the television.' I hadn't. I was good at French but Physics, Maths and Latin, don't even go there. My Latin master once said to me, 'I would rather try to teach the school roller [for the cricket pitch] Latin than you.'

Once I got into the rhythm of it, I really enjoyed my time at Wellington. The masters were cool – it's a horrible word, *cool*, but they were. They wore suede waistcoats and suede shoes or neat brogues. They were groovy and it was, after all, the fifties, the era of rock 'n' roll. When instructed to deliver a public speech, I addressed my fellow pupils with an audio-illustrated lecture about the life and times of Elvis Presley.

Then there was the mysterious case of the dirty magazine. My father had made me a wonderful wooden box for my fishing tackle, and the box also served as a seat. I went off to Sedgemoor Drain but instead of catching fish I found floating in the water some mildly erotic magazines called *Health and Efficiency*.

The pages contained photos of bare-breasted women, who were unattractive but who happened to be nudists in a nudist camp. Coincidentally, at school another pupil had been found with a 'dirty magazine', as it was called in those days, and after prayer meeting in the morning, the headmaster addressed the school about 'the circulation of these dirty magazines'.

And because of the association with my having found a completely unconnected *Health and Efficiency* magazine I blushed. The headmaster spotted my reddening cheeks and initially I was considered guilty of what I hadn't done, though a kind housemaster was given the chore of interrogation and believed me when I explained my innocent discovery of *H&E*

and insisted that I knew nothing of the dirty magazines that were doing the rounds.

I didn't want to leave Wellington. It was a life of playing fields and old-fashioned values. But my parents weren't able to maintain the fees that would have seen me through the sixth form.

I left in 1960 at the age of sixteen and it took me years to forgive them for taking me out of the school. It didn't cross anybody's mind that I should go to college to do A levels. In those days, at sixteen it was time to go and get a job. I did, however, do a night class in A-level English literature, but when I became a reporter I felt I didn't need the A level so ditched the course.

Just as I had got used to it and understood the rules, it was all change. I was dumped into reality. It hurt me badly for a long time and I never sat my parents down and openly shared my true emotions, my feelings of sadness at having to leave.

I doubt Mum and Dad would have understood the enjoyment that can be had at school.

They kept a station in life which was very worthy, I would say, but very old-fashioned. School, they would have agreed, wasn't to be enjoyed. It was an institution you attended in order to achieve qualifications to equip you for life so that you could get a job which would, in turn, get you a pension. Mum and Dad were intimidated by authority; the bank manager was called 'sir' and the headmaster was called 'sir'.

Many years later, when I was able to take my father for those wonderful lunches and dinners, we were at a restaurant table chatting away and the subject of Wellington came up.

Dad said to me, 'You've got to understand something.

Throughout your life, as a child, as a teenager, as a journalist, as an officer cadet, it's the first experience you've had of these things. But it's also the first experience I've had of them. I didn't know what it was like to have a ten-year-old son. I put you into public school because I thought it was good for you. I didn't know it would do you any harm.'

There was a pause. Then he added, 'And I never drank until I met you.'

And he didn't, except for Christmas, when the adults of my family had those funny sticky drinks, played cards in the smoke and gave each other tins of fifty Player's cigarettes.

While still at Wellington, and after observing Brenda pocketing the bus fare and then using her hidden bicycle to get to school, I thought I'd follow her example. Mum would give me the bus fare, but I'd walk to Wellington, thereby making myself richer by a few pence.

Some days I would leave home, and set off on the seven-mile trek to Wellington, trying to thumb a lift from a passing car in order to conserve my energy. And some days I would set off, and then a dark-green Bentley would pull up beside me, and I'd hear a voice: 'Jump in.'

The driver, the lucky owner of this magnificent car, was a doctor who lived nearby and whose journey to work took him right past the school gates. I would sit beside this kind man, take in the wonderful smell of leather, and say to myself, 'One day I am going to have one of these. One day I'll have a Bentley.'

Fast-forward to the spring of 1988 . . . By now I was making quite a few quid, having established myself as a success on television. The headmaster of Wellington contacted me to see if I'd be willing to return to the school to present prizes on commemoration day. Me? Me, who left Wellington with three and a half O levels?

I accepted the invitation and decided to go in style. If I have ever had aspirations or ambitions, then they are based on having a sense of style, and I like to believe that when I am at my best I have a great deal of style, in things I choose, the way I behave. You can't buy style but if I do have it then I think I inherited a bit of it from Wellington; that's when I read about style, as described by the likes of F. Scott Fitzgerald. As a boy I was outrageously precocious.

At the time of the headmaster's phone call I owned a Jaguar coupé, which was great fun but certainly not stylish enough for arrival at Wellington. I went to the Bristol showroom where I'd bought the Jag and asked the owner if I could borrow a Rolls-Royce for the day.

On a Friday in May, at nine in the morning, I turned up at Wellington in the Roller and was greeted by the sight of a massive marquee. There was a service in the Chapel of St Michael and St George, during which a soloist sang 'Jesu, Lover of My Soul', and it ended with an organist playing a toccata. I was not the President of the United States on the White House lawn, but I may as well have been. After the service, and as we stood on the grass by the Great Hall, a corps of drums did a march past in my honour.

I handed out the prizes, and gave the most bizarre speech which I based on Bob Dylan's 'The-Times They Are A-Changin'', the core of which was something like: 'If you haven't won prizes don't worry because your turn will come, as mine did.' The kids loved it and even the stuffiest members of the board of governors enjoyed my approach.

I returned to the showroom to hand back the Rolls-Royce

and said to the man who'd lent me the car, 'Thanks very much. How much do I owe you?'

He said, 'No, no, it's free.' Off I went.

I didn't particularly like the Roller. Also, there is an adage: 'Gentlemen drive Bentleys. Rolls-Royces are driven by chauffeurs.' It is one that left an impression on my strange mind. I didn't have a chauffeur so thought it would be correct to own a Bentley, but Zoe, my girlfriend at the time, believed that to own such a make of car was the mark of an ostentatious, pompous, pretentious man.

Whenever I raised the subject with her she said, 'If you get a Bentley I am going to leave you.' But there wasn't a long period of me constantly raising the subject.

Four days after returning the Rolls-Royce I was strolling past the same car showroom in Bristol, having just enjoyed a pint or two in a lovely little pub. Sitting on the showroom floor was a brand new white Bentley Mulsanne Turbo . . . resplendent, divine and unquestionably stylish, but with no price tag on it. I entered the showroom and spoke to the man who was by now a regular fixture in my life.

Pointing at the Bentley, I said, 'Look, I want that. I'll have it now.' I didn't ask the price, which was £88,000 (a couple of hundred grand in today's money). I'd arrived at the showroom by foot and left in the leather-seated, walnut-fasciaed luxury of the world's finest car.

Zoe has long gone. But the Bentley stayed. And when I later moved to Spain I sold it and bought another – a left-hand drive version – which loyally has remained with me ever since, even though it was once stolen.

SIX

So my dad never saw me make it.

He used to say, 'You ought to get a job at the Royal Mail. Earn £7 19s 6d a week and be a sensible person.' But I think he would have been satisfied that the sacrifices he made to send me to a fee-paying public school and then somehow twist it back into achieving something with my career in television . . . I think he would have very much appreciated that.

But he was a man without greed. I don't think he would have been impressed by my losing a cheque for £110,000 in a bar in a hotel in Sydney – money that I had collected from a week's work and that he had not been able to earn in a lifetime.

He'd say to me, 'Never a lender or a borrower be.' The words were lodged in my memory bank but I didn't follow the advice because throughout my life I have lent big and I have borrowed big.

I was leaving school and the Floyds were leaving Wiveliscombe. My father was made redundant but offered relocation in Bristol, which he took. We moved to a house in the Sea Mills area of Bristol, and for the first time in their lives my parents now had a home they could call their own, even though they had to pay a mortgage.

On my last day at Wellington, by which point I assumed

that I was like all the other boys, I went to the school shop and bought a worsted blazer and an old boy's tie, a pair of trousers, and an extremely nice pair of Church's black brogues.

I was not required to pay for the clothes there and then. Instead, all I had to do was sign a ticket, which I gaily did. When my school report came it included an end-of-term bill for extras. It didn't ask for settlement for the violin lessons, school trips or any of that, but just for the clothes shopping I had done on the final day. Everyone else was doing it, so I assumed I could too. I didn't know Dad earned seven pounds nineteen and six a week.

He looked at the bill and his face was filled with horror, and I mean real horror. It was like something out of *The Grapes of Wrath*, when they know the tank is out of petrol, the tyres have gone and California doesn't exist.

He said, 'I can't pay it.'

Somehow he managed to, but I needed to pay him back. I flitted in and out of admin jobs in order to raise the cash.

When I was sixteen I became a news reporter on the *Bristol Evening Post* and *Western Daily Press*. It was while working here that I was introduced to a wonderful restaurant which was without doubt inspirational. At the time food was nothing more than a commodity.

Food, you see, was just food. Olive oil was generally unknown and certainly not used, foreign ingredients were to be avoided, or tasted at your peril. 'Extra Virgin' would not have been allowed to appear on a bottle – far too rude. The term 'foodies', which I hate by the way, was decades away from being coined (thank goodness). Garlic? Forget it. Even if it was introduced to Britain by the Romans, it was deemed an acquired French taste and not to be found in most of our kitchens. You ate to live and did not live to eat. You ate but did not savour. If you want my advice then it is: before you can learn how to cook well you must first learn how to eat well.

Anyhow, my career as a reporter was short-lived and therefore I can take you through it with speed.

I was inspired by the film *The Day the Earth Caught Fire*, which was packed with disaster and journalists in trilby hats dashing around for their scoops. The film was partly notable because it featured Arthur Christiansen, the legendary post-war editor of the *Daily Express*.

One day I wrote to the *Bristol Evening Post* enquiring about vacancies and for some bizarre reason the editor, Richard Hawkins, agreed to see me.

To prepare myself for the interview I went out and bought a bow tie. It was the first of many, and bow ties would later become a Floydian trademark. To complete the image of a hack I also bought a trilby. If my intention was to look like a complete wally then I achieved it, but I was satisfied that I was just like one of the reporters in *The Day the Earth Caught Fire*, albeit a teenage version.

The day after the interview I began my brief career as a reporter, working for the *Post* and its sister paper, the *Western Daily Press*, and becoming colleagues with journalists who had to put together three daily editions of the paper. I was overwhelmed by the sight of the newsroom – the typewriters clickety-clacketing and the constant ring, ring, ring of scores of telephones. The rush, the buzz, the hurly-burly had me gripped.

The *Post* was printed in nearby Silver Street and you walked down criss-crossed metal stairs into the print room, where big rolls of paper were delivered and the air smelt of lead.

The front page carried the words 'The *Evening Post*. The paper all of Bristol wanted and helped to create.' It was an important paper.

The editor of the *Western Daily Press* was a man called Eric Price, who had worked for Christiansen. Eric despatched me to inquests and court hearings, and he sent me out on vice patrol to look for whores and drug dealers. Not that he wanted them for himself, but they might have a scoop to reveal.

Other members of staff included a young Tom Stoppard, who'd sit at the back of the newsroom in shades and smoking Gauloises.

The *Evening Post* had a children's column which for years had been written by one Uncle Bob before it was inherited by his son, Roger Bennett. Roger was a lovely man and a talented musician who played clarinet in the Blue Notes jazz band down at the Old Duke.

And the women's editor of the *Western Daily Press* was called Paddy and was in her late twenties. She was serene, gentle and incredibly beautiful with raven-black hair, high cheek-bones and a slender neck. I later learned she had been educated at Bristol University followed by the Sorbonne and spoke fluent French. Roger and Paddy lived virtually next door to each other in Clifton, and some nights I would babysit for their children.

One day, when I had been instructed by the editor to search for whores and drug dealers, a young boy fell in the canal. He nearly drowned but was rescued, and the incident was dramatic enough for Eric to instruct me to file a report. 'Today,'

I began, because that was the first word of all news reports, 'eleven-year-old Paul McMahon plunged off the lock gate into the canal. After the dramatic support of the fire brigade, he is being treated in . . .'

I typed out the story on folios, and happily filed it. Then Eric was beside me. 'What did the mother say?'

I said, 'Mr Price. The mother? She didn't say anything.'

'Yes she did,' he boomed, and then he took a folio and typed out: 'Paul's mother told the *Bristol Evening Post*, "I've said to that boy a dozen times never to play near the canal."'

I remember interviewing Eric Burdon and his band mates in the Animals. They were utterly unknown and playing a gig in the Corn Exchange in Bristol. In front of the Corn Exchange there are bronze nails and, in centuries past, corn merchants would stand there and buyers would come, fiddle with the corn, sniff it and do whatever you do with corn before making an offer. If the buyer approved of the crop, the merchant would say, 'Pay on the nail.'

The Corn Exchange had become a weekly music venue, run by a Chinese guy, where bands played and people danced to artistes like Lightnin' Hopkins, Sonny Terry and Muddy Waters. But on this particular night a band called the Animals were playing. They arrived in a beaten-up yellow camper van that had taken them from Scunthorpe to Gloucester to Taunton and Padstow and to who knows where.

They did a rendition of 'House of the Rising Sun' and made the one song last about fifteen minutes. It was electrifying. Afterwards, as the bow-tied teenager, I talked to Eric Burdon and said to him, 'That was incredible.'

Eric said, 'Man, we're fucked off. We're getting £10 a night.

There's five of us. And we've just recorded this song. The record company has shown no interest and we're going to quit. We've had it. Flogging up and down A roads, sometimes to play to twenty people in an audience, sometimes to a hundred. Squabbling all the way. Not eating properly. We're going to quit.'

Timing is everything. They stuck together long enough to see 'House of the Rising Sun' make number one in the following week's Hit Parade. Rock on.

My cub reporting days included an assignment to cover an under-fifteen football match at a ground in a suburb of Bristol. It was an important youth game and I didn't go. Instead I phoned the ground to get the result and then wrote up my story: 'Today in a very exciting match Eastfield Juniors swung to success in the final minute, with a header by . . .' I submitted the story to the news desk.

The news editor said, 'What about the fire?'

I said, 'Fire?'

'Yeah, the stadium burnt down.'

I covered several stories in Bristol Crown Court. I was hindered slightly as I couldn't do shorthand – the paper had offered to send me to college to learn the skill but I declined on the grounds that it was far too time-consuming and would take me away from the action.

One day an up-and-coming actor called Peter O'Toole turned up in Bristol to play Hamlet at Bristol Old Vic. We'd see him in the Naval Volunteer, which was opposite the theatre, and served a good pint of Guinness in the days when Guinness came in barrels from Dublin and wasn't brewed in Park Royal in London, as it is today.

One of the newspaper's executives, who was gay but legally wasn't allowed to be (as you weren't in those days), fancied

Peter to death, and whenever the actor walked into the pub with a lady, the executive would turn to me and hiss, 'I don't know what he sees in that girl.'

So I'd see Peter in the pub. And then one day I saw him in the dock.

He'd been nabbed for drink-driving and I can't for the life of me remember what happened to him, so I'll assume he was found not guilty as I am sure he would have been.

I dashed back to write up the story. Once done, I handed the folios to my editor. 'Were there other reporters in the court-room?' asked Richard.

I told him there was only me. In other words, I had an exclusive. I was the man – oh, OK, the bow-tied boy – with the scoop.

Then Richard ripped the pages in two and threw the paper into his bin. My story was 'spiked', as they say. Well and truly killed.

Why? Perhaps Richard had developed a soft spot for Peter. By keeping his name out of the paper, Richard had certainly done a favour for the actor. Peter was lined up to star in *Lawrence of Arabia* but had been told by studio bosses that if he found himself in trouble (even if he was not guilty) then he'd be out of the picture. The spiking of my story enabled Peter to go on and make the movie that would make him.

When I was working for Richard Hawkins I met Peter O'Toole a couple of times and was fascinated then, as now, by his charm and consummate skill as an actor. Peter once said sardonically that if he did something good in films or the theatre he was celebrated as a British actor. If he ever found himself in trouble, i.e. being pissed or in a brawl, he was described as an Irish actor. I encountered him as an adult too.

We've had drinks in the Dorchester and I remember a day in the pub, somewhere in London, probably Greek Street, when we were standing at the bar and he produced a pen from his pocket.

He said, 'Do you realize you can draw the face of a moon on the head of Guinness?' and proceeded to draw the moon's face, complete with smile, on the creamy white top of his pint of stout.

I might not have enjoyed watching my editor Richard rip up my report but I feel indebted to him, first, for giving me an opportunity, and second, for introducing me to food that I had never before seen, that I did not know existed.

Richard took a shine to me, and saw me as a sort of personal assistant. He would take me to his meetings with politicians and the so-called pillars of Bristol society, and my job was to take notes of what was being said. In fact, I wasn't really his personal assistant. That's far too grand a description. I was more like his servant.

A highly intelligent man, Richard was crucially a gastronaut; he loved fine cuisine, and as I was at his table with my notepad for his dinner and lunch meetings, I was also treated to meals in restaurants that I could never have afforded on my cub reporter's salary.

He took me one day to a restaurant called the Hole in the Wall, which was famous in Bath, and I remember vividly walking into the Hole for the first time and the sight before me.

There was a table of hors d'oeuvres, a veritable laden table – mushrooms à la grecque, ratatouille, taramasalata, three kinds of pâtés and terrines, as well as roasted red peppers with chopped garlic.

It was just amazing food that most British adults, let alone teenagers, would never have seen. It was exotic.

I had partridge braised in cabbage with a sauce of Gewürztraminer and juniper berries, and pommes dauphinoises (the dish of creamy layers of sliced potato that we take for granted these days, but in the sixties it was mind-boggling). The meal ended with chocolat Saint-Emilion, a chocolate mousse with biscuits that had been drenched in marc, and a dessert I would give to my own customers years later.

The Hole in the Wall became a favourite treat and it was run by a wonderful bearded man, George Perry-Smith, a former public school master. Just in case his happy customers didn't quite realize that he was an eccentric, George wore sandals and a long apron to drive home the point.

He looked biblical and indeed wouldn't have been out of place at the Last Supper (and his culinary skills would have made him a welcome addition). I found him quite intimidating – he *was* intimidating – but one day I plucked up the courage to ask him about the food he served. I wanted to know how he knew so much about gastronomy. 'Where does all this knowledge come from?' I asked.

And he replied with his usual supreme confidence, 'Oh, quite simple, dear boy. Just read Elizabeth David.'

We can go back to my father at this point. He was never particularly impressed that I became a reporter. The job involves total commitment, whether it be working in the newsroom late at night or having a rewarding pint with colleagues in the pub, again late at night.

The young, ambitious reporter strives for a byline and I considered it an achievement when I got my first at the age of sixteen: 'By Keith Floyd'.

Dad, however, did not share my enthusiasm for the life of a hack. It was a six-mile walk from the city centre to home, but if I came back after ten o'clock I'd find the doors locked. Cold and tired, I had to spend the night trying to sleep in the coal shed. If you're looking for a night of blissful sleep, don't do coal sheds.

Dad would say, 'You've got ambitions beyond your dreams, beyond your capabilities.' Though apart from the byline, my burning ambition most days was to get home before ten so I'd have the warmth of a bed.

Anyhow, I left. The pace was too much, I was overly ambitious, probably too precocious, and just couldn't hack it. I worked here and there for a while, before giving about an hour's consideration as to whether or not I should join the army.

Thoughts of cold nights in the coal shed remind me, incidentally, of filming *Floyd's Fjord Fiesta*. We've moved forward now to the turn of this century and we have zoomed from Bristol to the chilled border of Russia and north-east Sweden.

The snow was neat and deep. Overnight I had seen Arctic foxes and ptarmigans, which look a little like grouse. Ptarmigans moult three times a year, each time producing a different set of feathers to match the tundra and therefore provide camouflage. In winter, as it was when we went to film, the bird's feathers are white to match the snow; in summer, it has a new set of brown-grain feathers so that it is disguised among the rocks and soil.

My assistant, Scott, had dug me a trench and I had set up my fire. Behind me, in silhouette, stand the stalking watchtowers, the watchtowers that pervade Russia.

I had a leg of bear. I slashed its skin and stuffed little lardons of bacon and slivers of garlic into the incisions.

Over several hours sitting in my ice trench I cooked the beast. It tasted, since you ask, like a wonderful leg of pork. And with aquavit – meaning water of life, but dramatically alcoholic – and arctic berries I made a kind of cranberry sauce. In fact the berries were lingonberries and are related to the cranberry. They make a good jam, which the Scandinavians like to spread on pancakes.

It's funny, I remembered that song about Simon Smith and his dancing bear. Today the brown bear has become extinct in Spain, and in Eastern Europe, I do believe, is still used for sport and bear-baiting. And around the Arctic Ocean, the polar bear faces extinction . . . I had a passing twinge of guilt about cooking that bear, but I am not a platform for any environmental protest group. It is just what the people there did. I merely reflected that in my programme.

I've never kept any of my books, and don't have any videos of my shows. I *never* sit and watch myself on TV. But my mother kept my newspaper cuttings. They were not cuttings of my reports, my stories that appeared in the *Bristol Evening Post* and *Western Daily Press*. They were newspaper cuttings about me, rather than written by me. The stories were about Floyd, the television cook.

She kept them all; from the first articles about me, following my success with *Floyd on Fish*, right up to the day she died, a zillion or so programmes later. She carefully cut out the pieces – features, news reports, gossip stories, television reviews – and stuck them into scrapbooks. These were then put into boxes and eventually they ended up with me and I, in turn, put them into suitcases. I have a lot of suitcases.

A few years ago I was burgled – it was extremely nasty and I'll come to it later. The crooks made off with the suitcases of cuttings. Mistakenly, they thought the cases contained cash, jewels and gems. But scrapbooks of clippings that chronicle my career are not worth much on the French black market, so I imagine they ended up in the Rhône, which is half a mile from my home in Montfrin.

However, a box of cuttings remains and I've just been going through it, hoping to jog a few memories. One of the scrapbooks contains an article from the *Bristol Evening Post* but sure enough it was not written by me.

Instead it's a page-long feature written by a journalist called Rebecca Gooch, who interviewed me and whose piece was published on 31 July 1987. At the time I had separated from my second wife, Julie, and I am quoted: 'Quite a while ago I went and had my palm read and she told me that the woman I was waiting for was a long, long way off and that I was a very tortured person but that I would become famous and very successful and go and hide in the country in a lovely house, with chickens in the courtyard.'

Rebecca Gooch observes in her article: 'He says it with the longing of a man who knows that this is just what he wants to do, preferably with a skin-warming Provence sunset, a glass of fine wine, and a comfy chair to go with it. So what's stopping him? "It will happen . . ." he says.'

Hang on. Have the chickens been fed today?

SEVEN

Before becoming a reporter I had seen *The Day the Earth Caught Fire*. And now, for my next career, I was again inspired by a night at the cinema.

I went to see *Zulu*, the true story of the depleted British army regiment that fought a million or so Zulu warriors . . . and some of them lived to tell the tale so that decades later it could be turned into entertainment for moviegoers.

As with *The Day the Earth Caught Fire*, I was foolishly taken by the whole business. The following morning I put on my bow tie, trilby and a trenchcoat and walked into the army recruiting office, a definite spring in my step. 'I want to be a soldier,' I announced.

I had been fascinated by the First World War and I thought it would be a challenge. I thought it would sort of help me finish off my public school education; provide me with a sense of being someone. I am not a rebel, more of an adventurer, but only once I have made the plans. I don't rush in like a headless chicken, although it might look that way. I certainly didn't see it as a job for life. My parents were extremely proud of my decision to sign up.

I underwent a training period and at the time it was normal military procedure for soldiers to be put through the most punishing physical endurance tests. There were also interrogations during which we were grilled as if we had been captured by the Russians.

I underwent the training period, after which we were sent on exercise from Aldershot to Wales, to the Brecon Beacons. I said, 'Boys, on the way we'll stop at my mum's. She's quite a good cook.' The boys included Jamie Douglas-Home, who was nephew of the prime minister, Sir Alec Douglas-Home; the Honourable Kim Fraser, son of Lord Lovat; and Charles Blount, who I believe is the father of James Blount the pop singer. James changed the spelling of his surname because Americans can't pronounce Blount, just as Led Zeppelin were originally Lead Zeppelin but changed it because they thought Americans would pronounce it 'Leed'. Anyway, as usual my mother excelled herself, giving to me and my hungry friends her home-made bread, lamb and onion sauce, pea and ham soup, and coconut icing to finish.

I was selected to be one of the hundreds of soldiers to line the route for Winston Churchill's funeral, and it would be nice to say that I had done it. But before the occasion, in trying to do something clever I had inadvertently shot my bed in the barrack room with live rounds of ammunition, and was promptly barred from going.

My commissioning parade, meanwhile, had all the pomp and ceremony of such events. My parents came to watch and after the ceremony my father spoke to the platoon commander, the interestingly named Captain Kitchen.

I was embarrassed because throughout their brief chat my father referred to him as 'sir'. Afterwards, I said, 'Dad, you don't need to call him "sir". You are the boss here.' A man of humility, my father failed to get the point.

As with journalism, I did not have the longest career in army history. Perhaps it was one of the shortest. But again, I found myself in a position where I was reunited with the potential joys of food and the army is therefore pertinent to my story.

I was made a lieutenant in the Royal Tank Regiment, was in charge of three tanks, and was posted to Germany.

When you're a soldier and keeping fit, food becomes a pre-occupation. After sex, it's the main topic of conversation. What dawned on me, and would have been clear to anyone else with half a palate, was that in the officers' mess we didn't get the same quality rations as they received in the sergeants' mess or the soldiers' mess.

What's more, we had to pay sixpence a day towards the cost of our meals. I thought, here we are in Germany and yet we are having brown Windsor soup, plaice with a horrible cheese sort of sauce on it, and overcooked lamb. This is crazy. We have German cooks in the kitchen and we could be eating the local hare and country terrines.

At this point, George Perry-Smith's words came back to me: 'Oh, quite simple, dear boy. Just read Elizabeth David.' I had a word with the mess cook, who was appropriately named Corporal Feast. In fact, he wasn't appropriately named unless you consider brown Windsor soup and overcooked lamb a feast. His name was ambitious rather than apposite.

We devised a harmonious sort of partnership which worked like this: I told Corporal Feast how to cook terrine, which was information gleaned from my book by Elizabeth David, and in exchange he taught me how to cook the basics as well as training me how to use a knife when slicing and chopping.

It terrifies me that people are so casual with sharp knives. You should place your fingers on the chopping board and run the knife down your fingernails, which will prevent you from cutting yourself with the blade. As with so much in cooking, the key is simplicity and discipline. What good is a cook, or cookette, with bleeding hands?

Originally, I was supposed to organize functions on behalf of the mess and not set foot in the kitchen. But before long I was spending too much time at the stove with Corporal Feast and less time playing with my tanks.

High-level discussions took place between the war department and my people and it was decided that short of making me Major General Sir Mike Jackson there was little point in us pursuing our parallel careers.

In fact, that's not how it happened, though in the past I have always said something funny about my departure from the army. The real story is a little harsher.

I had a nervous breakdown in the second year of my three-year commission. Or rather, I was told that I was having a nervous breakdown.

My memory tells me that I was bored and frustrated with the army, so I sat in the mess most of the day, reading Evelyn Waugh and drinking German wine. I couldn't play in the tanks because we had no petrol!

All I can remember is that I had some sort of collapse and then I found myself in a military hospital in Germany. From there I was transported back to a psychiatric hospital on the south coast of England.

The hospital was Indian in its architecture, with the obligatory men in white coats pacing the wards, and the patients included an RAF pilot who had been flown back from Vietnam. People didn't know we were involved in Vietnam, but we had been. The pilot and other patients would play conkers with their Rolex watches. They had all gone completely loopy.

I think I spent several weeks there, constantly protesting my sanity and finally I was brought before a tribunal. My superiors who sat upon the tribunal were fair men with kind words and, having listened to reports of my obsession with the mess kitchen, one of them said, 'It's quite clear that you have a passion for food. Would you like to transfer to the Army Catering Corps?'

I said no because by then I had decided that I wanted to join a parachute regiment that was affiliated to a tank regiment. I was looking for excitement.

'Well, you have two choices,' said the officer leading the tribunal. 'If you would like to go into the Catering Corps we will transfer you straight away. Otherwise, you can leave the army.'

I chose the latter. I was given a medical discharge from the army on the grounds that I was 'temperamentally unsuitable'.

I came out of the army and decided to become a cook. I loved food. I had discovered I enjoyed cooking. And I liked eating. It seemed a sensible path to take.

So, dressed in my Chukka boots, a three-piece suit and regimental tie, I marched into the Royal Hotel in Bristol and asked to speak to the manager.

Why Bristol, rather than London or Paris? I'd done George Orwell, thank you. Besides Bristol, as we know, is the centre of the universe: ask anyone in Bristol and they will tell you that.

When the manager appeared at the front desk, I said, 'Hello, I'd like to be a cook and wondered if you had a job going.'

He took in the sight of the smartly dressed young man –

me – standing in front of him, and said, 'Sorry? What? Don't you mean you'd like to be in management?' The manager was astonished because in those days the bloke who became a chef was the bloke who had failed to get on to the bricklayers' course. There weren't – to use that nasty phrase – celebrity chefs to inspire middle-class young men and women to take up a career in the kitchen.

I was taken to the kitchens of the Royal and introduced to the head chef, who was like Swelter from Mervyn Peake's novel *Gormenghast**, and so rigid in his starched whites that if you bent him he'd suddenly crack. We had a brief chat but he had a look of disdain in his eyes, his body language sending the certain message that he didn't really want to hire a second lieutenant, public-school-educated chap to be a cook in his kitchen.

Behind him were coal-fired ranges and on the stoves grey liquid bubbled away in huge cauldrons. Pimply-faced youths with scruffy aprons and runny noses were burning things and killing things. To me it was exciting.

Chef tutted, 'Oh, I don't know,' but I wasn't budging – I am not a quitter – and eventually he said, 'I'll tell you what. What is the difference between a waiter and a bucket of shit?' This was a life-changing question and I knew it.

I stood with my hands behind my back to show that I had no fear. And then I said, 'Sir, I think it's the bucket.'

It's always nice when you answer correctly, and Chef was suitably impressed but I still had a way to go before landing the job. My next feat, the second challenge, was to obey his command, 'Go and cook this beetroot.' He handed me the vegetable and really wanted me to mess up. He thought I was

---

* I'm going to write another book soon, called *Gourmetghast*.

going to peel it, but because I had been brought up by my mum, I know that you cook beetroot in its skin and peel it after it is cooked. I boiled and then peeled, rather than peeling before boiling.

I was hired.

The Royal was Bristol's most prestigious hotel and the signature dish – though dishes had yet to be called signature dishes – was roast duckling in orange sauce. This excited me as I had never before seen roast duckling.

I stood in utter astonishment, astonished in a bad way rather than a good way. The runny-nosed, spotty-faced youths put about twenty free-range ducks into the ovens and cooked them to buggery so that the skin on their legs was almost peeling itself away from the once glorious bird.

Then the overcooked ducklings were put in the cold room. Hours and hours later, when the order was called for duck à l'orange, half of the bird was cut and dumped into the big cauldron of grey liquid to be warmed through. The duckling was then removed and placed under the grill.

Little white paper ruffles were put on the bird's feet, and it was placed on a silver platter. Then in a beautifully burnished, copper-lined saucepan the chef ladled out a dollop of brown liquid and covered the meat with it. This brown liquid was sauce espagnole, traditionally a slowly cooked sauce from the days of Escoffier (and also known as brown sauce). In this kitchen it was a multi-purpose sauce, used in the preparation of most of the menu's dishes.

The finishing touch to the duck was three tablespoons of Cooper's Oxford marmalade, which were heaped on to the sauce espagnole that was on top of the meat.

The cloche, that bell-shaped silver dome, was placed over the dish and there you have it. The plate was whisked away by the waiter. As chefs don't like waiters and vice versa, an essential requirement of duck à l'orange – and all other dishes for that matter – involved heating the cloche to such a high temperature that when the waiter appeared at the guests' table and went to remove it, his fingerprints would be scorched away.

As blisters formed on the waiter's fingertips, he was then required to pour some form of lethal alcohol over the food and set alight to it at the table in front of the guest.

My job was to peel vegetables but, somehow, one Sunday night I was put in charge of the kitchen. Sunday was traditionally a night when there weren't many customers in the restaurant. Suddenly the order came through for lobster bisque. I thought, Christ, what do I do?

In a panic I turned to the kitchen porter – the man who does the washing-up – and said, 'Someone wants lobster bisque.' I envisaged having to find the lobster, boil it, slice it and remove the flesh.

The kitchen porter pointed to a corner of the room and said casually, 'Oh, it's in the cupboard over there.' Sure enough, the cupboard contained magnificent soups . . . all in tins. It was heartbreaking.

EIGHT

I became disillusioned with the kitchens at the Royal Hotel. This wasn't the stuff of George Perry-Smith. Yet I had no intention of quitting the business.

And so began a nomadic existence, and I'm not quite sure if it has ever ended though I dearly wish it would. I toiled away in one kitchen after another, on the way to having my own place several years later.

Bristol happened to be the place where omelette bars were invented. Omelettes had been served in French bistros for centuries, of course, but as far as Bristolians were concerned the omelette bar was born in their city. There were probably ten of them in Bristol, each serving thirty different types of omelette. There was, the menu told customers, 'the Royal Imperial Bristol omelette containing five eggs and seven further ingredients; the Bombay omelette with curried shrimps and eight spices of the Orient'. It was all rubbish, but brilliant and successful. I got a job as an omelette chef, making thousands of omelettes a night.

I also did a couple of seasons feeding summertime tourists in the restaurants of Cornwall. There, I worked for a man known as Wheelhouse Willie, who had a place in Port Isaac.

He ran a beamed waterside restaurant that sold clotted-cream teas in the afternoon and dinners in the evening. Wheelhouse Willie had exceptionally high standards of hygiene and you actually had to polish the bottoms of the saucepans after washing them up. If you didn't then you were in for a whack because Wheelhouse Willie was also a man with a fierce temper.

From time to time he'd get very drunk and then bash whoever happened to be closest to him at the time. We cooked lobsters and funny things like chicken Maryland with fried bananas and pineapple, and we also served prawn cocktails. It was all typical of the time, and actually they are all wonderful things. I like them.

My stint with Wheelhouse Willie included an episode when I had the living daylights knocked out of me.

One night the waitresses and I had a night off and they said, 'Fancy coming to the dance in Wadebridge?'

I said, 'No, I don't.' Wadebridge was a nearby town and frankly I wasn't up for country dances in the town hall. So of course I went. At least it would take me away from Wheelhouse and his flailing fists.

The boys from Port Isaac didn't like the boys from Wadebridge and vice versa, as I discovered when I was attacked.

One of the Wadebridge lads believed, incorrectly, that I was going out with one of the waitresses, his girlfriend. I was completely innocent. I hadn't even danced with her. I hadn't danced with anybody for that matter. I just sat at the bar drinking and thinking, I wonder who Wheelhouse is thumping at the moment. There were shouts of 'Leave my girl alone', and all that and I was beaten to a pulp.

It didn't take long for the Port Isaac boys to find out that I'd been smashed up. Now, the Port Isaac boys were all fishermen and very tough and one of them, Cyril Spry, was as hard as nails. He considered me a bit of a gentleman, something of a novelty and utterly harmless. 'Leave it to me,' he said and then he went off to find the bloke who hit me, who was well known for being a thug.

The lad who'd beaten me up was now, in turn, beaten up and had his arm broken in the process. Before long a mass fight had erupted and the police swarmed in. We all got arrested.

While waiting for the court case I lived in a caravan and worked at a restaurant called the Erenincan at Tintagel. It was run by a Frenchman, Marcel, who had been a waiter at the Savoy and here, in his own restaurant, he oversaw front-of-house.

His cockney wife was the cook and she worked like hell in the kitchen. My job was to help her, perhaps plucking pheasants or peeling spuds, and to wash up. Even though I'd worked in a few kitchens, at Erenincan I was not allowed to create at the stove.

Every night Marcel put on his dinner jacket and single-handedly silver-served the customers, doing all old-fashioned stuff like flambé on a lamp at the table. In his mind, Marcel was still in the dining room of the Savoy Grill in the fifties.

He was financially astute enough not to take on too many staff but once or twice, when he could do with a hand, he allowed me to put on a white shirt and a clip-on bow tie and assist him by pushing the trolley around in the dining room.

It was a bizarre and wonderful experience but it got to me in the end and when the season finished I felt I'd had enough, but I had certainly learned a good deal by observing Marcel and his cockney missus.

Meanwhile, there was the court case to face charges of causing an affray and the like. A motley crew were gathered before the magistrates, the tough nuts from Port Isaac, the hard cases from Wadebridge, and me in my bow tie.

By now I had set my sights on owning a restaurant and was anxious because, while I didn't know much about the business, I knew that if you had a criminal record you wouldn't be able to get a licence to serve alcohol.

Marcel found me a solicitor and in court I was treated very nicely. I was completely exonerated of any blame and the magistrates could sense my anxiety. One of them asked if the episode had deterred me from ever visiting Cornwall again. 'Not at all,' I said. 'I love Cornwall so much that of course I'll come back.' In fact, I had no intention of setting foot in the place ever again.

Marcel did have one other member of staff apart from me. He was a lad who came from Worcester and was a student out to earn a little money during the summer break from college. He was, therefore, in Marcel's eyes, cheap labour.

When we were reaching the end of the season it dawned on me that I had nowhere to go and didn't know what to do. In those days Cornwall shut down when the summer ended – that was the season done – so I would have to move on. The student said, 'Come to Worcester.'

Kindly, he suggested I stay with him for a fortnight – but not any longer because his landlord wouldn't like it – and I could use that time to find a job and a home of my own. We travelled to Worcester together and within a few days I presented myself at what was at the time the city's premier hotel, the Gifford. I now had a degree of experience and knew the culinary terms.

The kitchen at the Gifford operated within the traditional rankings of a kitchen in a restaurant in France. There was Chef, the master of the kitchen. Then there was his sous-chef, and then the head chefs of each department – from Fish, Sauce (which looks after meat dishes) through to Pastry and Larder. Each section had commis chefs who aspired to be head of a section.

I was hired as chef tournand, which meant that I had to fill in the gaps when other chefs had a day off, not in the executive positions as head of a section, but the deputy position of say Larder, Grill or Sauce. Effectively, I moved around the kitchen: hence *tournand*. However, one of my major jobs was to do breakfasts, cooking eggs, bacon, sausage and all the rest of it for 150 people.

The other young chefs were taking diplomas in cooking, taking a day off each week to study at college, and I was seen as jollying along because college wasn't for me. They took it very seriously and looked down on me, but I got on very well with the head chef.

I lived in the hotel and didn't like that one bit, partly because kitchen staff were instructed not to enter and leave via the front door of the hotel. It wouldn't be right to have pimply chefs in soiled aprons spoiling the grandeur of the place. By contrast, when eventually I would have my own places, my cooks were constantly on view to the customers in the dining room. But here the fun being had by guests was not on view to the brigade in the kitchen. (Apparently and incidentally the Gifford's pianist-singer in the bar was a young

man called Dorsey who turned into Englebert Humper-
dinck.)

There must have been some inner trauma or unhappiness
because other members of staff would find me wandering the
corridors sound asleep. I don't think I have sleepwalked since,
or if I have, then those who have found me have either not
told me the following morning or had no idea I was fast asleep
when they saw me.

I stuck at it for six months, when I was in my early twenties, and then a funny thing happened.

I was in touch with friends back in Bristol and one day I
got a phone call from a chap called Teddy Cowell. He was an
architect in the city and worked with David Bilk, brother of
the highly successful jazz musician Acker Bilk.

Over the phone and in his North Country accent, Teddy
explained to me how he and David had formed a company
called the Bilk Marketing Board, leaving a pause for me
to laugh because they both thought it was a terribly funny
name (there was, at the time, the Milk Marketing Board, you
see).

I continued to listen to Teddy's tale . . . He and David had
opened a coffee bar in the Mall in the Clifton part of Bristol.
'I've heard lots of good things about you,' said Teddy. 'Would
you like to come and run it?'

'Yes.'

I went into my room, packed my suitcase and within an
hour of Teddy's call I had left the Gifford. I didn't even say
goodbye, didn't hand in my notice and didn't collect my wages.
I just left. I told one of the other cooks, 'Please tell Chef I've
gone,' and no one ever pursued me.

*

I met up with Teddy at his restaurant, Number Ten (so named because it was 10, The Mall). Teddy was quite short, had a little pointed Sir Walter Raleigh beard and a head of reddish hair. He was slightly plump, had sparkling blue eyes and was full of energy and enthusiasm. His mantra, I'd quickly discover, was 'We're all Renaissance men here.' Full steam ahead, no job too big; that sort of thing.

The restaurant itself was nicely done and quite innovative for what must have been about 1967. It had a curved ceiling, there were posters depicting Spanish life, and on Saturdays a flamenco guitarist came to entertain the customers. By day it was a coffee bar, and in the evenings it tried to serve food, though the most popular dish was tinned ravioli.

Furthermore, it was in the right location because if you were a would-be Bristol restaurateur in the sixties, Clifton was the place to be.

The area was undeniably trendy, and had folk clubs, a jazz pub, and an old-fashioned French restaurant called Le Boeuf sur le Toit, known to its regulars by its English translation, the Ox on the Roof. It served *petites marmites Henri IV*, snails and frogs' legs. Steak Diane was flamed in the copper frying pan at your table. It was highly thought of, but not really that good I discovered with hindsight.

Across the road was a mean Swiss man, Guido, who cooked behind the bar of an open kitchen, pleasing his customers with Italian dishes of veal with mushroom and cream sauce, and kidneys with mushrooms in a cream sauce; everything was in a cream sauce in those days.

But he did make the most fabulous zabaglione.

At the time Clifton had real tailors, real antiques shops and real delicatessens. It was like a little Hampstead; really proper.

Now it has bouncers on the doors, Café Go-Go, if there is such a thing, and Est, as well as shop windows full of ladies' green shoes. I hate it.

As we stood together, looking at the dining room before us, Teddy said, 'The fashion is the bistro, lad. Turn this into a bistro.'

So I turned Number Ten into Bistro Ten, serving mostly French food.

I got rid of the tins of cannelloni and the scones, a move which annoyed everybody to death because they had previously regarded Number Ten as a cheap den: customers would stagger into the restaurant, having been kicked out of the pub, and order a bowl of tinned cannelloni between four of them; total cost was six pence.

So the tinned cannelloni was off the menu but I continued to serve omelettes – the ham ones were called Hamlets – and added dishes like beef stroganoff and scallops wrapped in bacon and grilled on a skewer.

Gradually, I built up a small but loyal clientele but could never get it right with that party of four or five men who regularly came together for lunch on Saturday. They were members of a gentlemen's club called the Clifton Club, which was just up the road and whose members were made up of estate agents, solicitors, auctioneers and businessmen. It was a very posh place, and to my amazement on Saturdays this clutch of Clifton members would turn up at Bistro Ten in their very well-cut suits and ties denoting the public school they had attended or the rugby club for which they played.

Every time I served them there was something wrong. A waiter would come and tell me of the problem: a slug in the lettuce, perhaps, or a cigarette end in the boeuf bourguignon.

I forever had to leave the stove, go to their table, hold my head in shame and say, 'Oh, I am terribly sorry. You can have it for free.'

They always took the table by the front window and one day a friend of mine was on the pavement outside and glanced in to the restaurant. He saw one of the Clifton club members take a matchbox from his pocket, and then remove a crunched snail from the box. The snail was then dumped on to the salad before the waiter was summoned to hear, 'I have a complaint. There's a snail in my lettuce.'

My friend came into the restaurant and then to the kitchen, and told me what he had just seen.

Enraged, I marched up to the table, effed and blinded and threw them out. '. . . And don't ever come near this place again . . .' So began a reputation that I had of being unreasonable. They were older than me and sharper than me and they had me on the run, so yes, that's when I started getting tough with customers.

It was here that I would gather experience of hiring staff.

I took on a waiter who had served for twenty-five years at the Royal Hotel. He came dressed in his dinner jacket, bow tie and all the rest of it and said, 'I do silver service.' He could do silver service up to about half past eight, by which time he would just collapse drunk on the floor. The next morning he was back, pleading for his job, and I'd always give in.

I took on a chef, a Dutchman called Peter, who was lovely, fast and quick at the stove, but was also wild and shagged anything – everything – that moved. He too liked a drink and after service he would go and get drunk and beat somebody up. Or he would arrive in the mornings badly bruised, having gone to a nightclub and been beaten up because he had mis-behaved terribly.

Then there was Enoch Hunt, one of Clifton's most famous characters, and in fact a man who has a bench in his honour in Clifton's park; the seat was bought by the city's residents.

Enoch was a frightfully large man, in his thirties and weighing eighteen stone at least. He always wore a three-piece suit and tie. Underneath the suit he wore his pyjamas (even in the summer).

On Saturdays he'd often sit on the pavement outside Bistro Ten playing his euphonium and passers-by tossed a coin into the hat beside him. His wealth was the subject of debate. He'd been a lawyer but something had gone wrong there, and along the way his rich family had decided he was the black sheep.

Enoch was pompous but highly intelligent, and I was in awe of him. I'd been in the back bar of the Greyhound pub and heard him pontificating in Latin. I used to think, my God, what an incredible brain.

One day I was in the bistro when the huge bulk of Enoch filled the doorway and the room simultaneously darkened, sunlight blocked by his substantial girth. He shuffled towards me and said in his amusingly pompous way, 'Good morning. I noticed in the window that you are advertising for a *plongeur*.' The ad in the window had said 'dish washer'.

He went on, 'I wonder if I may present myself as a suitable applicant for this position.'

I said, 'Surely a man of your calibre wouldn't want to wash up.'

'Oh well,' he said. 'I am on vacation for the summer.' He was unemployed.

So I hired him and that was the beginning of a long

relationship. He completed his first night's washing-up and said, 'I wonder if you could see your way clear to advancing me a few pounds against my stipend for the week.' This was to begin a pattern which one way or another didn't stop for the next five years.

The Bilk Marketing Board was expanding. Teddy and David Bilk had taken over a huge warehouse, the old granary, right on the waterfront in the docks of Bristol, and wanted to turn it into what was going to be Europe's premier jazz venue, and Bristol was a city full of jazz and famous for it.

I was called in to help design and run the large restaurant within the warehouse. The place opened with a spectacular fanfare. International jazz stars came to the party, as well as David's brother, Acker. It was an ambitious venture and, as it turned out, it was too good to be true.

Teddy did not have the best grasp of reality. He'd say, 'Just go up to the butcher's and say you want a hundred lamb chops at a shilling each,' when they weren't a shilling each. They were one and nine each. I couldn't battle with a butcher with fifty years' experience telling them they were a shilling each. But Teddy being North Country saw it that way.

Meanwhile, somehow Enoch had got into a position of now being, God help us, the financial controller of the bistro, which wasn't good news. And rapidly the Bilk Marketing Board was turning sour. I don't know the details but the bistro was in financial difficulties, which meant I didn't get any wages and was out of a job. David Bilk was last seen heading off to live as a wild man of the woods in Cornwall.

At this stage, you might have thought I'd quit the business. But no.

I had a friend, Mark Benson, who ran a little sandwich bar,

the Apple and Charlotte, in Park Street. Mark was very trendy and a minor aristocrat – the Honourable Mark Benson – and he used to tell me, 'I was brought up in the back of a Lagonda with a bottle of lemonade and a packet of crisps outside every pub in Gloucestershire.'

He was very dry and cool and a great backgammon player. He suggested we turn his sandwich bar into a night-time bistro, but then his father exerted pressure on him and the next thing I knew, Mark had to give up the Apple and Charlotte and take a course in architecture. So that was the end of that.

Time to take a plunge.

Off Clifton there was a one-storeyed, long, narrow building which had been a laundry. It was to let and so I scrabbled together some cash, heavens knows how, and rented it. I set up a kitchen and turned it into a takeaway. I put up a sign – Floyd's Feasts – and there I was, in business.

I sold home-made steak and kidney puddings and coq au vin, which customers could buy cold and then take home to heat up. I was also selling what I considered authentic kebabs. Just behind Floyd's Feasts was one of the medical colleges for the Bristol Royal Infirmary, and many of the medical students were Syrians and Jordanians. They started to come in for food, but disapproved of the kebabs. 'That's not a kebab,' they said.

I said, 'Well, you show me what a kebab is then, please.' And they did. While I had been leaving the fat on the lamb, they showed me that the essential thing is first to cut the fat from the lamb and second, to cut that fat into cubes. The fat is then pushed on to the skewer, making alternate layers between segments of the meat and vegetables. So now I really was serving authentic kebabs and authentic or not I was the first person to sell them in Bristol.

I also pioneered the dial-a-dinner service. Customers could phone up, order a meal and then I'd deliver in my newly purchased van.

The dial-a-dinner service failed. The phone would ring and there'd be an order for a dozen roast pheasants. I'd cook, load the food into the van and then set off to deliver the food. Far too often, the orders were to be delivered to a tower block of council flats in north Bristol, the occupants always wondering why I was standing on their doorstep with a dozen pheasants.

Obviously somebody was winding me up, most likely another restaurateur. So I had to abandon it.

Meanwhile, there was a great buzz about the Bristol food scene. The city's Italian trattorias were absolutely wonderful, and invariably housed in old wine cellars and ancient buildings with stone arched roofs.

Inside, waiters in white-and-blue-hooped shirts were singing 'O sole mio' and dashing from table to table with huge pepper mills. They served pasta dishes and salads of white haricot beans with tuna. The chefs were mostly former bus drivers and taxi drivers who'd been made redundant in their homeland and who'd come to England to pick up the social security and pretend they could cook, which of course they couldn't.

But they had grown up with mum and dad and knew that every day granny used to more or less make her tomato sauce. And how they did it in the south of Italy was to prepare their tomatoes raw with garlic and basil and whatever else they wanted to flavour it with, and then put the flavoured tomatoes into what we would call a Kilner jar.

The jar was left out in the sun, and the tomatoes cooked (much as they do in Jaipoor and Bengal, or wherever, to make their chutneys by preparing the fruit and letting it cook in the sun). That is what I call putting sunshine on a plate. That is beauty.

I went to the Café du Commerce this morning; sat and drank hot chocolate and watched the comings and goings around the town square. I was thinking about beauty. A friend in the bar had asked me to define it, to give my definition of beauty.

The first thing that comes to mind is a field of Provençal lavender under a Van Gogh sky. Beauty, the way I see it, is also a field of sunflowers. It is the snow-covered Blackdown Hills in Somerset.

It is a May morning at the shimmering waters of the Sedgemoor drain where I used to fish at the age of ten, or eleven, or twelve; when I caught a thrashing tench, jerked it from the water, and tossed it behind me, into the dandelions and nettles. Beauty is a freshly ploughed field that looks like glistening turned chocolate.

When it is spring and summertime I love to wander the markets, and I'll overshop for asparagus or cherries, or artichokes, or strawberries because they look so beautiful. Then there are the fishmongers' stalls along the Vieux Port in Marseilles: trestle tables laden with lobster and crayfish, snapper and octopus. Again, beautiful.

On the subject of markets, with very few exceptions farmers' markets in the twee shire villages of Britain are, to my mind, largely a scam. Bring back the WI. Too many gardeners or, in some cases farmers, are obsessed with the size rather than the quality of their produce. Who wants to eat organically grown leeks the size of a baseball bat? *Pas moi.*

When I became a professional chef and when I did things to my satisfaction, I think I saw beauty on the plate. They say that people eat with their eyes but few can see the real and intrinsic beauty of a piece of haddock on the plate.

But what of the plate? No matter what the fashion dictates, I will never serve food on decorated plates. The food is the picture and the plate is just the white canvas (if that doesn't sound too pompous).

I hate it the way that these days the food is assembled. It's not cooked. It's sort of created and assembled like Lego, and on square plates. I can't stand them, and I know the people who employ chefs hate them too because fancy square plates cost about a hundred pounds each and are out of fashion in four months. Then they have to be replaced. Square plates are ugly.

Yet beauty isn't necessarily a visible thing, is it?

It is half past five. I have decided to interrupt this book to send it some letters. On the still Spanish *jueves* of the 9th day of *Julio* of Our Lord, my typist, AKA Celia Constanduros, interrupted my siesta. She wanted to know, despite having been educated at Millford and many other reputable establishments for the fashionable young ladies of the suited and booted and horse-riding privileged society, 'Why do they say sick as a parrot?'

Dear Reader

In Provence there is a drink which is called 'a perroquet'. Paul, our host here in Andalusia, has several parrots of which Celia is much enamoured – but to return to the bar, where I wish to God I was – the French drink 'perroquet' in long glasses.

This is a mixture of scarlet grenadine syrup upon which floats a verdant green dose of mint syrup which is then stirred with pastis.

As they say absinthe (the original pastis) makes the heart grow fonder. And when you have had several perroquets you will know how it is to feel as sick as a parrot. Although of course, the origin of the phrase does not come from inarticulate football managers but from the rich lexicon of the once mighty, but still esteemed, British navy.

Another phrase comes from that huge lexicon: 'He was three sheets to the wind.' This meant that the ropes that held the sails had come adrift, craft out of control, ergo three sheets to the wind means as pissed as a skunk and, possibly, as sick as a parrot.

Floyd

NINE

Her name was Celia and she was beautiful, and she dreamed that one day she would be an actress.

Celia was a couple of years younger than me and was a barmaid in the back bar of the Greyhound pub in Princess Victoria Street. She'll tell you it was the front bar, but either way she worked at the Greyhound and she was the Celia I mentioned in the first chapter of this book, when I flew out to Sydney.

The front bar of the Greyhound was run by Henry, a Pole who had flown Spitfires during the Second World War. Then, if you walked through a passageway you reached the windowless back bar which was run by Henry's wife, Barbara. She was as hard as nails and her raven-black hair was piled high above her head in a beehive style.

Barbara oversaw the kitchen, which produced food that was predominantly Spanish and extraordinarily good for the time. I am sure that Barbara loved her husband, but she also adored the Spanish bartender and he was the inspiration behind the dishes.

Celia, meanwhile, was funny, exceptionally bright and any question of her being a decent person could be well and truly established when I tell you that she was cool enough to have been expelled from Millfield School (and every other school to which she went). You'll recall that as a schoolboy I played Millfield at rugby and we beat them – a feat that is worthy of repetition.

Celia was the daughter of an accomplished writer, Denis Constanduros, and she was the wife of a soon-to-be accomplished writer. Her husband, David Martin, was one of the regulars in the back bar.

David and Celia had met at Bristol's Old Vic, where she had another job in the costume department. He had a failed marriage behind him, and he and Celia went on to have two children, Thea and Leo. David would also go on to create television programmes.

I cannot recall whom I met initially – David on one side of the bar, or Celia on the other – but they were both lovely. They would become dominant figures in my life, though to begin with they were merely drinking partners and in those early days, when the pub closed, it was all back to theirs for a party.

There were two Davids who played a significant role in my television career, and David Martin was the first.

But I also played a role in assisting him with his television career. I was in the Greyhound one evening, chatting to David and his writing partner, Bob Baker, about my days in the army. I told them about the troubles I had as an officer, the boredom I suffered, the grief I got and my nervous breakdown.

It was heartbreaking stuff, all of which they found completely hilarious. When they had finished howling with laughter, they said they thought my stories would make an excellent television series. Over the next few pints, they scribbled notes and then went off to write up a proposal for a series on the BBC.

The proposal was despatched and a letter came back from the head of drama at the BBC: 'Come in and have a chat.' David and Bob arrived for their meeting with the department head, but he glanced over the proposal one more time, shook his head and said, 'It's great but it won't work. We can't afford tanks.'

As I had been a tank commander, the series would have seemed a little sparse if at least one tank had not featured.

However, and this is where it gets better, the department head asked the Bristol Boys (as they would later become known), 'Fancy writing some *Doctor Who*s?' They certainly weren't going to say no. They had walked in expecting to sell a series about a despondent soldier who didn't know how to spend his time, and they left with a deal to write about a doctor who travels in time.

It was David, incidentally, who created the K9 character, Doctor Who's metallic pet dog. One night David was having dinner chez Martin, when he glanced at the family dog. It was always hovering by the table, begging for food and David thought, wouldn't it be nice to have a dog that was a robot because then you could tell it to get lost and it would? Bob Baker, meanwhile, has done well. He is the scriptwriter of the *Wallace and Gromit* films.

David was doing a lot of work for Harlech Television (HTV), as well as other television and film companies, and one day he got in touch to say that he'd heard the resident HTV television cook was ill (probably eaten some of his food). They were desperate to find a replacement. 'Can you do it?' asked David, and I agreed.

It was a four-minute piece, which of course takes an hour

and a half to shoot. At the time I was particularly fond of a very popular dish of my own, which was roast guinea fowl with kumquats. I proudly did this in the studio at HTV, and finished off the segment by saying, 'To serve it you cut it open . . .'

As I cut into the bird I saw, to my utter horror, that I'd left a plastic bag of gizzards inside it. Amazingly, not one member of the crew noticed. There they were, about eighty-seven of them all sitting up in the gallery, scrutinizing how I looked and sending messages like 'Your bow tie's crooked' or 'Your hair's not quite right.' They'd forgotten to look at the food.

It wasn't until the segment was broadcast that someone wrote in to say, 'Hey, you can't do that. He cooked the plastic bag in the bird.'

From that experience I discovered the terrifying thing about television is that there's no one to get help from. You can't phone a friend and say, 'How do you suggest I do it?'

Jesmond, too, was a barmaid in the Greyhound. She had worked at HTV but it was in the pub that we first met. While she was serving me, we'd chat and then one thing led to another and sure enough I was in love.

I have not mentioned romance much because I did not have much of it.

Throughout my youth I suffered from severe acne, that most ancient form of contraception. But my complexion was OK when I met Jesmond and I fell in love with her. This was the late sixties, a world of Peace and Love, but a world that still frowned upon Living in Sin.

Jesmond was a year or two older than me, was dark-haired and charming and possessed a wit as dry as the Sahara sands.

We went out for just a matter of months before deciding to get married.

We were married in a register office, with just close family, and about six friends – a few of hers, a few of mine – to witness the nuptials. I was twenty-four years old. Jesmond and I celebrated the event by holding a small reception lunch for the crowd at the Hole in the Wall.

At the celebration, Jesmond's father, whom until that day I had not met, took me to one side. He was Irish, wore well-cut sports jackets and was I think the son of a former governor of the Bank of Ireland.

I thought he was going to say, 'Well done, son,' but not a bit of it. Instead, he brought his face close to mine and told me, 'Do anything wrong to my daughter and I'll be after you. Don't you worry about that. I'll have you sorted out.'

Young – but so what? – we lived in a huge rented flat not far from my takeaway shop, Floyd's Feasts. And we worked together, as I set about building a mini-empire of restaurants in Bristol.

At the bottom of Princess Victoria Street, not far from the Greyhound, there was a woman called Paula Huberner who was in her thirties and who had been a school mistress. Paula had opened a pottery, from which she sold her hand-made pots, and beside the pottery she had a little coffee shop, with nailed-together rickety cheap furniture. She took her pottery very seriously, though she was more of a businesswoman than she ever was an artist.

She had eaten at Bistro Ten where I was the cook, and she had also tasted my food at my bistro venture at Mark Benson's Apple and Charlotte. We were chatting one day, when she explained that she wanted to give up pottery and she won-dered whether I'd like to rent her shop. 'You could turn it into a bistro,' she suggested.

I said, 'I can't afford to do that.'

But Paula was generous and said she'd let me have the property rent-free while I converted it into a bistro. In other words, no rent until the business was up and running. We shook on it.

And so I transformed 112, Princess Victoria Street into what would be my first restaurant, Floyd's Bistro. Tongue and groove was put around the walls, as was the fashion, and the interior was painted maroon.

The carpet came from the Bath and West Country Show. It had been used in a marquee and with the help of Jesmond and friends we cleaned off the mud and the crushed sparrows, and spread it on the floor of the bistro.

From a second-hand shop I bought three old-fashioned speckled, enamelled gas stoves, each with a pair of gas rings in the middle. They cost twenty-five shillings each and I had them linked together, thus providing me with six burners. I had a chip fryer, though not to make chips; the bistro didn't serve them. Instead I used the fryer to make whitebait and aubergine fritters and courgette fritters. I also had a great big microwave oven, which no one had ever heard of.

The dining room consisted of five tables: the small ones could seat four; the large one took eight. And I bought thirty-two authentic bentwood chairs, each costing one pound. Toulouse Lautrec posters went up on the wall, and in the middle of the dining room sat the till on top of a marble-topped, bow-fronted cabinet with 'Fry's Chocolate' written on it. All we needed was that bistro requisite – the gingham-checked tablecloths – which were laid on to the tables and, hey presto, Floyd's Bistro opened for business.

We served whitebait, onion soup, potted shrimps, mushrooms à la grecque, taramasalata, terrine de campagne, and that classic French dish, boeuf à la bourguignonne, in which cubes of beef are cooked with red wine and bacon (or salt pork), and garnished with little onions and mushrooms. There were kidneys in red wine, and oxtail aux vignerons – oxtail with grapes. Desserts included chocolate mousse, syllabub and sorbets. There was ice cream and hot chocolate sauce with toasted almonds.

And I mean hot chocolate sauce, not something squeezed from a plastic tube. In a small bain marie, I melted dark chocolate with butter, freshly squeezed orange juice and cognac, and served it in a pre-warmed jug so the diner could really enjoy this exquisite, hot – and I repeat, hot – chocolate sauce.

To begin with, customers brought their own booze because the business had been set up in such a rush I had yet to be granted a licence. Otherwise, either I or a member of staff would get the booze for the customers: they came in, sat down; I'd take their order – drink included – and then dash across the road, to the Portcullis pub, and buy their wine. Once I acquired the licence, the house wine was a lethal Moroccan red served in carafes or, for the brave, there were litre bottles of the stuff.

After just a few days I had achieved success.

At six in the evening, I'd open the door and see a queue of thirty people on the pavement and waiting to be fed. The queue became a nightly sight, and lasted as long as the bistro. People would come bursting in and stare menacingly at diners at the tables, trying to get them to move.

Customers had to share tables and the clientele was mostly made up like this: there was the crowd from the Bristol Old Vic, including actors who would go on to make *Brideshead Revisited*; there were the law students and solicitors in their pinstripe suits, who were terribly pompous; there was the indigenous artistic colony who hated what I called the Young Thrusters; and then there were the Young Thrusters themselves, who were the people who drove Ford Cortina Es with go-faster stripes, and were all twenty-six, probably in property and earning lots of money. The Young Thrusters were very superior and they drank lots in the Portcullis before weaving across the road to get a table at the bistro.

The Thrusters, the lawyers, the artists, the actors . . . They'd all clash and have arguments. The music played on – the Beatles, the Kinks, the Stones and Loving Spoonful – and I just rocked on, frying away at the stove. I could see them and they could see me because then, as with all my restaurants, I had an open kitchen, so there were no barriers between me and my customers. Not like the Gifford, where I'd previously cooked. Front-of-house, Jesmond worked tirelessly as a waitress.

She fell pregnant and our son Patrick was born on 12 November 1968. Becoming a father was the most exciting thing. He seemed to be such a big baby and so advanced, even in the early months of his life. It is one of my regrets that I wasn't able to see fatherhood through the whole way.

We used to take our newborn baby in a basket in the well of the front seat of my Volvo P1800 – just like the one driven by Roger Moore in *The Saint* – and we'd whizz down to Padstow or Port Isaac to pick up fish and other ingredients for the bistro.

Although I had fatherhood to think of, I was absolutely obsessed with the restaurant, my own little business, and that obsession was about to intensify.

One of the regulars at the bistro was what I considered to be a lonely man because he always dined alone. He was very proper, wore a three-piece suit, a striped shirt with stiff, starched collar and a spotted polka-dot tie. If I was front-of-house when he was on his way out, he'd nod at me and let me know he approved of what he'd just eaten. 'Very good, very good.'

Then there was the night when he did the 'very good, very good' line and hovered for a little longer to tell me that he owned a property in Clifton and it was available to rent. 'I think it would be very suitable for you if you wanted to open a restaurant.' I went to have a look. Number thirty-six Oakfield Road had been a pharmacy.

I found a backer, the Bristol wine merchants, Howell's, who agreed to inject some money if I sold their wine. So I rented the site and set about turning it into Floyd's Restaurant, a thirty-two-seater with a bar as well. The kitchen was downstairs in the basement and somehow Jesmond and I raised the cash to buy the house next door: we created a flat for ourselves and rented rooms out to the Bristol Boys, David and Bob, for office use.

It occurred to me that the restaurant's dining room was quite small, but could be doubled in size by knocking a hole in the wall between that room and the ground floor of the back part of the house in which we lived.

So one night, after we'd seen out the stragglers, I got a

couple of friends round and overnight we smashed a hole through the dividing wall. One of my mates who had a rough idea of plastering, plastered up the jagged edges of the wall – not very well – and we painted the plaster while it was still wet.

We painted the walls of the room in the house to match the walls of the dining room. First thing in the morning I went out and bought a carpet. Then I popped in to Habitat and bought another six red tables and six red wicker bentwood chairs and that night we laid it all up.

Voilà! How to double the size of a restaurant in less than twenty-four hours.

When we opened the doors for business, customers just walked in, sat down, and didn't notice they were in a room that hadn't been there the night before.

The restaurant had a massive wine list, fantastic cheese-board, and to get the best ingredients I'd make a weekly drive to Cornwall to buy lobsters, sole and the like. In winter I specialized in game. I was really cooking on gas now and was still doing hours in the kitchen in the bistro, where I'd also installed a chef, Neil. His previous job was making chicken Maryland for gamblers at a Bristol casino.

Neil was fine, but I went berserk when I caught him adding tomato and paprika to boeuf bourguignon and then passing it off as Hungarian goulash.

I have been going through my bookshelves and unearthed *The Good Food Guide 1971*.

It describes Floyd's Bistro as 'Tiny, crowded, happy-go-lucky bistro. Moussaka, sweetbreads, goulash are good.' Three courses à la carte, £1.

There is also an entry for Floyd's Restaurant:

Floyd (of the Bistro) has gone up in the world, and you sit more comfortably at this new place. There is a terrace, too, for the summer. There is a substantial list of hot and cold first courses, and main dishes range from Moussaka at 75p or so (we have not seen the latest menu) to beef Wellington at £3 for two.

The shellfish soup, a member reports, was thick with shellfish, and a waiter considerately advised that no potatoes were needed with the seafood pie, but that some could be quickly obtained if he changed his mind. An inspector had a huge sole poached in cider with shellfish, accompanied by leaf spinach. Jugged hare, however, was a little dry, though the sauce itself was rich. Sweets, mostly ice-cream based, vary from day to day.

You pay 20p for cheese but there is a fair choice. Wines begin at £1.18 and rise to Ch. d'Yquem at £5.

The canned music is more obtrusive in the bar than in the restaurant. A la carte, three courses £2. Service 10 per cent. Seats forty. No dogs in the dining room.

A year later I'd added another restaurant, the Chop House in Clifton's Mall. By then we had the bistro and the restaurant in Oakfield Road. The same property developer who had rented me Oakfield Road had acquired Guido's Swiss Gourmet. The developer said, 'You seem to be doing very well. Would you like to have this one?' And I thought, why not? It was moderately successful. I'll let the *Good Food Guide 1972* tell you about it.

Floyd's Chop House. It is hard to get away from Keith Floyd in the tiny world of Clifton's noteworthy restaurants. One member's comments on this new chop house are worthy of Mr

Jingle: 'Home-made pâté, good. Whitebait, crispy. Pigeon, excellent. Service, good. Atmosphere, great. Seats, hard. Also had tripe and onions at 50p.' Other wordier visitors for the most part agree, especially about the seats. As in Floyd's restaurant (q.v.) the main offering here is a five-course dinner, which some find excessive in these surroundings, when they are looking chiefly for an informal supper.

The staff do not always draw people's attention to the alternative option, a 'cook's special' with soup or crudités for 75p. The original intention to serve English dishes only has been diluted since opening day, and an inspector's Hunters-style game pie was not in fact the most exciting dish he had had from Mr Floyd – but the proprietor is a busy man these days, and standards tend to slip a little wherever he is not. However, Susan Dutch's cooking (of Curries too) is reckoned competent. She used to be at the Black Bull, Reeth. And one visitor says he was served by an ex-Rag queen (not to be confused with a drag queen).

Add up the bill: in the 'biblical gloom' they may rob either themselves or you. Litres of ordinaire are £1.25 (30p by the glass, or should it be tumbler?). If you want anything better, go to the Restaurant. There is recorded music sometimes. Table d'hôte lunch 50p, dinner from £1.25. A la carte dinner two courses, from 75p. No dogs.

The guide lists a few people who contributed reviews of the restaurant. One of them, I see, is a certain David Martin.

The same 1972 guide describes the bistro as a 'rough, noisy bistro in the early Floyd manner' and is also quite positive about the restaurant.

Many people who sat under Keith Floyd's sauteuse at the bistro have graduated with him to this chocolate and green restaurant in a quiet Victorian terrace, where there is more choice, better food, and outdoor eating in the summer. His chef, Colin Waterton (sometimes assisted by the proprietor), is now doing a five-course dinner with quite a wide choice in three of the courses.

The price ranges from £1.75 to £3 according to the main course chosen. One visitor's favourite is the loin of pork with calvados (£2.50). Another mentions Dover sole poached in cider with shellfish sauce, adding that 'the sauce was unprofessional with large chunks of crab' – a more welcome symptom of amateurism than some we can think of. An inspector who knows the place well chose the scallop and bacon pie because it was new to him: both it and the apple, lemon and sultana tart that followed were delicious.

The first course of these dinners is simply crudités: then may come an iced soup, mushrooms à la grecque ('good' says one report) or pâté (less good, and served with poor toast on occasion). In winter there may be hare, pheasant or oxtail with grapes. Many puddings are now made by a home cook outside the restaurant: this seems to be a success.

Mr Floyd says people are expected to occupy their tables for two hours at least, but one member says his party was moved to the (comfortable) bar for coffee. The wines (from Howell's of Bristol) include Moroccan red at £1.25 a litre but after that you pay over £1.50 for most things, and £4.90 for Ch. Rausan-Ségla '61. There is no music now. Table d'hôte £1.75 – £3. Seats 32. No dogs. Closed public hols (except Christmas Day).

Contributors on this occasion included Patrick Dromgoole, head of HTV, and another loyal regular. Patrick employed David and Celia.

In a small way I was huge, if you get my drift. I would be eachwhere and everywhere. To give you an idea of the food culture in those days, I would have to keep a close eye on customers who'd ordered artichoke. Invariably, they'd pick up their knife and fork and so I'd dash over to their table to say in a friendly way, 'We don't bother with knives and forks here. We just pluck off the leaves and eat them with our fingers.' It made them feel comfortable.

Then there were those who ordered snails and looked horrified when the dish arrived with callipers to pull the meat from the shell. I could see that coming so I'd drift over and engage in chit-chat and then pick up the callipers and say, 'Oh these things are a bloody nuisance. Be careful . . . Look, I'll show you, this bit can spring out . . .' I'd find a way of putting them at ease.

What was the enjoyment? As much as I was very serious abut the food, it was the overall ambience that was important to me. I wanted great food, great wine and great music. They all had to come together as one. It was like one of those Terry's Chocolate Oranges: if one of the segments is missing it can't be described as a whole. Everything had to be right.

TEN

I was fixated with my three restaurants, and Jesmond and Patrick occupied second and third places in my life. It's a harsh statement for the average decent person to absorb, but any man in this business will tell you that his restaurant is like a mistress, forever demanding. I was just obsessed by the restaurants and thought everybody else should be too, which was very unfair of me.

I have always fallen in love easily. And I have never entered a relationship which I didn't believe in, which I didn't firmly believe could work out. I never expected any of my relationships to end in tears and when they do I ask myself the question, 'When am I going to learn?'

In terms of my marriage to Jesmond, the rows became more and more frequent and increasingly fierce.

I used to have a siesta in between lunch and dinner service and one day I was in my clogs – I always wore clogs – and clomping up the uncarpeted stairs to our flat beside the restaurant. I'd done the prep for the night and was looking forward to a snooze before coming back down again at six to start service. Out of the bedroom a woman emerged, saying to me, 'Would you be quiet? My children are trying to sleep.'

I said, 'Who are you?' Then I realized she was David

Martin's first wife, Ruth. She was a good friend of Jesmond, and Jesmond had allowed her to move into the flat without telling me. I swore at her, telling her to get out, and then Jesmond appeared and there was one of those screaming matches that went in the shape of a pear.

I was also carrying a burden – a secret – that I could not discuss with Jesmond. On the day that Patrick was born, Jesmond had gone into labour and was taken into the maternity hospital in Clifton. Meanwhile, I went to the kitchen of the restaurant and when there was a break in service I phoned the hospital to see how everything was going. Today, fathers are there with the mother-to-be during childbirth, but back then the paternal presence in the delivery ward was unusual. The ward sister said chirpily, 'It's all going splendidly,' and then she added, 'Mrs Floyd is very comfortable. And anyway as it's her second child she will have no problems.'

Second child? I didn't know that Jesmond had previously given birth. It sounds stupid now, but I didn't discuss the matter with her. It weighed heavily on my mind, it was a constant preoccupation, and during rows it would have been a good one to lob in. Yet I did not mention that chirpy ward sister and her revelation. For ages I felt that my wife had betrayed me. Who was this first child? Where did it live? Why on earth hadn't Jesmond told me?

Eventually, the truth came out. One day, in a by-the-way fashion, Jesmond happened to mention that when she was in hospital there was another expectant mother in the ward ... and her name, too, was Mrs Floyd. Jesmond did not have two children; Patrick was her first. By then, it was all too late.

We had been in love, but now that was gone. Chances are

you have been in a relationship that crumbles and you think, there's no going back. We were at that stage.

Despite being popular, Floyd's Restaurant wasn't making much money. There was a huge amount of theft going on.

I'd taken on a barman whom I'd seen working in the Greyhound for many years and he was really good. He fell out with Barbara, the Greyhound's beehived landlady, and when he turned up in a smart suit and looking for work I had no hesitation in giving him a job there and then. He was excellent.

The sales rep from Howell's wine merchants – the people who'd lent me the money to open the restaurant in return for selling their wine – often used to drift in to see how things were going. He'd sit at the bar having a glass of wine which, incidentally, he'd pay for. One day the sales rep said to me, 'That barman of yours is doing you.'

He explained how I was being fiddled by my excellent barman and when the accounts, the dockets, the bills and the tabs were scrutinized I discovered that this wonderful employee had ripped me off to the tune of many hundreds of pounds. He was prosecuted, but the money had gone and would not return.

Then I got involved with the local branch of NACRO, the organization that tries to help with the rehabilitation of criminals. They persuaded me to take on two young offenders. I was assured that the lads had reached the point where it was considered 'safe' for them to have jobs. They had learned their lessons, they were willing to make a fresh start in life and I was to assist them in this bold challenge. I gave jobs to the duo. They worked at the restaurant, lived in a hostel and I bought clothes for them because they couldn't afford much.

You don't need to be Sherlock Holmes to hazard a guess at what happened next. The burglary was committed one night, and the thieves' stash included money from my office and then, from my flat in the neighbouring house, they also pinched the stereo, the television set and more cash.

I was stupid to have given them work. But they were daft, too. They had the keys but in order to make it look like breaking and entering, they had smashed a window. However, the glass was on the ground outside rather than inside, thereby confirming that it was an inside job. There's nothing like as thick as thieves.

The two lads had enlisted a third member – the washer-up, who was a very smart, cool young man and who before hooking up with this pair hadn't committed anything more serious than breaking a dish or two while at the sink. They all disappeared, and were never found.

Drinks were on the house for regulars when the mood took me, and it often did. I let out one of the rooms in the neighbouring house to a chap called Barry. He had the most gorgeous girlfriend but they fought incessantly and Barry was often in a state. He'd come into the bar of Floyd's Restaurant and say, 'OK if I have a drink, Keith?'

I'd look at the messed-up Barry and say, 'Yes, of course you can.' That would be at six o'clock in the evening. He'd still be there at one o'clock the following morning and that's when he'd fall off his stool in my elegant restaurant, or create a fight with somebody so vicious that police would have to be called. Or perhaps his girlfriend would walk in and then they'd be at it again.

*

Around about 1974 I received a letter from Kenneth Bell. He was an established force in the business, owning one of the best restaurants in the country, Thornbury Castle. He wondered whether I'd like to sell Floyd's Restaurant. I didn't ponder for too long. We met and he offered me £17,500, a huge amount of money.

I recall the lunch with Ken at Thornbury Castle. And by the by, the crunchy fresh green beans I was eating had been grown and picked by my friend, Celia Martin, from the gardens of her sixteenth-century eerie house, Morton Grange. Her husband David, with his high literary ambitions, was reduced (and I jest with the greatest affection and respect) to writing a TV police series with Bob, and was cavorting, against his will, with some truly great actors, and sometimes actresses, and Doctor Who.

Meanwhile, back at the table the head waiter approached the one next to mine with his pepper mill and said to the lady, 'Can I grind you?' Elizabeth David, a smoker, a drinker, a cook, a writer, with appetites that extended beyond the plate and perhaps into a bed, in, maybe Egypt, maybe Provence, maybe Sardinia, looked up at him and his mill and imperiously said, 'Take that thing away.'

Whoever the actress was that played with Dan Aykroyd in *My Stepmother is an Alien* (in the film she drank battery acid by the way) is – when I think about women – probably the woman I most fantasize about. However, Elizabeth David was, and is, my all-time heroine. She got ripped off too.

The first thing I ever cooked that I was proud of was her chicken, gently roasted in oodles of butter. You took the chicken from the pan and laid it to rest on a tray or a platter, so its juices would seep gently out. Then with the roasting pan on a very low heat, you whisked into the golden butter the ochre yolks of eggs, so gently, so carefully, that the result was an unforgettable unctuous creamy sauce. Thank you, the late Ms David. Actually it should be Dame.

So back to Ken, who offered me £17,500 for the restaurant. This is when complications arose. I had a partner in the restaurant, a man I shall call Trevor. I'd made Trevor a partner when the business was going through a rough patch, and in return for an injection of cash had given him 20 per cent.

Of course Trevor would have received his rightful share from the sale of the restaurant. But in some way I've never fully understood – but perhaps because Bell was told the restaurant wasn't mine to sell – the deal fell through.

However, Trevor told me not to worry. I believed he would buy the restaurant from me for the same amount of money.

After a series of meetings I was handed a bundle of documents which I didn't have time to read. I signed. Yes, like a fool, I signed without reading the large print, let alone the small print. Trevor gave me what I assumed was a £2,000 deposit with the rest to be due in six weeks' time.

I waited six weeks. Then I went to see Trevor to collect the remaining fifteen and a half grand. 'Oh,' he said, 'I am not paying you any more. You've already signed over all the shares to me.' I didn't know I had done that.

A year or so earlier the property developer who rented the Chop House to me had suggested I incorporate it into the same limited company that owned the restaurant. He said it would enable the deal to be done quickly, which was no doubt true. However, I had overlooked the fact that Trevor had 20 per cent in the restaurant.

Now I realized that I had merrily signed away all the shares of the company. In return for £2,000 cash, Trevor not only ended up owning the restaurant but he also got the Chop House.

So that was it. Finished.

When I punched Trevor, I did so with all the might of a man who felt thoroughly and utterly well and truly stitched up.

Instead of being a respectful and mute scribe, the ghost, James Steen, has just asked me, 'Why don't you ever read contracts?' If I knew the answer to that I'd be a very rich man and wouldn't have to go through the painful process of writing this goddamn book.

But seriously, the reason is: I have always trusted people. If everything could be done on a handshake, I'd heartily approve. Signing on the dotted line is such a pain.

Of course, I should have paid heed to one of my father's homilies which ended with the line, 'So pay me today and tomorrow I'll trust.'

By now I had sold the bistro, making a few grand in the process. It was a good sale, and I used two thousand of it to buy a yacht called *Flirty*, a 1912 Norwegian eight-metre.

For years, I felt constrained by the daily grind of peeling courgettes, and putting out the bins at two in the morning. Everyone else I knew – the David and Celia Martins of my world – were, meanwhile, travelling off to Greece in camper vans, having a ball and wearing bright ties with flowers on them. I need a break, I thought. I haven't had a life, I reckoned.

Jesmond and I wouldn't get divorced for another decade or so, but our marriage was over. I was about thirty and had got to the point where our relationship was insupportable. We weren't living in the same worlds. She was more attracted to the arty side of Clifton society, while I was more attracted to trying to run my restaurants. I can no longer remember what we rowed about. I just can't.

I simply packed my bags and left. So I was restaurant-less and marriage-less.

One morning I climbed on to my boat with a few friends – David Martin and Peter Gardiner, who was quite a cynical Scotsman and a brilliant engineer and very interested in sailing and motor racing. Like me, Peter loves his rugby.

We set sail. My friends returned soon enough, but I stayed away, exploring the Mediterranean for some eighteen months. I was completely foolhardy, didn't have enough money to go sailing, and hadn't thought of the future; not at all.

Perhaps I'll come back to that period, but for now just imagine that you have been with me on *Flirty*, along the way getting into scrapes, cooking, sailing, making friends, drinking, smoking and meeting women.

I had vanished without thinking much about Patrick, a confession that sounds too cruel. I was on a voyage of utter selfishness. As time went by, I would come to think of him all the time and then the nightmares started: nightmares that any absent parent might have about the safety of their child.

When I returned to England, I brought with me a woman, Dolores, and a child who had a really beautiful African name which I just cannot remember. I had met her in Spain, where she made beautiful clothes and sold them at a local market. She was a kind of sub-Mary Quant, and with her raven-black hair she was outstandingly attractive.

I remember one day in Spain when this huge black man, a tribal chief of Somalia, appeared and stood in the doorway of her bedroom, pointing at me and saying to his friend, 'Look, that's what she's done to me.' Then he turned and walked away. He was clearly a gentleman otherwise he would have put a machete through me.

The child, aged about three or four, was not mine but from a previous relationship; perhaps she was the daughter of the tribal chief.

I thought it would all work out, but when we set foot in England we went to live in a rented house near Wiveliscombe rather than heading for the more cosmopolitan Bristol. To be the mother of a half-caste child in rural Somerset did not ensure a hearty welcome from the community, at times stuffy and racist. She was uncomfortable, to say the least. What had seemed like a damned good plan when we were in Spain now appeared to have been the worst idea that a young couple ever came up with.

My parents, however, welcomed Dolores: any friend of mine was always welcome in their house. If they had reservations about any of my friends or lovers, they would never express those reservations to me. They were good, hospitable people.

Perhaps romance, like wine, doesn't travel well. Within a few months of moving to Somerset we decided to go our separate ways. Translated: she went off, leaving me on my own in the village that derived its name from *wife-less-combe*.

I'd come back to Britain with another plan: to write a novel. I told Jesmond about my ambitions to become a writer and, characteristically funny, she sent me a cartoon from *Punch* magazine.

The drawing showed two men in conversation, one saying, 'What are you doing at the moment?'

The other replies, 'I'm writing a novel.'

And the first then says, 'Me neither.'

The cartoon appealed to Jesmond's wicked sense of humour and sending it to me gave her another chortle. The idea that I was like the man vowing to write a novel yet never keeping the promise amused Jesmond.

She and I agreed that Patrick, who was about six or seven, would come to live with me, and so I was reunited with my son. We lived together in the cottage down a remote track, and each weekday morning, I'd put him on to my shoulders and we'd march off to Wiveliscombe Primary School, where I, like my mother and uncles and aunts before me, had been a pupil.

In the evenings, I'd collect him from school and carry him home on my shoulders. We cooked together and fished together. Apart from having a great sense of responsibility, it was also a bit like being a child again.

I recreated for Patrick the pastimes that I had enjoyed at his age – going fishing, collecting chestnuts, making bows and arrows from a piece of ash cut from the hedgerows and Red Indian headdresses from duck feathers.

We always had a proper supper together and then I'd take him to bed and read to him, *Swallows and Amazons*, perhaps. As he slept, I would write, watch television or sip a glass of wine. It was an extremely contented period of my life.

We spent days with my uncle Ken, my mother's brother. I've not mentioned him in detail until now, but Uncle Ken was a prominent figure in my childhood. If I had heroes – which you know I don't – then he would be one of them.

*

When I was a child I was in awe of Uncle Ken. He was a ferreting, cricket-playing, rugby-playing, hard-drinking smoothie. His hair was slicked back by Brylcreem and his usual attire was a blue blazer, underneath which was a white shirt; the collar stood like a tent over the jacket collar.

His friends called him 'Maggots', which came from his surname, Margetts.

Uncle Ken seemed to spend his life swaggering around and ripping off my grandfather in the latter's second shoe repair shop in Milverton, a few miles down the road.

In winter, when the snow was on the hills and it was freezing, he'd take me ferreting. In summertime, we'd go rabbiting; the combine harvester had cut the corn down to a square in the middle of the fields; me and my friends stood round with sticks while Uncle Ken was in the thick of it, driving out the rabbits and hares for us to clobber. We'd catch rabbits and cut them on their wrists and hang them on the crossbar of our bicycles. Uncle Ken sold them to Mr Murdoch, the butcher, and often gave me half a crown.

At lunchtime he'd say he was going to the nearby farm, to pick up cheese and onion sandwiches and a flask or two of tea. He'd be gone for hours. What I didn't realize for years was that he was giving one to the daughter of one of the farmers, or maybe his wife.

Then to the absolute horror of my very puritanical family he carried on – and *carrying on* was an important phrase of the day – with the barmaid of the White Hart Hotel in Wivey. She was at least twelve years older than him and, worse, she was a divorcee. That was more shocking than anything you can imagine.

My grandfather's business had managed to get a contract from the Somerset and Wilts Light Infantry to repair the regiment's boots. It was a huge contract, but once Uncle Ken inherited the business from my grandfather, he single-handedly managed to bankrupt it. He thought he'd become a publican so he took over a pub, which, predictably, he ran completely illegally, staying open all hours of the night and setting up a gambling den.

One day he said, 'Can I borrow your van? I've got to take some cornmeal over to Bertie's place.'

I said, 'Sure,' and didn't think any more of it.

So he went up to one farm and loaded about six sacks of animal foodstuffs into my van. Then he drove to another farm and filled it up with the carcasses of two dead pigs. Then he drove the lot back to his pub. He'd stolen it. He was never convicted of any of the many crimes he committed: far too charming to be charged.

Eventually the pub went completely bust, of course. He was an extraordinary man, and a great companion, but I thought it best to leave Wivey.

Meanwhile, Jesmond wanted to take back Patrick, as was her right, and it seemed normal that he would return to his mother in Bristol, though I would miss him, of course. I thought I'd better return to Bristol to try and find a job of some kind.

Jesmond was wrong to mock me about the novel because I finished the manuscript. I submitted it to a couple of literary agents. They sent it back with letters that said, 'Thanks but no thanks.' So I gave up . . . or rather, put it on hold.

Alas, it was never published and was among the haul taken by the burglars who visited me a few years ago at my home in Montfrin. The novel, incidentally, in which I was the protagonist, was about a sailing trip and I threw demons overboard. I murdered quite a few.

Although it was written as a novel, entitled *A Long Road South*, it was an autobiographical account of how I had been stitched up in Bristol by people who I felt had ripped me off. It had a food theme: the main character (me) wanted to reach the Mediterranean, its olives, its red peppers, and try to understand what the Med was all about.

I needed to earn money and so I returned to Bristol to see what it could offer, though I would not be near Patrick because Jesmond was making plans to move to Teignmouth with our son and her boyfriend.

ELEVEN

Once back in Bristol (and we're now in the mid-seventies, by the way) I hooked up with old friends, like David and Celia and Bob Baker. These reunions involved revisiting all of the city's pubs.

One night, in all the pubs in all of Bristol, someone just happened to walk into mine.

I hadn't seen her for ten years but we recognized each other instantly and chatted as if we were long-lost friends. She was Paddy, the sophisticated women's editor at the *Western Daily Press*, for whom I had babysat in my days as a cub reporter.

Over drinks that night, and over subsequent weeks, we fell for each other, head over heels as they say.

By now her life had changed completely. She had three children but was divorced. Paddy had ditched journalism and was now running what could loosely be described as a free school, housed in a large Edwardian mansion close to the downs of Bristol.

The method of education was based on allowing children to do whatever they liked. If the kids wanted to murder rabbits or smash windows, then so be it. I didn't understand it, though this style of schooling was a genuine, passionate and thoughtful attempt on Paddy's behalf to give children a real break, a proper upbringing. It was completely at odds with my theories of how children should be raised, but nevertheless, it wasn't an issue at all because we were in love.

Together we went on holiday to France and to stay, incidentally, at the farm near Saint-Didier that belonged to our former editor, Richard Hawkins. Paddy's young children were enchanting and we played *Swallows and Amazons*, albeit on dry land. Out of branches and twigs I built a table. I made a tent. And I drew maps of the area, sending the youngsters on exciting expeditions in the woods.

It was around about that time that I hit on the idea of buying wine from this region of France, the Vaucluse, and taking it back to Bristol, where I could supply the city's wine bars and restaurants. I bought a three-tonne, crew-cab lorry, and Paddy and I formed a company called Walker Floyd (Walker was her maiden name).

The first trip was a nightmare. After all these complex negotiations with the *caves*, I bought the first 3,000 litres of wine and turned up at the *cave* to collect it. I expected to find the wine in cardboard cartons, each containing twelve bottles. No. They were in rough wooden crates, all of which couldn't fit into the lorry. I had to pay a deposit for the crates and then I had to find a way of loading the wine into the lorry.

In the end I made a couple of trips to Richard's farm, where the wine was unloaded from the crates and then repackaged in cardboard boxes originally intended for transporting melons. It was autumn, which was the only good omen: in order to limit breakages we used recently fallen leaves as layers in between the bottles. Then I drove back to England grinding along like a tortoise in this ancient truck.

Paddy came on one of the wine trips, and it was then that

she said, 'I'd like to live here.' And I said, 'I'd like to live here, too.' You know me by now. I like to be spontaneous.

She had 6,000 quid and I didn't have a penny. So we – she – bought an old grocery shop in L'Isle-sur-la-Sorgue in the Vaucluse region of Provence and we started to live there with the three kids.

The *cité* of L'Isle-sur-la-Sorgue is, as the name tells you, an island on the River Sorgue. It is a maze of narrow, ancient streets and canals, and over the centuries the islanders have produced wool, silk and paper. At one stage many of the inhabitants were fishermen who every day hauled thousands of crayfish from the river.

The island is also home to an antiques market, and Paddy and I came up with a brainwave. The lorry was full on the way from France to Bristol, but empty on the way from Bristol to France. Wouldn't it be a good idea, we thought, to do the jumble sales in Bristol, fill up the lorry with bric-à-brac, bring it back to L'Isle-sur-la-Sorgue and flog the stuff at the street market? The market, at this point, was selling mostly crap and if we chose correctly we could do well.

So it developed into a trip up to cross the Channel with wine, which was then sold in Bristol, followed by twenty jumble sales and a trip or two to the auction rooms, where we bought pieces of Spode, wickerwork bedroom furniture and veneer-fronted chests of drawers. Back in France, we sold out every time; it went great.

I had time on my hands and thought I'd turn the downstairs of our home – previously a shop – into a restaurant. And I did.

It had about six tables and it was joyful. In the mornings I would walk up to the square and see pyramids of aubergines and peppers that could be used in dishes. The bakery was just opposite and when I made daube provençale I'd borrow the baker's oven. I'd prepare my marinade and my beef and when the baker had finished his morning's work, the daube went in and was cooked by the heat of the dying embers.

It was easy to cook well and bit by bit this new and French Floyd's became a cult restaurant.

Paddy was an absolutely wonderful woman but I couldn't handle the children.

I'd bought a big hearse, an old Daimler-Benz, and we moved around in it en masse. If I wanted to go to the local markets in Aix-en-Provence then we all had to go. If I was due to make a trip back to Britain then we all had to go. If the children, aged between eight and twelve, wanted to eat at six or nine, then we all had to eat at six or nine. If they wanted to stay up all night, then . . . you get my point. It got to me.

Having been raised into free thinking, they could say what they liked and do as they wished. If they wanted to go to school they went, if they didn't want to go then they didn't.

What had seemed blissful in the freedom of young love was now a completely different story. Inevitably we all fell out big time. I was going slightly mad and felt I was being dominated by Paddy and her children. We didn't share the same values. She was very altruistic and progressive.

One day we climbed into the lorry and drove back to Britain. We simply abandoned the house, didn't even sell it. It was just abandoned. We all drove back to Bristol.

Paddy and her children went their way, I went mine. I never heard from her again. I don't stay in touch with people after things like that. They'd have plenty of complaints about me,

I'm sure. Lots of divorced couples have lunch with each other, but I don't do that. In fact, I can't understand that. Once they're gone, they're gone.

But what had started off, as on so many occasions, full of optimism, romanticism and tenderness just cascaded into some bloody storm.

Again, I was back in Bristol. I went sailing to the Scilly Isles with (among others) my son Patrick and Howell Price. Howell was a sort of Welsh mystic and master craftsman who lived for sailing, with twinkling eyes and soft stories about the pleasures of the ocean, delivered in a lyrical, captivating way. His love of wood and how it could be used was on a par with the way I think about food.

David Martin also came on the trip. Celia and the other wives – not one of mine because, unusually, I didn't have one at the time – flew out by helicopter from Penzance to join us in a rented house. After the bust-up from Paddy, I was like a wounded leopard, wanting to curl up and die. My French dream was shattered and I had returned to England full of despair, not knowing what to do next.

One day David and the other men went out for the day while I stayed at the house, saying, 'Do you mind if I don't come? I just want to stay in bed.' Celia, too, remained at the house as she was the one charged with cooking that night's dinner.

When David returned he and Celia had a row, though it was not fierce enough for Celia to stop cooking kidneys in a red wine sauce. 'And another thing,' shouted David. 'You've been screwing Floyd.' I do not know why he thought that, but it was not true.

*

When it was time to sail back to the mainland we went to Padstow. I knew it well because it was near Port Isaac and not that far from Wadebridge, the town where I'd been beaten to a pulp in my youth.

We went into a restaurant which had fishing nets on the ceiling and Chianti bottles with candles on the tables. It wasn't that bad, really, but it was a pretty tatty-looking place.

However, a blackboard outside the restaurant told passers-by that it specialized in seafood, and it did. It had lobster thermidor with a floury sauce and Death by Chocolate, which was fashionable at the time.

It wasn't very good, but you could clearly see that the bloke who ran it was trying very hard. We all thought, this is great.

The chef-patron was Rick Stein, then in his mid-thirties. When he came over to say hello, I thanked him for a wonderful meal but said that next time maybe he should leave the floury sauce off the lobster. 'Just have a fresh lobster instead. Why ruin it?' I said.

He just hadn't made a very good sauce that day, but we all enjoyed ourselves, got rollicking drunk and Rick and the rest of us had a jolly fine time. I liked him immensely. Of course, Rick and I didn't know – because we couldn't have known then – that one day we would both become famous through television series made by David Pritchard.

The Five Hundred Club has to have been one of the world's smallest clubs.

It had a membership of six, each member being a friend of mine and wealthy (and willing) enough to pay the sign-up fee of £500. The money was then given to me, and with a total of £3,500 I was able to open my next restaurant, called – surprise, surprise – Floyd's.

Once a small corner shop, the property was in a typical Victorian terrace in Chandos Road. It had big plate glass windows on two sides, an open kitchen and about eight tables. The restaurant was very small, but nicely light and airy.

My approach to food, my style if you like, had developed as a result of my life in France with Paddy. I was now cooking what was effectively nouvelle cuisine in the true sense of the phrase: freshness whenever possible, and lightness – try to avoid the heavy, flour-based sauces and use only the lightest possible sauces; let the ingredients speak for themselves.

In France I had used the baker's oven and now I was confident that if I had ingredients and if I had heat then I could cook. This would become the theme of my television cookery programmes.

If you ordered wild duck in Chandos Road I didn't cook until I saw the whites of your eyes. There were few pre-prepared sauces and I strived to cook *à la minute* so that the dish was freshly vibrant. My menu, as ever, contained a good deal of fish and a lot of game in the wintertime.

There was, however, the perennial nightmare of trying to obtain top-quality ingredients. They were so difficult to find. Even when I thought I'd found a terrific supplier I depended upon him to be reliable with deliveries. I shall never forget the night of the Glorious Twelfth, waiting for the man to deliver the bloody grouse; sweating at six o'clock when they still hadn't arrived.

Supermarkets were pretty basic, and good-quality olive oil was hard to come by. You couldn't even buy a decent lamb chop. Ingredients that we take for granted today were mostly unavailable unless you searched and searched . . . There was a brilliant supplier called Vin Sullivan, based in Abergavenny, and he could get langoustines, scallops, guinea fowl, and all kinds of stuff. So he'd drive over twice a week with all these wonderful things, but on those days when Vin's van was late then I was stuffed.

This may have been when the nightmares started. They are terrible, awful recurring dreams about food and cooking. Even though I no longer have a restaurant these nightmares still wake me at night and they keep me awake.

They might have started then, in Chandos Road, or they might have started earlier. But they go way back.

I dream that I am in the kitchen of my restaurant. Sixty customers are about to arrive for dinner but I can't feed them because I don't have food. 'The fish hasn't arrived,' I am saying to myself. 'What am I going to do? I'm stuffed.' I am pacing up and down, becoming more and more anxious, frightened because I don't have a clue what to do. The clock is ticking, they'll be here in a minute; but where is my food, where is that man with the fish? What can I do? And then I awake but the horror of it all – and it was horror for me – prevents me from getting back to sleep.

Or, and this is another mad dream, I am standing in the kitchen and this time I have all my ingredients. The food is there and the customers are in the restaurant, so that's all right. But now the stove won't work. I turn the knobs. Nothing. I check the gas supply. That seems fine. But the stupid stove still won't work. Again, what am I going to do? And as with the other nightmare, the clock is ticking.

*

Of course, all the trendy Bristolians frequently visited London and returned to brag: 'Oh, in London, in the Two Three Five, they're cooking so and so . . .' With a group of friends, I formed a dining club and we made monthly trips to the capital.

We ate in Borscht 'n' Tears, Nick's Diner and, yes, the Two Three Five in the King's Road, their menus all chalked up on blackboards. There was a dreadful place in Beauchamp Place called Parks. They used to serve soufflés with dahlias on the plate. We all thought that was amazing. The soufflés were made from Campbell's condensed mushroom soup, though we didn't know that at the time.

The members of the Five Hundred Club received something in return for their cash. They were allowed to 'eat off' their investment. They could come in, stuff their faces, and not have to settle a bill. Obviously, they always chose to come on Saturdays, which was the busiest night of the week, thus depriving me of profits.

I was well known in Bristol, appearing on local radio to share my knowledge of cooking and food. Customers would arrive at the restaurant and introduce me to their friends with the words, 'Oh, this is my friend Keith.' But when they saw me – the cook – at the Bristol Old Vic watching *The Cherry Orchard*, they couldn't quite get it. 'Oh, what are you doing here?' they'd say in a rather pompous tone.

I wrote my first cookery book, *Floyd's Food*, which was published in 1981, and it included recipes for dishes which I now served to my customers in Bristol.

They were simple, easy-to-follow recipes for oxtail with grapes and beef in red wine, as well as monkfish with paprika sauce, bass with Pernod, hot onion tart and a dandelion salad: 'Pick, young, small, un-flowering dandelion leaves. Wash and dry them carefully. Serve with olive oil, salt and sherry vinegar and cubes of hot fried bread.' Simple, eh?

Desserts in the book included pears in red wine, peach pancakes, chocolate mousse and a dish called the Strawberry Alternative: 'Fill a glass bowl with strawberries. Cover liberally with caster sugar, squeeze over the juice of two lemons and pour over half a bottle of red wine. Leave in the fridge for several hours. Don't for heaven's sake pour cream over them.'

The foreword was written by one of my regulars, the comic actor Leonard Rossiter, by then well and truly a star following his performances in the TV sitcoms *Rising Damp* and *The Fall and Rise of Reginald Perrin*. Whenever Leonard came into the restaurant – accompanied by David Martin or Patrick Dromgoole, the boss at HTV – he was always on top form and very funny. He loved his oysters and Chablis. Leonard's foreword read as follows:

'What about lunch, Pat?' I said. We were making a television film in Bristol, my favourite city, and as we were to be there for more than three weeks catering arrangements were going to be important. Normally a film unit is fed by strange men who follow you around in a small lorry. 'Ah,' said Pat Dromgoole, our director, 'we're going to Keith Floyd's in Clifton.' This was in the early 1970s. The first meal was so good that afterwards I remember saying to Pat, 'Never mind the filming, let's just make sure Keith can fit us in every day.'

From that time on whenever I have visited Bristol a meal at one of the Keith's restaurants is a pleasure to which I have always looked forward. Obviously his food is good or I wouldn't be writing this, but above all there is always that one essential quality, you are made to feel that the meal you are having is Keith's most important job of that day. I can think of no higher praise.

Upstairs was great but downstairs, in the earth-floored basement, I was sleeping on an army camp bed. It was tough trying to get the place going.

One Sunday morning – a freezing winter's morning – I awoke, wandered upstairs and opened the front door. To my horror, I saw there was a young boy of about fourteen or fifteen lying semi-conscious, huddled in a T-shirt and jeans. In his hands he held a bottle of glue – glue sniffing was a sad fad among teenagers of the day. I thought, this is awful.

I called for an ambulance, but when the ambulance arrived I pretended that I didn't know who he was. In fact, I had realized that the boy was the eldest son of an ex-girlfriend. It was wrong, I know, but I had troubles of my own and didn't want to end up in another mess with his mother.

TWELVE

It was about midnight when a waitress came into the kitchen and said to me, 'There's a gentleman on table five who wants to have a quick word with you.'

I thought, oh dear, here we go, there's going to be a complaint. I walked from the kitchen to the dining room and glanced around. There was a couple on table five, a man and a woman. I cannot tell you much about the woman because my eyes were fixed mostly on the sight of the man, and yours would have been, too.

He was large and balding, with a red moon face and wearing a leather jacket and Communist Party scarf. And he was slumped, half asleep on a pile of lobster and mussel shells. When I got to his table – clocking his Doc Martens boots as I got closer – my primary concern was how many staff it would take to heave him from his chair and send him on his way.

Miraculous though it seems, he managed to lift his head from his bowl of shells, and began to talk as if entirely sober (well, almost). And he was smiling, which signified there was no complaint coming. Quite the contrary. He said, 'I think that was a very good meal. How would you like to be on television?'

At that point I realized he was one of the BBC People. I

have mentioned the Young Thrusters, the artists and actors who made up the clientele of most restaurants in Bristol. But I have so far failed to mention the BBC People who worked at BBC Bristol. I've been saving it for now.

These particular jungle animals bore certain characteristics that distinguished them from the other beasts. They tended to book a table for five, which would excite any hard-working restaurateur with an eye on the profits. When they arrived there were not five or them, but three or two – an instant slash in the size of the potential bill. And they were physically incapable of arriving at the restaurant at the time they had booked. If they wanted the table for five at eight, three or two of them would come in at 8.30 or even later. BBC People were always a nuisance but generally they were lovely and they lifted the ambience of the dining room. They worked hard and played hard and at the table they were chatty and enjoyed themselves.

David Pritchard explained a programme that he was making and thought I could feature in it. I did not take him seriously. Surely it was the wine talking. I finished the brief conversation by saying, 'Yes, great, thanks a lot. I'll do that. Fine. Would you still pay for your meal?'

The following day he phoned, but not to apologize for his drunken promises. Instead, he was just as enthusiastic about putting me on television, and talked me through a programme he was making for BBC Bristol. It was called *RPM*, a sort of arty-crafty programme that went out in the early evenings and featured music and people doing brass rubbings and other arty-crafty things. By my understanding, RPM stands for revs per minute and to this day I have not managed to work out its relevance to the series.

'I was watching you cooking last night,' said David, 'and it would be fantastic to have you on *RPM*.' What did he want me to do precisely? 'I just want you to do a little cooking slot to show on the programme. Do you think you could show viewers how to cook a quality dish for four people for a pound?'

Sometimes by mistake I switch on the TV and see some dreadful daytime cookery programme in the twenty-first century where household name chefs are asked to cook for some C-list celebrity, creating something exotic for a fiver. This is thirty years after Pritchard conned me into cooking a meal for four for £1. What are the producers up to? I don't want to napalm the cooks (as Pritchard has accused me in his book *Shooting the Cook*). I want to napalm the producers.

But back to *RPM*. I thought the publicity would be good for my struggling restaurant and, what's more, David insisted, 'It will only take about five minutes.' That was my first experience of David Pritchard's unusual sense of time. It took all day.

My dish was rabbit with prunes flamed in Cognac, though I never gave any serious consideration to the cost of the ingredients. A pound; ten pounds; who knows? Viewers who did the dish at home might have ended up skint.

David arrived with the entourage: cameramen, sound men, a team of production assistants and as for David's promise that it would only take five minutes, they spent the first five minutes doing a recce – short for *reconnaissance* – of the place to establish what they would eat and drink for the day.

In between shooting me at the stove, they used my telephone, drank my cellar dry, rearranged the furniture, and thumbed through my collection of cassettes to ensure that they were listening to their favourite music. In return, David said, 'That was fantastic,' and gave me a tenner.

I reckoned, it doesn't matter that they've come in and trashed the place because when the finished product is broadcast millions of viewers will come to my restaurant. I also believed that I would feature in not just one programme but each and every programme of the series.

I'm not sure why I thought that. Perhaps it was because the crew had spent so long with me, and I didn't know that a day of filming – constant retakes while you're worried that a production assistant is raiding your wine cellar – often equals just a couple of minutes on air.

The series was broadcast. Was I in the first programme? No. The second? No. The third, fourth, fifth programmes? No, no and no. I appeared, cooking my flaming rabbit, in the final programme. Coincidentally, the same final programme also featured the Stranglers, whom people seem to think I know really well. I don't. I only know Hugh Cornwell, the lead singer. (I forgot, until recently, that he used to play classical Spanish guitar in my Oakfield Road restaurant. Bloody good he was too.)

I can't remember it doing anything to boost bookings in my restaurant, which by now was spiralling uncontrollably into debt.

And I had a new wife; my second.

Julie was a regular at the restaurant. She played squash a couple of times a week, and after smashing balls on court she and her opponent would come for lunch at Chandos Road. She was blonde, bouncy, vivacious and about ten years younger than me. She was engaging, witty and funny and stood out from the crowd, not least because she was the only customer in a tracksuit and wearing a headband.

Our romance was of the whirlwind variety. We swiftly fell for one another and when, a few months into the relationship, I proposed, Julie said, 'Yes.' The breakdown of my marriage to Jesmond I attributed to the foolishness of youth. Now, in the early eighties, I was approaching my forties and had the benefit of hindsight and the wisdom of maturity from which to draw.

The day before our wedding in 1983 I headed for London with my friend, Alisdair Cuddon, to buy pearl earrings for Julie.

Alisdair and I thought we'd make a day of it. By then we had done quite a few booze-ups in London, all of which seemed to follow a ritual and the search for Julie's earrings was no different from our other outings to the capital.

We began with 'breakfast' on the train. Breakfast did not involve food, but instead was the term, the code, we used for vodka and orange – the *screwdriver* that got everything working first thing in the morning.

When we arrived in London we headed for the West End, and to Bentley's in Swallow Street, just off Piccadilly. Bentley's was very much an Establishment place and, having been through its troubles over the years, it's still there and now being run very well by Richard Corrigan.

At Bentley's Alisdair and I would have a bottle of Chablis and – this is when food hit our stomachs – a dozen oysters each. After that, it was a short stroll to Richard Shepherd's restaurant (and my favourite in London), Langan's. Buzzy, brasserie-like and with walls crammed with great works of art, Langan's is a great restaurant.

With lunch finished, we had to focus on the object of the exercise, which was to buy the earrings, wasn't it? From

Langan's we weaved our way to Asprey's, one of the most expensive jewellery shops in the world.

We were both well spoken and smartly dressed, and when I said, 'I'd like to see some pearl earrings,' the manager raised a nose at the jewels under the glass of the counter as if they were worthless and therefore not for me. Then he escorted Alisdair and me to the vault, which contained the gargantuan gems only available, surely, to rich sheiks, princes and moguls.

When the manager turned his back to retract a tray of pearls the size of footballs, I whispered to Alisdair, 'Get me out of here. I've got 115 quid to spend, not 115,000.'

Eventually we escaped from Asprey's with some tiny pearl earrings, each a speck of white on a gold setting. It was time for afternoon tea, so we staggered off to the Ritz. And afternoon tea drifted into cocktails. It often does.

When it was time to catch the train back, we found ourselves sharing the buffet car with the singer Gary Glitter. There was a time when everyone raved about Glitter. In his weird spangly get-up and high-heeled boots, he was an iconic performer of the seventies.

Then he was exposed and imprisoned for being the vilest paedophile ever known to show business.

Anyhow, Alisdair and I met him in the days when everyone still raved about him. The three of us ended up getting completely pissed. He loved the West Country and a few years later, when I owned my pub in Devon, Glitter would often pop in for a drink. Or I'd bump into him at Langan's. Like others who knew him, I never saw any sign of the evilness that lurked within him. He was positively adored by the British, a seemingly indisputable national treasure.

When Julie and I got married in early 1983 we weren't very well off, but we were determined to be married in what had been her local parish church in Bristol. My restaurant colleagues, particularly Michael McGowan, created a fantastic wedding breakfast in his Bristol restaurant, Michael's.

Barry Yeuille, who ran the highly popular Bonne Auberge in Clifton, acquired a Bentley to take us from the church and he disguised himself as a chauffeur. It was a sumptuous party, all paid for by Michael, Barry and other friends.

Someone had organized a cash whip-round and booked us into the Ritz in London for our wedding night. The only dark shadow over the proceedings was that Julie's mother and brother refused to attend. Outwardly, I was phlegmatic about their lack of approval in me. Inwardly, I was very hurt.

Poppy was born shortly after Christmas, 1983. Julie had the most terrible long labour. I was in the restaurant and called round to the hospital at about eleven o'clock on 28 December, my birthday. She was going to be born imminently. But it wasn't to be and I had to return to the restaurant to lock up.

We had long prepared a cradle and all of the baby things and Julie and I brought our child home. She was a great big baby and she was very red – that's why we called her Poppy. It just seemed to fit. Her second name was Thea, after Celia and David's daughter.

A year after the *RPM* programme I was still running the restaurant in Chandos Road, and it was even closer to bankruptcy than it had been when David and his crew had come to film me twelve months earlier.

A waitress came into the kitchen and said, 'There's a chap called David on the phone. He wants to speak to you.'

I'm sick and tired of waking up feeling sick and tired.

Me at Wellington School in 1959.
I am top row, second from the right.

My father in 1938.

Mum in her beloved garden in
Sea Mills, Bristol.

A rare photo of my sister Brenda, Mum and me in 2000 at Brenda's home in Henley-on-Thames. Mum was by then very poorly.

My mother was a life-long socialist. She said, 'When you see that Neil Kinnock make sure you get a picture of the two of you.' Hence this shot of me and the Labour leader, taken at BBC TV Wales.

With David Pritchard, food lover and talented director. Our relationship had a profound effect on television and cookery programmes.

I first met Marco Pierre White in the late 1980s.

From top left: Poppy and friend at Creek Lodge; Poppy, Major and me in Kinsale; Me and Taoiseach Charlie Haughey, aboard his yacht in those halcyon Irish days.

Creek lodge, Kinsale, Co Cork. Bought for £16,000
whilst filming *Floyd on Britain and Ireland*.

The auctioneer's brochure for Creek Lodge, after the slight improvement.

My son Patrick and I at Floyd's Inn (Sometimes), Tuckenhay, Devon, circa 1995.

Being forced to pose again.

Wedding day, January 1996. Tess and I celebrate with two of my very best friends, Trish Winterbottom and Hugh McHardy, aka Huge Bacardi.

Me in my Spanish kitchen.

I picked up the phone, assumed it was David Martin on the other line, and said, 'Hello, everything OK?'

He said, 'It's David.' It was not the Brummie accent of my friend David Martin. 'David Pritchard. Do you remember we did that programme in your restaurant?'

I had on my mind the preoccupations of what might be happening in the busy kitchen and at first I hadn't a clue what he was talking about. I quickly whizzed through the memory bank and then I recalled my cameo on *RPM*. 'Oh yes, hello.'

He said, 'I am now Features Editor of BBC Plymouth. Would you like to come and make a pilot programme about fish and cooking fish?' He told me how his BBC remit was only to make programmes that reflected the local industry and community. This would be a one-off programme, but called 'a pilot' because if it did well, then, let's hope, it would lead on to a series.

I had a minivan, which would get me to Plymouth, but I had no money. I was well and truly broke.

However, I wanted to look my best. I 'borrowed' some cash from the till, and had myself a double-breasted blue blazer made. I bought a pair of smart trousers, and a pair of Church's shoes. I'd been wearing bow ties since my mid-teens, when I was a cub reporter, and wasn't about to stop now. I loaded my new clothes into the back of the minivan, along with a picnic of food that would see me through. If I learned anything from my days in the army, then it was to ensure I always had food close by. You never knew when you might need it.

All packed, I drove to Plymouth in the evening ahead of filming the following day.

I was due to meet David at seven the next morning but hadn't booked a hotel for the night, mainly because paying for a room was an unaffordable luxury. It hadn't occurred to David that I might want to stay in a hotel, and therefore it should be on BBC expenses, and I hadn't pushed it. I parked the car, hit the pub, and then maybe another pub, and ended up in a salubrious haunt in Union Street, where all the prostitutes and the drug addicts hung out.

Chucking-out time coincided with my arranged 7 a.m. meeting with David, which was pretty neat as I didn't find myself wandering the streets, looking for warmth and a coffee in a greasy spoon café. David explained the plan. We'd go out on a fishing boat, catch some pilchards and then cook the fish aboard the boat. There were about eight of us: me, David the director, the cameraman, the assistant cameraman, the lighting man, sound man, a production assistant and a couple of other bods.

What I was to discover – in fact, it took me some while to discover – was that BBC film crews, like other television film crews, sometimes know nothing about food and locations and people.

They had found a nice Cornish fisherman who had told them, 'I'll take ye out and get those pilchards for ye.'

BBC crew: 'Great. How much?'

Wrinkled Cornish fisherman: 'To catch those pilchards from them there seas will cost ye £150 for the rent of the boat. That be my best price for ye folk from the telly.'

BBC crew, handing over cash: 'Wow. Thank you. Great.'

We stared at the boat. I said to the director, 'David, this is not a pilchard boat.' Remember, I had sailed around the Med for about eighteen months. I knew about boats.

He said, 'Yes it is.' He glanced away and then looked back at me. 'What do you mean?'

I said, 'David, I went sailing around the Med for about eighteen months. I owned a yacht. I know what a pilchard boat looks like and this ain't one of them.' We all clambered on to the fisherman's boat and sailed out into the Atlantic.

Two hours later we were bobbing around. Freezing cold, wet from drizzle and waves, hungry and still without having caught one single fish, let alone a pilchard. The tide was going out and it was beginning to dawn on the least seafaring among us that we were in danger of being stranded or, worse, swept away on a course to America.

The fisherman, meanwhile, continued to toss his net into the sea and then haul it back in, feign surprise and say, 'This be a black net.' It was an empty net, in other words. A net full of flapping silver fish would be 'a silver net'.

This was the point at which to produce my picnic. When I met the crew a few hours earlier, they looked at my picnic with some amusement. Then, they were intrigued. Now they watched in envy – seven pairs of eyes on stalks (eight if you count the Cornish fisherman) – as I started to unpack my lunch. It included Marmite sandwiches and some fruit, a Thermos flask of steaming tea and a quarter bottle of Johnnie Walker whisky. I also had a tin of John West pilchards in tomato sauce.

'I told you, David.' I tossed a forkful of tinned pilchards overboard and then said, 'I've just put more pilchards back into this sea than have been taken out of it for the past fifty years. And on the strength of that, boys, let's have a little whisky.'

After six hours on the waves, our expedition to catch a pilchard came to an end and we motored back to shore. The fisherman rubbed his weather-wrinkled forehead with the back of his weather-wrinkled hand and gave us: 'The pilchards won't come t' ye if they don't like t' look o' ye,' or some such superstition and we all went and had a drink to work out how we would find a fish for *Floyd on Fish*.

The next morning, we struck gold, though not with silver nets. We found an Italian fishmonger who was based in Falmouth and who sold pilchards. His pilchards were imported from Sicily and while David was keen to feature local produce, he reasoned that the fishmonger was local and his business was local and, after all, the pilchards might have started out in the Mediterranean but they were now firmly on West Country soil.

However, the birth of our innovative and fresh television style – much copied since, I might add – happened quite by chance when we filmed at the Horn of Plenty, the hotel near Tavistock, set in five acres of the Tamar Valley in Devon.

The kitchen was overseen by Sonia Stevenson, who was unusual in that she was one of the few celebrated female chefs in Britain. Years earlier I had eaten there with David and Celia Martin, and jolly good it was, too.

This time round, David Pritchard, the crew and I arrived at the hotel and we all sat in the garden with Sonia, chatting about this or that. It was extremely nice and pleasant but I became increasingly curious about what we would do. After all, we had to film *something*. Didn't we? Was there a plan?

Eventually, I said, 'So David, what's the plan? What's going to happen?' He looked at me, mystified. 'Oh,' he said, 'I think it would be nice if you go and cook something with Sonia.' In other words, there was no plan, let alone idiot boards and certainly not autocues.

We all traipsed into the hotel's kitchens, Sonia being assured that 'it will only take five minutes', and because she was a decent person who did not understand television speak she didn't know that five minutes means eight hours.

When David shouted, 'Turn over' it didn't seem to work. Sonia had decided to cook hake with a hollandaise sauce and I was expected to be the presenter, standing at her side and saying things like, 'And now, Sonia, tell me, what you are going to cook for us?'

It quickly became clear that she hadn't prepared her ingredients. So when she said, 'I am going to cook hake,' she then walked off to the fridge, straight out of shot. The camera was left focused on a chopping board. Sonia came back into shot, clutching the hake. I said, 'And what happens next?'

Sonia replied, 'Now I need some lemon,' and off she went again, wandering off to the fridge, straight out of shot. She returned, eventually, but when she needed the frying pan she was off again, the camera unable to follow her. It was disastrous, although I must say that it was not Sonia's fault. She had not been told what to do. People in TV don't tell you what to do because they don't know what to do.

David was soon desperately bored and he left the kitchen and strolled into the garden, what to do I do not know. 'Hold on a minute Mrs Stevenson,' I said. 'Let's stop everything.' I found David in the grounds and suggested that Sonia and I reverse the roles. I would cook, while she would observe. He liked the idea.

Back in the kitchen, I gathered together all the ingredients and put them on a table, as if I was preparing to cook for customers. When we came to film, I took off my blazer and laid it on the floor, like Sir Walter Raleigh laying his cloak on the ground for Queen Elizabeth. I beckoned her to step onto the blazer and away, out of shot, so that I could cook.

So I set about cooking the hake with hollandaise, but soon realized that there were periods, albeit brief, when I needed to think about what I might say next. Although I was petrified, I couldn't simply stare at the food or into the camera in silence. I had to do something.

I had a bottle of wine on the prep table intended for cooking. But in the absence of any direction from Pritchard, when I ran out of inspiration and words, I said, 'I think I'll have a quick slurp,' to buy valuable seconds to recompose my thoughts. I now realize I borrowed that fantastic phrase from the great Graham Kerr, the Galloping Gourmet. Thank you, Graham.

At one stage onions were frying in the pan and I noticed that Clive's camera was aimed at me, rather than the food. 'Clive,' I said, looking straight into the lens, 'if this is a programme about cooking then surely the camera should be on the food.' He moved the camera from my face, down to the frying pan. Again, my remarks to Clive would become a major part of the success. (To this day, when I am in airports or roaming around, the most common question I am asked is: 'Where's Clive?')

When it was time to do the voice-overs, I reckoned they had to be done as sort of postcards written to an imaginary friend. Instead of doing the conventional voice-over, which was both wordy and worthy, I wanted a narrative that was down-to-earth, friendly and familiar. I addressed them to Hector, the name of a chap I'd sailed the Mediterranean with.

These criteria – the wine glass, Clive and the 'postcard' voice-overs – became the essential ingredients for our recipe for success.

The pilot, which was broadcast in October 1984, showed me, on the fishing boat, consoling myself with a snifter of Johnnie Walker. Followed by me, buying Italian pilchards and then frying them for the viewers. And then me drinking wine in Sonia's kitchen. Oh, the drinking. That dram and that glass of wine would not bode well . . .

THIRTEEN

David Pritchard had a really excellent wife, Judith. I don't know what she did. She might have been a nurse or she might have been a council administrator, but whatever, she was an impeccable lady, smart and correct, and I liked her a lot.

I think Judith sometimes found David's behaviour unacceptable but she was old school, one of those wives who tolerated a husband's poor points while keeping the house going and checking the bills. She was a lovely woman.

It occurred to me that while I had happily agreed to make the pilot for *Floyd on Fish* I didn't have a contract, and it won't surprise you to know that I hadn't even asked for money. In fact, money hadn't been discussed.

In other words, David didn't need to pay me a bean. This grated and as David hadn't raised the subject of cash and because I was skint as usual I said to him one day, 'I haven't got any money. When are you going to give me some?'

David glanced away, staring into the middle distance, as if I had asked him a question he couldn't answer. And he didn't answer.

The subject continued to come up, but each time David failed to say when he would actually pay me for presenting the programme and would forget after we'd gone our separate ways. Eventually, I said, 'David, if you do not pay me I am going to tell your wife.'

David was stunned. 'You wouldn't dare,' he said.

'Yes I would.' I knew I would and you know I would, but David didn't know me well enough to know I would.

I was having dinner with the Pritchards one night when, around about digestifs, I decided the time was right. I said to Judith, 'I don't quite know how to say this, but I have not actually been paid yet by David.'

She was alarmed. 'You have not been paid?'

'No.'

'David,' she said, with immense authority, 'you are so irresponsible. You must pay this man.' David's bottom wriggled uncomfortably on his chair.

The next morning I had a cheque and we never argued about money again.

The pilot was a success. It had to have to have been, I suppose, or else I wouldn't be doing this autobiography. The *Western Morning News* ran a review under the headline 'A Star is Born'. And as a result of the programme BBC Plymouth was inundated with sackloads of mail and had to hire a couple of temp secretaries to read and respond to the unpredicted amount of letters.

However, the controller of BBC Plymouth would not allow the programme to be submitted to the network so that it could be broadcast nationally. And here's a curious thing . . . The controller did not consider the programme worthy of a wider audience because I was, there on film, drinking alcohol. I told you that whisky and that glass of wine would get me into trouble. And I should also add that in that programme and throughout the *Floyd* series that followed I was never drunk when I stepped in front of the camera, even if I did have a drink in my hand.

David, however, was not a quitter. He travelled to London, met the head honchos at the Beeb, and a couple of months after the screening of the pilot, we'd negotiated a contract to make a series, *Floyd on Fish*, for BBC2.

He phoned me to say, 'We've landed a deal.' I thought, wow, that's great, I'll do it, it'll be fun. I didn't think any more of it or what it might bring. Quite simply, I had no idea how it would change my life.

Let's look at the main characters, the crew – invisible to the viewer – who were there for most of the *Floyd* series.

David Pritchard, director and producer: depending on his mood he saw himself as either Billy Wilder (the legendary American director of Hollywood greats *The Odd Couple* and *Some Like It Hot*) or David Lean (the legendary British director of the classics *Doctor Zhivago*, *Lawrence of Arabia* and *The Bridge on the River Kwai*).

Clive North, cameraman: tall, short hair and a very straight man. His wife was an impassioned goat breeder who didn't really approve of Clive going off for weeks at a time with reprobates like Floyd and Pritchard. But his photography was outstanding, ceaseless work.

Tim White, sound man: the youngest member of the crew, he was – I thought at first – a little obnoxious. I quickly grew to love and admire him. Like all sound men, Tim couldn't stand the sound of gas. 'The gas is making a spluttering noise,' he'd say. And I'd say, 'Tim, I can't cook without it. It's gas – it splutters.'

Sound men want 'clean' sound. They want to exist in a

world where there is no noise on the streets; there are no other people talking, shouting or doing noisy things that people do; there are no cars, no buses, no bicycles with rink-a-tink bells on their handlebars; there is nothing; most important of all there are no aeroplanes flying overhead and certainly no helicopters. I quickly learned how to overcome the problem, so if we were filming and I saw a helicopter approaching I'd say, 'Oh no, not another noisy helicopter' and Tim would know to cut his sound accordingly.

Andy MacCormack, assistant cameraman: a bit of a hippy, handsome, laid-back and dead cool. When David and I rowed, Andy would hippy talk the arguments out. 'Come on, man,' he'd say.

Frances Proudfoot-Wallis, production assistant: adorable and everybody's mother. Looked after us all, but would become very distressed about everything. She couldn't drive cars in foreign countries and do other essentials that production assistants would ordinarily be required to do. But she always did her best, often in very difficult circumstances.

In times of trouble, she'd say in her Scottish accent, 'David, what have you done now?' She was lovely and gentle. When we were filming in Taunton I sent her off to buy some food props. I said, 'Get some cheese, or tomatoes, something to decorate the set.' She returned with a tin of tomatoes.

Steve Williams, lighting man: hailed from the theatre. Wore silk suits and flowing scarves and was always having crises. You might have thought he was gay, except he absolutely was not. He lit things exquisitely and carefully.

Steve was about the only one who would ever stand up to David but then he would collapse as well. He would have a crisis, phone home and then he was in tears because something terrible had happened at home. I gave him a hug when he needed it. And when I needed it, he gave me a hug.

I wrote a book, *Floyd on Fish* (published by BBC Books), to tie in with the series. It was an A to Z of recipes.

So you had A for Anchovies, H for Haddock and Herrings, P for Paella . . . and so on. B was for *Ric* (yes, misspelt) Stein's Baked Bass, which involves stuffing bass with stir-fried celery, carrot and turnips, before baking it in white wine for half an hour at 220°C. I often borrowed other chefs' recipes for my books, giving due credit of course.

Having committed myself to compile an A to Z, I found myself stuffed because I couldn't think of a fish dish that began with Z.

The deadline for delivery was fast approaching and the Z fish dish was becoming a nagging preoccupation. I asked around, but no one could help out. Then, one evening, I found myself on a train from London to Bristol and I met Miles Kington, the brilliant writer of satire. Miles asked what I was up to, and I told him, 'I have to deliver a book about the A to Z of fish dishes, but I'm in trouble.'

'Why?'

'Because I can't think of a fish dish that begins with the letter Z.'

'Oh, that's easy,' he said, as if I had just asked him the sum of two plus two.

I said, 'Sorry?'

Miles repeated, 'That's easy. Zarzuela.'

I'd never heard of it. '*Zarzuela*?'

'Yes. Zarzuela.'

He then produced pen and paper and wrote the book's entry

for the letter Z. You should know before reading on that zarzuela is a Catalan fish stew; there is no such thing as a zarzuela fish, and Miles gave the whole thing the typical Kington touch, complete with ridicule and heaps of imagination. It was duly published in my book . . .

Zarzuela

I have only ever come across this fish in Spain, so I can't tell you the English name for it – I doubt if there is one. The first time I tasted it was in Tarifa, the small town which is even further south than Gibraltar and just across the water from Africa. There was a competition going on, featuring a game not unlike boules, *but instead of being played with metal bowls in French style, it was being played with the empty husks of sea urchins – a sort of* boules marinières. *The locals told me that way back in Moorish days, the Moors used to play it with the skulls of conquered Spaniards. I was persuaded to enter and managed to get through two rounds before it got too painful.*

Anyway, they were cooking fish over an open fire, a delicious large fish with firm white flesh called zarzuela which is so rare that is only found at the very beginning of April. Curiously, I found it the next time in the north of Spain, but at the end of September. The locals explained that the schools of zarzuela drift slowly up the Portuguese coast during the summer and land in the north of Spain at the end of the season before returning south for the winter. What was never explained to me was why the fish was now, not big and white, but small and red-skinned. I can only assume that we were eating the off-spring of the ones I had seen in Tarifa.

They are best grilled over an open fire and washed down with good local wine. Don't forget – it's pronounced tharthuela.

As a footnote to 'Zarzuela', I wrote: 'Miles Kington kindly gave me this recipe – when he was a judge at the Bridport Scallop Festival (I was a judge, too, actually).' The Bridport Scallop Festival was a product of my own imagination. It did not exist.

Yet after the book was published I received letters from readers who had also attended the festival. Then one night I was at a gathering in London and a food critic came up to me and said, 'You don't cook zarzuela like that, you know.'

Sadly, Miles died not so long ago. I didn't know him well but he was a funny and gentle man and I have a vague recollection of spending what must have been a good night at his house in London.

I went on to continue the mischief in my future cookery books. In *Floyd Around the Med* I invented a restaurant with its noted vineyard called Château Palombes – Doves Château. I gave specific directions on how to find it: 'Up the D127, off the RN7 . . .' and all the rest of it. I was in Dubai a few years ago and met a man who said, 'You bugger. I drove all the way there and it didn't exist.'

I invented a restaurant in Tunisia in a charming, non-existent place called Place des Prostituées – Prostitutes' Square.

In *Floyd on Britain and Ireland* I invented coaching inns between York and heaven-knows-where. They didn't exist, just like the Bridport Scallop Festival didn't exist, but I'd receive letters from readers telling me they'd enjoyed going to the inns and they had a thoroughly good meal.

It's crucial to emphasize that for most of the time I was terribly serious about what I was writing. But every now and again I thought it would be funny to put something in and couldn't resist.

Floyd on Fish was broadcast in the summer of 1985 and was an instant triumph: a hit with viewers and critics alike.

It is a strange feeling to experience success of that sort, and what sticks in my mind is that David and I had never imagined the reaction. What had just been us, you know, on a Cornish coastline, or a Devon trawler or in the shadow of a tin mine, or something like that, in the pissing rain, or in the howling wind, or in the sunshine, or on a riverbank . . . What had just been a few of us playing at filming suddenly became public on a national scale.

David and I set out to have some fun and create programmes, but we hadn't taken into consideration that at the time British television only presented studio-based cookery programmes and they were fundamentally dull. Yes, they were dull and worthy and akin to a secondary school lesson in modern home economy.

But David and I hadn't spent our time groaning about other cookery programmes. We just did our own thing. We simply went out on the road and thought, let's go and get a fish and cook it, and fish aren't covered in breadcrumbs and don't come in packets. Fish come out of the sea or out of the river, so that's where we'd better go to get them.

We had no idea of the enormous impact that the series would have on people but we'd not had ambitions to achieve that impact. We didn't do it deliberately. As you know, there were no rehearsals, no scripts and everything was done in one take . . . unless a noisy helicopter flew over and I didn't spot it in time to warn Tim White.

If you were to set out nowadays to achieve similar success the rules would be entirely different. The crew would comprise scores of people, rather than about a dozen, and there would be constant reshoots and retakes.

It was the impromptu feel of our programmes that would help to capture the hearts of the British public, as well as the feeling that anything could go wrong at any time. I mention rules, yet I don't think we had any, and if we did, then we most certainly would have broken them. The success of *Floyd on Fish* was followed by another hit, *Floyd on Food*, which was broadcast on the BBC in the spring of 1986.

A lot of people thought I was an actor. I didn't like that because actors dress up in other people's clothes and faces. They are not themselves. So many times you hear an actor – dynamic on stage and screen – being interviewed on the radio, and how boring are they?

While filming *Floyd on Fish* I left the restaurant in Chandos Road in what I believed were capable hands, but during my absence things had not run smoothly; let's put it that way.

My relationship with Julie was deteriorating, so much so that before filming I had packed a suitcase and moved out of our home, the house next to the restaurant. I moved into my mother's home. So there I was, pretending to be a film star shooting in Devon, when the reality was that my life was a mess. And, now in my early forties, I was living with my mum, which remained a secret from viewers and the press.

I thought it was time to sell the lease to the restaurant. The new owner was an ex-accountant, the same man who bought the bistro some years earlier.

The ex-accountant was paying a very modest sum for the business and on the agreed day of sale I went round to his home, as requested, to pick up the cash. He lived on the top floor of a Georgian five-storey property in Clifton. I rang on the bell, and he opened the window five storeys up. He shouted down, 'Hello, Keith, I can't come down, I don't feel very well. I'll throw the money out of the window.'

As I was trying to absorb the absurdity of what he had just said, he threw a great big bundle of cash out of the window. I stood on the pavement and gazed up dreamily as a wad of notes was tossed outwards. I don't know if they had started out held together by an elastic band. But there was no elastic band when a few feet out of the window, the notes were caught by the wind, separated into a rainfall of pounds and were blown all over Clifton. Notes scattered and notes flew. I managed to retrieve about £3,000; the rest ended up on rooftops or God knows where. Maybe you found a fiver that day?

For my new career as a television star I started out in debt.

FOURTEEN

There had been strong signs of chaos during the making of our television series, but life with Pritch really took on new meaning when we crossed the Channel to film *Floyd on France*.

By now, I'd established a thoroughly organized way of travelling in an effort to minimize stress and avoid catastrophe.

I had my Go File – a folder that contained all the essentials: passport, tickets, diary, notes and other miscellaneous but required documents.

I travelled with lots of suitcases that contained items I considered absolute musts for an enjoyable life. I had a little portable radio, and one or two books I'd read ten million times before. I took maps and a first-aid kit, and clothes to suit the occasion.

I also packed a knife, some kind of heat source like a Primus stove, and a piece of string which had a magnet tied at the end in case I dropped my keys down a drain and had to retrieve them. I didn't once drop my keys down a drain, but I had the magnet-on-string nevertheless.

I took stacks of notebooks and a tape recorder. In terms of food, my luggage included a jar of Marmite, a few dozen Mars bars, apples or other fruit, mineral water (still) and a bottle of

Scotch. There was also a collapsible walking stick or foldable chair, so that when I wanted to sit and eat I could.

This drove members of the crew insane. They hovered around me and my picnic, like buzzards waiting to pick, and said, 'Can we have some of yours?' I said no because they should by now have learned their lesson – they should bring picnics, too. 'A Mars bar?' No. 'An apple?' No, get your own. 'But we haven't got any food. Please can we have some of yours?' No.

I also packed a small plastic jug so that if we found ourselves in a place where water was scarce, I could just fill the jug and keep it with me, either for cooking purposes or for washing my hair.

I always took precautions. Almost like having safe sex.

So we agreed to meet in France, and I packed all my cases into my Volvo and with a driver to take me (at my expense, rather than the BBC's), drove to our rendezvous in France. I arrived at the hotel, carted my luggage to my room, and waited for David. Compare what I had brought with the sight that greeted me when the director came through the front door: David was carrying a child's suitcase, a picture of Mickey Mouse on it. It was, I later discovered, a case that he had borrowed from his young daughter.

David said he could murder a cup of tea, and what followed would become a pattern that was almost comical in its repetition during our tour of France. Of course, David wanted what we know as builder's tea – a cup of Tetley's or something similar. But they cannot make tea in France. I know this and David should soon have known it, but he never seemed to grasp it.

Me to the waiter: *'Deux thés, s'il vous plaît.'*

The tea arrives with either a slice of lemon and no milk, or a pot of steaming hot milk.

David: 'I don't want that.'

I'd tell him that was how the French served tea and you'll never change it, but if he wanted to try then he should learn to speak French. Time and again, we endured the tea-ordering ritual: order it, stare at it and then say, 'I don't want that.' Strangely, even when he ordered coffee he was frequently served tea with lemon.

We went to Colmar, in the Alsace region, to film at an impressive hotel-restaurant called La Maison des Têtes, originally a house built in the seventeenth century. Frances had failed to book us into a hotel, and as it was the middle of the day David was optimistic that he had the time to find a B&B. 'Can I take your car and driver?' he asked and I agreed.

He did not come back until ten o'clock at night. I said, 'Where have you been?'

He replied, 'Oh, I've just been to see *Full Metal Jacket*.'

Things weren't going to get any better. Clive, who was meticulous about his work, was always the first up in the morning and he'd head off to film what we called 'the pretties'.

The pretties were cut-away shots that were weaved into the final cut of the programme. They might show the surrounding countryside or a chateau or a few birds – herons skimming across the water – or, for that matter, a few birds in bikinis and walking along a beach.

All of these sights are pretty, hence 'the pretties'. Later on, when the programme was broadcast, viewers would see me cooking and I'd say, 'And while we're waiting for the boring onions to fry have a look at this bit of architecture . . .' Cut to Clive's pretties.

We were in the Dordogne, in south-west France, and David went fishing. I'll say that again. The director-producer just buggered off and left us, to go fishing. I didn't believe it myself when a member of the crew told me.

When he returned, I said, 'David, where have you been?'

He said casually, 'I was tired. I went fishing.'

'David,' I said, as if talking to a child, 'your job is to tell us what to do. Not to bugger off.'

We had a chat about the Dordogne and learned about the vast chateaux that were built by the English in the fourteenth and fifteenth centuries. David and I both share an interest in architecture and I said, 'I don't think it would be a bad idea if you just took a couple of pretties of the chateaux.' So the next day David and Clive squeezed themselves in David's beaten-up 1966 Renault and drove off to shoot a few of the English castles that were about fifteen miles down the road. I was in my hotel room having an afternoon siesta when the phone rang. It was David. The telephone conversation went like this . . .

David: 'We've run out of petrol.'

Me: 'Run out of petrol?'

David: 'Yes.'

Me: 'Where are you?'

David: 'We're in a bar.'

Me: 'Well, can't you buy some petrol and put it in the car?'

David: 'We haven't got any money.'

Me: 'Well, if you haven't got any money how are you going to pay for the drinks in the bar?'

David: 'We can't.'

Me: 'David, let me get this straight. You have no money, do not have a car that works and you are sitting getting drunk in a bar buying drinks with money that you do not have.'

David: 'It's not our fault we ran out of petrol. Can you send your driver with some cash?'

Me: 'I think you should speak to Frances. She is the production assistant. She is there to help the director when he runs out of petrol and does not have the money to pay for drinks in a bar. I really think you should speak to Frances, David. She can get into a car and drive over with the petty cash, pay your bill and put petrol in your car.'

Frances would not drive in France. She didn't like driving on 'the wrong side of the road'. She refused to go. I said, 'Well, can you somehow get some francs over to David in the bar?'

She said, 'I haven't got any francs.'

I said, 'Can you change some travellers' cheques?'

She replied, 'I don't know how to change travellers' cheques.'

I'd had enough. 'Stuff them,' I said of David and Clive. 'Let them be. They can stay there for eternity as far as I'm concerned.'

I don't remember how they managed to get back to the hotel, but when the programme was shown the English chateaux were there in the film. How had David achieved this? He'd bought a few postcards and with clever editing slipped them in as the pretties.

As it was, I was the one who took the 'rushes' – the unedited film – to the airport every day so that it could be sent back to the BBC for editing. I was the one who took the travellers' cheques to the bank and got them cashed for expenses.

I tended not to eat with the crew because I quickly realized it can be frustrating. A dozen people sit down at a table, look at the menu and choose what they want. When the waiter arrives to take the order they all decide to change their minds and choose a different dish. When the food is being cooked by the chef in the kitchen they all change their minds again, usually reverting to their initial choice. When the food is brought to the table they cannot remember what they ordered. 'I asked for no olives,' one will say to the waiter, and another will add, 'I wanted it well done.'

The experienced members of the crew, I discovered, carry a guidebook that tells them where to find the best curry in that particular country – it's a bit like the taxi driver's Knowledge. Essentially, they are mostly talented people who work hard and want to end each day with a damned good curry before retiring to their rooms, where they wash their underwear in the sink and polish their lenses. Frequently, I spent evenings alone in my hotel room preparing for the following day.

I thought through what I'd say and, of course, what I'd cook for the following day's cooking sketch – those bits of me at the stove we called 'cooking sketches'. For instance, when I cooked for the master chefs in Dijon I decided to serve perch in Gevrey Chambertin, one of the finest wines of Burgundy. I used my bedroom and bathroom as a storage unit full of pots and pans and full of the ingredients in the red wine marinade.

Increasingly, however, I found myself staying up all night, unable to sleep because I was worrying about how it would go the next day. Slowly and, it seems, inevitably a bottle of whisky was becoming my crutch: a companion that would help me through the hours from midnight to dawn.

I did have an assistant to help me prepare the food. David

had introduced her and said she was an intelligent Cambridge graduate who loved food and was fluent in the language. She did love food, but only if it was vegetarian cuisine. The language in which she was fluent was Russian, not French. I said to David, 'How can you do this to me? I want a proper person who can eat meat.'

He shrugged, 'Oh she'll be fine. She's got a degree in Theology.'

One day in France, David appeared and told me about his plan for the day. He was extremely excited about it, even though, he too, had been up all night, but in a bar rather than a bedroom. He'd met a multi-millionaire who owned a hot-air balloon. David was forever meeting people in bars who would ultimately be dragged into the chaos. 'We're going ballooning,' he said, and I nodded. 'OK, I can do that.'

We drove to Alsace to meet the multi-millionaire. He was one of those rich hippies. You know the sort: long hair, scruffy jeans and a T-shirt, but with a Ferrari sitting in the long, gravel driveway leading to a mansion, and a hot-air balloon down the road. Of all genres, David much prefers rich hippies.

This was the plan, and as we stood by the balloon in a field I worked it out with military precision. The hippy, Clive and I would go up in the balloon, fly high and gracefully over the Vosges mountains and I'd try to cook something while up in the air.

The crew down on the ground were divided between three cars, and they'd follow us. I produced maps by, I think, the Institut Géographique National (the French version of the Ordnance Survey) and plotted out the routes. We weren't quite sure where the wind would take us so to compensate I studied the maps and told the driver of each car exactly which roads and dirt tracks to use.

'David,' I said, 'we are here and according to your lunatic friend we'll probably land there.' These sorts of maps, incidentally, were items that the director and rest of the crew had never previously seen, possibly didn't know existed. They didn't know where they were from one minute to the next.

The three of us climbed into the balloon. Lift off. I looked down to earth and saw the three cars heading off in completely the wrong directions, the blind mice scurrying. The points of the compass had become an irrelevance. I thought, Christ, they are incompetent. No, they're not. They don't have a leader. They don't have someone to tell them what to do and then make sure they know how to do it.

To fly in a hot-air balloon is an exhilarating experience and I thoroughly enjoyed it . . . in the beginning. As we sailed through the skies, the mad French hippy said, 'I've been told you like to have a drink.'

Wow, I thought, has he got a drinks cabinet on board? 'Yes, I do,' I said. 'Pastis or something?'

'I've got some champagne,' he told me and I nodded with approval. From a hippy-ish rucksack he brought out a magnum and said, 'Do you know how to chill champagne instantly?'

I said, 'No, I don't,' although I do know that a good way to chill drinks is to fill your ice bucket with salt. But I didn't know that the other best way, if you are in a hot-air balloon fuelled by butane, is to unplug the butane gas container and spray the bottle with the gas so that it frosts up.

That is what he did, and that is when I also learned that this chilling technique deprives the balloon of any motivational power.

So we ran out of gas. Oblivious to the fact that the butane

gas which a minute earlier was working was now not working, the hippy blasted the cork off the bottle and poured me a glass of champagne.

He then demolished the remaining contents with rapidity, and in between gulps told me things like, 'Here in the Vosges, where the ceps are collected in the autumn time . . . and you know the hares are the finest . . .' Forgive me if I can't remember precisely what he said, but as he was talking the balloon was losing height and my life was flashing before my eyes.

The rich hippy's voice was a perpetual hum, and he laughed as well, as Clive and I looked out over the edge of the basket, and down to see where we would crash.

It wasn't that bad. We were heading towards a motorway so it would all be quite quick – as we'd hit the ground a juggernaut would squash us instantly and we'd feel no pain. Otherwise, we might hit those high-tension pylons and would be electrocuted. Alternatively, we'd plummet into the lake over there, and drown. The hippy laughed. I thought, we haven't got a chance. At the very least, we'll break every bone in our bodies. Never mind *Around the World in Eighty Days*. We were starring in *See the Vosges and Die*.

As it was we went down on the motorway. The drivers had seen us coming down, and they had slowed and then come to a halt so that we landed on the tarmac in front of a queue of lorries and cars. We hit the ground with a thud and the basket toppled but we remained alive.

Clive and I were shocked and dazed. The hippy was uncharacteristically quiet and clearly shaken. The traffic started to drive around us and then a battered Renault pulled up. It was David. He marched up to Clive and the first thing he asked was, 'Were you turning over [filming] as you crashed?'

There are two ways of looking at it. You could say that David didn't give a damn about Clive and me (or his hippy friend). Or you could say that he was brilliant at his job. That he was putting the film – rather than the presenter and cameraman – first. It's what television producers do and why shouldn't they? I don't criticize them for it, but it makes me feel sorry for them. They seem to have missed out on something. Like life.

David found me difficult and stubborn but he was amused by me. And still is.

We were filming in France – in Saint-Malo, to be precise – when the letter arrived. It was a divorce writ.

These days when you want to divorce the reason you give is all-encompassing – 'irretrievably broken down', for instance. There's no need for details. Back in the mid-eighties the divorce writ was a catalogue of errors on the part of the spouse who was being divorced. All the crimes were listed.

My list of crimes went on for two pages. As I remember, it was gambling, whoring and drinking ad infinitum. It was terrible, absolutely terrible, but it was a little exaggerated I have to say. The whoring bit was nonsense. The late nights gambling and drinking may have seemed suspicious but I have never been unfaithful to any of my wives.

I hadn't seen the writ coming. I knew we were going to get divorced but I didn't know it was would happen like this.

I should explain the gambling accusation. The restaurant scene in Bristol had undergone a dramatic change, with an alternative sect of restaurateurs taking business from the likes of Berni Inns and trattorias. This sect included me, and two chaps previously mentioned. One was Michael McGowan, whom I had taught to cook at Bistro Ten, before he opened Michael's restaurant, which was extraordinary – homely Victorian decor with comfortable chairs beside a fireplace. It was where Julie and I held our wedding reception.

Then there was Barry Yeuille, who'd been the Bentley-driving chauffeur at our wedding. He had the Bonne Auberge, which served moules frites and steak au poivre. Barry was Jack the Lad. He had curly blond hair and was usually dressed in a white silk suit and white silk shirt which was unbuttoned to just above the navel, so that he could show off the medallion that hung on a chunky chain around his neck.

We'd meet up after work, usually at the Tiberius casino, which was above Barry's restaurant. There, we played roulette and grumbled about the day. Our little group was something of a self-preservation society. We all disliked the Young Thrusters, who thought London was the Premier Division – the place where it was all happening – and saw our restaurants as Second Division. The Thrusters would book all of us for dinner on a Saturday night and then meet in the pub and decide where to go. It was messing us all up. They were screwing us.

So the likes of Michael, Barry and I said to one another, 'Have the Hendersons booked your place tonight?' When we discovered the Hendersons had booked all of our restaurants for the same evening we said, 'Right, let's black them out.' The Hendersons were banned from all of our restaurants.

If you work in an office you might finish at five or six in the evening and then head off to a wine bar or the pub for an hour. You'll have a cigarette and a glass of wine, talk to someone about the day, and then go home. You'll bath the kids, have dinner with your wife, watch television and tomorrow you'll start all over again.

The restaurant business is not like that. If the restaurateur finishes at two in the morning he doesn't necessarily feel tired. He might want to go out but where does he go?

This is why the Tiberius served a purpose. Gambling is rife in the restaurant business. Think, for example, of that period in between lunch and dinner service. I always had a siesta, but others who worked in the profession might be miles from home and didn't know what to do in that spare time. That's when they'd hit the bookies.

My nocturnal trips to Tiberius caused Julie great distress. I wasn't an extravagant gambler: I played roulette and won more than I lost.

Gambling was Julie's problem with me, or at least one of them. My problem was her mother, who had not attended our wedding. She lived in Guernsey and wrote to Julie saying that I was a bigamist and had lied about being a pupil at Wellington School. I was not a bigamist and had been a pupil at Wellington School.

Her mother's animosity towards me was intense and I believed Julie was steered, was heavily influenced, by her mother. When Poppy was born I took our baby by plane to Guernsey and arrived on the doorstep to introduce grandmother to her granddaughter. 'You're not coming in,' she said.

A few hours later I was at the airport returning home, mystified. Julie didn't have a bad bone in her body, but she was unable to disregard her mother's feelings about me. Her brother, too, really disliked me. I found it peculiar. My parents would say, 'Come in, whoever you are.' But not Julie's mother.

The divorce writ instructed me to be at court on a certain date, which I couldn't make because I was filming. As it was,

I'm quite pleased I wasn't there because I was completely wiped out and wouldn't want to have witnessed it.

Julie got the house beside the restaurant, which in all fairness she had paid for in the first place (though I had maintained it and restored it). If I was entitled to a small slice of it, then I didn't get it. Julie also walked away with quite a large financial settlement, based upon my future earnings.

Now, imagine if I had gone into a bank and said, 'I think I am going to be a TV star. Could you advance me fifty grand?' They would have thrown me out of the door. Somehow Julie's lawyers managed to achieve that.

Julie found a new man, Jean-Jacques, and together with Poppy they went to France to start a new life in Toulouse. I didn't like that one bit because the first I knew of it was when I received a legal document informing me that a hearing about their proposed move would take place at the High Court. I felt desperately unhappy. My attempts to create a home for my family had so far been unsuccessful.

Again, I was filming so didn't receive the letter until I returned to Britain, by which time the hearing had taken place. Had Julie written to me to say they were going to live in France, I would have said, 'Terrific. Good for you.'

I knew Poppy was in good hands because whatever Julie might have been to me she was unquestionably a first-class mother. With hindsight her French husband Jean-Jacques has clearly been an outstanding stepfather, there's no doubt about it. I salute them for that.

FIFTEEN

After the regional screening of *Floyd on Fish* I had become famous overnight in the south-west of England. People were asking me to open fêtes, make speeches to Women's Institutes and all sorts. 'Will you come and judge our Cornish pasty contest?'

It occurred to me that I ought to charge for such things but since I had no agent, I didn't know how to go about it. However, at the time in the BBC Plymouth studios the local news was fronted by a very popular presenter called Chris Denham. We'd meet in the bar of the BBC Club in Plymouth, for a few drinks after the day's work.

He was something of a local hero, forever opening fêtes, taking part in pro-celebrity cricket matches and probably judging Cornish pasty contests. Chris knew the form. So I sought his advice and he said to me, 'You want to get your petrol money, be sure you don't have to pay for any drinks and try to hit them for about fifty quid . . . in cash.'

Incidentally, when Chris later left the BBC he formed his own production company, Denham Productions. It was with Chris – but without his close friend, David Pritchard (who by that time was working for Denham Productions) – that I made *Floyd Around the Med* and *Floyd On Africa*.

Requests for personal appearances grew quite steadily and I became busy, opening supermarkets and attending those fêtes. But one day I received an intriguing phone call from a chap at a local airline, Bryman Airways, which was starting a service from Plymouth to Cork in the Republic of Ireland. He invited me, along with other local minor celebrities and the press and media, to go on the inaugural flight.

He also wondered whether I'd like to attend an event of which I had never heard, the Kinsale Gourmet Festival. The whole trip would last from a Friday to the following Monday. He told me that Kinsale was a charming former fishing village some fifteen miles from Cork City, and I would later discover that he was not wrong.

I had always wanted to go to Ireland, mainly because of the influence of books by J. P. Donleavy, Flann O'Brien, James Joyce and others, so I was immensely excited by the prospect. However, Bryman Airways were offering only a free return flight. No accommodation and no fee.

Frankly, I could not afford to go. I could not afford three nights in a hotel in Kinsale. I didn't have enough money to buy drinks or meals. The whole thing was completely out of the question. I was still struggling with my restaurant in Chandos Road, and going through the death throes of my marriage to Julie. The £2,000 fee that the BBC paid me for making the series *Floyd on Fish* had long been swallowed up.

So regretfully and with great disappointment I had to decline Bryman Airways' offer. A few days later, I got a telephone call from a certain Maureen Aherne, the PR officer for Cork airport. She was charming and friendly and said, 'We're so sorry you are not coming over to the gourmet festival.'

I didn't know until Maureen's call that in the extreme

south-east of Ireland they had all been watching *Floyd on Fish*. I was quite a celebrity there, as well, although my mother living in Bristol could not receive the programme.

'I can't afford to come, Maureen.'

'Don't worry about that,' she said. 'We'll fix all that up for you.'

'But I haven't got enough money to buy a round of drinks.'

'You won't have to buy a round of drinks. You won't have to buy a meal. You won't have to pay for a hotel. Just come on over and have a fantastically good time.' Just the sort of woman you want to know.

I arrived in Cork airport, which in those days was more like a pub with an airstrip rather than the sophisticated international airport that it is today. Maureen and a bevy of local reporters met me off the plane, and she whisked me straight into the VIP bar, where we drank several pints of Murphy's (Cork City being the home to Murphy's stout, whereas Dublin is home to Guinness).

Maureen outlined the itinerary. On the Friday night all the restaurants of Kinsale opened their doors to the media – and of course, to the general public – and we were paired off into small groups. I was with a fabulous Irish journalist called Miles McWinney, a cultured man who specialized in writing about food and who worked for the *Irish Independent*. Also in our group was the legendary Irish journalist Stan Gebler Davies, who sadly has since passed away.

On this Friday night, the three of us were given a table in the Blue Haven hotel in Kinsale. They brought us fresh Dublin Bay prawns followed by roast goose, Irish cheeses and as much as we could drink. We were given an extravagant dessert but more detail than that I can't remember.

The following day the Gourmet Festival was officially opened in the ballroom of Acton's Hotel by the American Ambassador to Ireland, a lady who was a member of the Kennedy clan. After rambling speeches and a champagne reception, the doors were opened to the public.

People came in and sampled the local delights of Irish food set up on stalls by the area's restaurants, hotels, fishermen, oyster catchers and cheese makers. It was just huge fun; tasting and eating wonderful seafood, cheeses, Irish stew, all of it washed down by pint after pint of Murphy's stout.

Stan, Miles and I fell naturally together and spent the entire weekend as a terrible trio.

Saturday night had the same routine as Friday but in a different restaurant, and afterwards it was back to Acton's Hotel to listen to Billy Crosby and the Cork City Jazz Band. They played until about three in the morning and most of the guests stumbled drunkenly home. A hard core of about thirty men and women remained, including Miles, Stan and me.

Billy Crosby, the pianist in the band, was now stripped to the waist with a towel around his neck. The top of his piano was covered in pints of lager and smoking ashtrays and he played and sang until dawn. There was no sleep.

We had the classic Irish breakfast of rashers, eggs, Clonakilty black pudding and wild mushrooms, fried bread and Black Velvet or vodka and orange juice.

On Sunday, at noon, a huge buffet was laid out for the press and local notables and again the Cork City Jazz Band performed. Although he'd been up all night, Billy emerged freshly scrubbed, his hair still wet from the shower, and he wore a crisp white shirt, looking for all the world like the head chorister (although indeed he was about thirty-five). Lunch finished at about 6 p.m.

I can't recall how many people I met during that fabulous weekend but all of them were lovely and funny. I certainly met Stanley and Heide Roache, whom I shall come to later.

Until I had been to Ireland I thought I was quite a good talker but after a couple of days with Stan and Billy Crosby and others, I realized I was a novice.

I should point out that on Friday, when I had met Stan for the first time, he was wearing a striped shirt with a stiff white collar, a neat silk tie and a white linen jacket with a gardenia in the lapel. He was looking as if he had stepped straight out of the pages *The Onion Eaters* by J. P. Donleavy.

He was still wearing the same clothes when he bid us farewell on Monday morning but by now the flower was dead, the jacket was crumpled and the tie was splashed with wine and stout. The man was a mess. But then, who wasn't?

With a heavy heart and endless embraces in the bar of Cork airport, I carried the mother of all hangovers – described by Stan as the 'wrath of grapes' – on to the plane that would take me to the relative sanity of Plymouth and onwards to Bristol.

The weekend had such a pleasantly profound effect on me that I said to David Pritchard, 'The next series we make has got to include Ireland.' And thus it was.

A year or two later, in 1987, we made *Floyd on Britain and Ireland*, and found ourselves staying in Acton's Hotel, filming at Myrtle Allen's famous Ballymalloo House, fishing for prawns, curing salmon, recreating classic Irish dishes like bacon and cabbages, as well as Irish stew, and filming the bustling Victorian central market in Cork City, bizarrely known as the English Market.

We went on to film in the Long Valley bar in Cork, where we ate the finest salt beef sandwiches prepared the Irish way, which involves the beef being marinated in an almost explosive mixture of saltpetre and other spices. It was still the time of the Irish troubles and saltpetre – which is used to make bombs – could only be bought from a chemist. How many dishes need a chemist?

Et tu, Heston Blumenthal? The man is quite clearly a genius, but someone told me – and I don't know if this is true – that when he serves a particular dish of scallops you have to put on earphones so you can hear the sound of the sea while you eat. Can we go back to Elizabeth David, who would not have approved of listening to the sea while eating scallops? She would have sensed it instead. She famously said that the once sublime quiche lorraine, a savoury egg and cream tart, had become a culinary dustbin. My god, she'd turn in her grave if she had lived to see the creation of a chicken tikka masala pizza. Roll over Curnonsky, and tell Escoffier the news (Chuck Berry would have understood this).

Back to Ireland. At the time I was living in a flat in Bristol. I really wanted to move down to Somerset or Devon but property prices were so high there was no question I would be able to afford a cottage in those areas. But the morning we drove into Cork to film at the Long Valley bar we went on the road that ran alongside the estuary and we passed a small cottage on the banks.

I said to David, 'That's the sort of house I'd like to have. A little place like that in Devon or Somerset.' I thought no more of it.

During a break in filming I wandered around the streets of Cork and stopped and gazed into the window of an auctioneer's, which is Irish for an estate agent. Lo and behold, tucked away in the far corner of the window, away from the grand castles and huge farm houses for sale in the region, there was a tiny black-and-white photograph – curled at the edges – of that self-same cottage David and I had driven past that very morning.

On a slightly Murphy's-inspired whim I strode boldly into the office. They recognized me immediately and assumed I was interested in one of the derelict stately homes. 'No, no,' I said. 'It's that little cottage in the corner I'm interested in.'

They shuffled around for a few minutes until they found the details. 'Two rooms, two bedrooms, electricity but no water, half to three quarters of an acre of land on the estuary, in need of total renovation. Price: £16,000.' Such a place in Somerset at that time would have been about £90,000.

I made arrangements to meet the owner. He was a very serious farmer on the other side of the road from the little house that in former times was part of a larger estate and was the gamekeeper's cottage.

Clearly, he was reluctant to sell the cottage to a foreigner, especially an Englishman. He didn't seem to think much of me and showed no real interest. But I enlisted the help of my Irish friend, Billy MacEsey, another larger-than-life chef-patron whom I met a couple of years earlier at the Gourmet Festival.

Billy came to meet the farmer with me and as we talked I promised the farmer that I would restore the cottage to its former glory. There would be hollyhocks by the front door, there would be a vegetable patch and there would be chickens.

I recounted my fifties childhood in Somerset and explained how I would like to recreate that here in Ireland.

On about our third meeting inside the cool and gloomy farmhouse, with only the glow of the wood fire for light, Billy and I were sitting around a coffee table and I was by now quite anxiously waiting for the farmer to decide whether or not to sell me the place.

His wife, whom hitherto I had not seen or met, emerged from the shadows and placed a huge Bible on the coffee table. She did not speak and left the room. She returned a few moments later with a tray, upon which were three glasses and a bottle of Middletown twenty-year-old Irish whiskey. She put the tray on top of the Bible and then withdrew back into the shadows. It was surreal.

The farmer carefully and slowly unscrewed the bottle and poured three fat glasses of this amazing whiskey. We lifted our glasses and as we chinked them, he said, 'Sláinte' – good health. 'Sláinte, good luck and God bless.' I wrote him a cheque for 18,000 punts, the equivalent then of about £16,000.

We shook hands and over the next ten or twelve years that I either visited the cottage or lived there I never saw him again. He had not sold up and moved out, but was just a quiet, religious farmer who didn't stray from his land.

Over the next couple of years I set about restoring the cottage and the garden with two mates, Geoff and Biff. Geoff, an ex-marine, was a good all-rounder, while Biff was a carpenter and yet another good all-rounder. I also brought out of retirement a jack of all trades called Old Bob. I never knew his surname.

He was just Old Bob, but he knew everything. I bought a

wrecked Fergusson 220 tractor – the grey sort from the 1950s
– and Bob restored that for me. He built the pigsties in the
classic Somerset way, rounding off the tops of the walls and
painting the walls in white lime. He put a balcony on to my
bedroom window overlooking the estuary.

We built a boathouse with a slip for my eighteen-foot, varnished, classic River Dart bass-fishing boat, the *Wet Dream*.
There was a caretaker's apartment over the boathouse, and
next to that I built an office with guest bedrooms above. We
created what I called an Italian water garden with a terrace
and barbecue. We put in a lawn, filled the coop with rare-
breed chickens and golden pheasants and had a classic
dovecote built.

I bought a pair of Jacob's sheep, a pony and some Vietnamese pot-bellied pigs, a few ducks, some turkeys, and in
the evenings I'd feed the swans that glided up this mystical
estuary to the end of the jetty, where they gobbled pieces of
stale bread. I grew raspberries, runner beans, broad beans.
(And my tip, by the way, when faced with the daunting task
of shelling peas or podding beans on a Sunday morning, is to
always have more that you need so you don't have to do them
all.) I built a greenhouse. And I planted sunflowers, chillies,
garlic and ginger.

And true to my word, I put in the hollyhocks. I had recreated my childhood in Somerset, and then some.

Every time I returned from a filming trip or a busy schedule
of personal appearances or book-signing tours I'd sigh with
relief as the plane took off for Cork. At the airport I was met
by Jim, my gardener-cum-minder and a former policeman.
He took me to what was truly my spiritual home.

Here, I was able to escape the falseness of showbiz. It was

such a relief to get to Creek Lodge and then maybe wander down to the pub. The boys would come in, with all their pockets full of money but no visible means of support. They'd say, 'Let's go west. There's a great pub down in . . .' So we'd all pile into somebody's car and set off for lunch, which sometimes lasted for two days.

I built the rugby club in Kinsale, with much help from Hugh McHardy, and Saturdays might be spent up at the rugby ground, in the driving rain and the howling wind, cooking sausages on a burner on the tailgate of my Land Rover. Every Sunday there was jazz at Acton's. Sometimes I made a trip up to Dublin, for the all-Ireland final of hurling or Gaelic football. Sometimes I went to Lansdowne Road to see a rugby international, or attend the endless religious charity events which raised money for nuns in strife-stricken places in Africa.

I remember one day, before the ban on stubble-burning, when a black cloud hung beneath the blue sky and in the *Wet Dream*, laden with friends and booze, we negotiated the shallows of an abandoned river and stopped to have a strawberry cream tea. As we passed the Old Head of Kinsale, and the first drinks had been poured, my friend Michael said, 'It's another shitty day in paradise. I wonder what the poor people are doing today?' And as I dictate this to the editor of this book, we are munching, beyond our means, a peach meringue and toasted almond gateau. *Malgré tout*, it is another shitty day in paradise.

During that halcyon, hedonistic time women came and went, but no hearts were broken and no blame attaches.

I had a huge model railway based on the Wiveliscombe and Taunton Great Western railway region. It cost me over £20,000 to have made. Sadly, later, after I had gone bankrupt I needed to raise some cash and had to sell it. It made £500 in auction.

I held the most amazing parties at Creek Lodge, particularly at Christmas, when I'd make a hot mulled wine but didn't tell them I'd filled it with the illegal poteen made by the local garage owner. There were mountains of prawns and oysters and parties went on for two or three days. People left and then came back a day or so later, to join in the fun of the continuing party.

Heide and Stanley Roache, whom I met at the Kinsale Gourmet Festival, quietly reprimanded me for keeping the wrong company and for being too hospitable to people whom, in some cases, I barely knew.

But what the hell? After the bullshit of making television commercials and attending chat shows this was life with a roaring heart and blood pumping through it. Good friends came but it was a sacrosanct place and I didn't invite my television colleagues.

However, I did once make the mistake of inviting David Pritchard to stay. Before I tell you about his visit, I should say that down the creek four bachelor brothers lived. They had terrible wrecked fishing boats and though they lived in the same house they didn't speak to each other. But for some strange reason the brothers befriended me. Every now and again I'd come back to the house and on the back step there was a bucket containing two or three lobsters. It was understood that when I met them in the pub – individually, as they didn't hang out together – the drinks were on me.

Anyhow, when David came to stay I had just received my occasional back-step bucket of lobsters. I had a busy day ahead of me, so in the morning I boiled a couple of lobsters which I thought David and I could eat cold for supper that evening.

I was off to a social engagement in Cork for the day and David said he'd spend the time fishing.

I returned from Cork at about seven o'clock, not having eaten and really looking forward to the lobster. As I walked into the kitchen I saw them on a plate. All that remained were the sucked out red shells. 'I couldn't help it,' said David. 'I was hungry.'

And of course he couldn't help it. When it came to treats, food and drinks, David had the breaking strain of a hot Mars bar. Or as Oscar Wilde said, 'I can resist anything except temptation.'

Louisiana
Sunday morning

Dear Reader

My driver, a petite blonde American who I
hired from an agency and renamed Jo-Jo instead
of Rosabella or whatever, had said the night before,
'Hey, you look good in suspenders.' We were having
a drink in my hotel room, probably tequila sunrises.
Or in my case, sunsets. She was referring not to my
underwear but to my red felt braces.

It was early morning, we gassed up. I bought a
bottle, a bag of ice, and surveyed the shotguns and
the rifles, pistols and machine guns that were on sale
in the gas station on this sad Sunday morning,
thinking with no need for a licence, and with the
swamps and the everglades nearby, I could shoot
Pritchard, feed him to the alligators and have a
celebration dish of jambalaya, crawfish pie and filly
gumbo. In fact, I didn't buy the gun. But I ate
the food, drank the Jack Daniels and did another
one of my outstanding TV cookery programmes.

Floyd

SIXTEEN

We landed a deal to do *American Pie*, in which David and I and the crew would spend a few months of 1988 travelling across the States, cooking, eating and meeting. I don't know why I agreed to do it because, much as I loved David, I hated him, too.

He was great at his job, whether he was being Billy Wilder, David Lean or even just David Pritchard. But he really knew how to wind me up, Like, for instance, that incessant need of his to fill his stomach. Granted, we were meant to love food. We were, after all, making programmes about the stuff.

Yet wherever we went, David would suddenly say, 'I've got to stop. I *must* get something to eat.' It didn't matter that he was always on a diet. 'I thought you were trying to lose weight, David,' I'd say, and he'd come back with, 'I am but I'm absolutely starving. I've got to have something.'

One day we were invited to a grand lunch in Cornwall. We were to meet some people who had helped with a series and to thank them on behalf of the BBC. I was driving and picked up David and we set off on the journey. Lunch was in an hour or so, and on the other side of the Tamar I stopped at a service station to fill the car with petrol. David said, 'I'm just going for a pee.'

I filled up, bought a packet of fags and went for a pee myself. Then I went and sat in the car. David wasn't there. I waited for five minutes. I waited for a further five minutes. I thought, where the hell has he gone?

When I went to investigate I found David sitting at a table in the service station's cafeteria. In front of him was a half-eaten plate of steak, bacon, eggs, grilled mushrooms and tomatoes. 'David, what are you doing? We're having lunch soon.'

'I felt a bit hungry.'

In America it was the same thing, though the steaks are far larger than the ones they serve in any service station in England's West Country.

I'd had T-shirts made that were emblazoned with the words 'Floyd's American Pie', and wherever we went we were mobbed by people who wanted to meet us, touch us, shake our hands, kiss us and hug us. They thought we were Pink Floyd on a tour. 'Can we have your T-shirts?' they'd say.

Mind you, the Pink Floyd confusion continues to this day. Not so long ago I was a party at the Serbian Embassy in London with Bill Padley, a friend, songwriter and musician. I managed to deliver a short speech, confusing Serbia with Siberia, which confused everyone. And then a bloke came up and said, 'You are Floyd, aren't you?'

I nodded and then he turned to Bill and said, 'What do you do?'

Bill replied, 'I'm a musician.'

'So you're still in the band then.'

We went to Memphis, most famous for Graceland, Elvis Presley's home to which millions of fans flock every year. I said to David, 'When are we shooting at Graceland?'

'We're not.'

'What do you mean, "We're not?" We can't come to Memphis without going to Elvis Presley's house.'

David said, 'Whose programme is this?'

I said, 'It's mine.'

And he said, 'Oh, all right then.'

At the height of our dispute, I phoned my agent, John Miles, and begged him to come out to America to sort it out. John arrived and over breakfast said, 'I'll have a word with David. Leave it with me.' Whatever he said to David smoothed things over for a few days before hostilities broke out again..

The communication barrier between David and me was well and truly established on the day we were due to film in a Native Indian reservation. David, by now, seemed to have lost interest in the film-making but had gained an interest in a new companion, a young lady who seemed to be 'hanging out' with us all the time.

We arrived at the reservation, where I discovered that we did not have a location. Nothing had been arranged, nothing had been set up and there was nothing that would work in filming terms. 'Not again,' I said. 'When are you going to learn, David?'

In the middle of filming *American Pie* I was flying to and from Britain by Concorde to make a television series for London Weekend Television (LWT). The series was entitled *Floyd on Television*, and I took over from Clive James.

I do not know Clive James but at the time he was an established wit and raconteur who wrote newspaper columns on the subject of television. His writing style was indisputably hilarious and universally admired. He got the gig on LWT off the back of his column and he managed to pull it off well.

I was asked to step into the great man's shoes. This was a particularly daunting challenge for two reasons: first, I didn't consider myself to be as cerebral as Mr James and was therefore likely to fail; second, my existence was so crammed with opening and running restaurants and then filming I didn't have time to watch television. While the Australian wit James was paid to watch the box, I was paid to make programmes for it.

'It's going to be great,' said John Miles. Then I was introduced to the executives from LWT. They said, 'It's going to be great. We've already worked out the set.'

'Which is what?' I asked.

'You'll have a bar behind you, and you'll sit in a chair with a drink beside you and come out with very funny lines.' I thought, I get it: they're trying to turn me into Dave Allen, the Irish comedian who used sit on a chair, glass of whisky in one hand, cigarette in the other, recounting funny stories and lengthy jokes. And then one of the executives said, 'You'll be like Dave Allen.'

As John and I left the plush office we walked through a corridor, the walls of which were covered by framed photographs of LWT's famous presenters. 'You'll be up there one day,' said one of the executives. Oh no I won't, I thought.

I'd tried to tell them I couldn't do it, and I couldn't. The theme of each thirty-minute programme was simple enough: a team of LWT researchers had scoured the world to find the worst television programmes and commercials; these clips were supposed to be so bad as to be belly-achingly funny; my job was to deliver hilarious lines about what we'd just seen and what we were about to see – I did the 'links'.

I arrived on set and was strapped into something that resembled an electric chair. Then I had to read the autocue of the script, nothing that I had contributed to in any way (which might have been a blessing).

The clips tended to be vulgar and edging towards soft porn. There were semi-naked women advertising a deodorant for a Brazilian television commercial, and that sort of thing. Researchers had trawled Japanese telly searching for pouting Oriental ladies advertising . . . deodorant. If it wasn't a clip of a large-breasted woman posing with an aerosol can, then it was a clip of a large-breasted woman advertising a bra.

I reckon the viewers were the sort of people who would have watched not *Strictly Come Dancing*, but *Come Dancing* with the sound off because they were after lust rather than a laugh. It was all rather distasteful, I concluded.

I shot the first series and when I was released from the electric chair I told John Miles that while I was signed up to do the same series the following year, I would not do it. In fact, I was so angry about agreeing to do *Floyd on Television* that when the shows were finished I could not bring myself to watch a single one of them.

Somehow the message never reached the bosses at LWT. A year later I had a call from them saying, 'Are you all ready to turn up next week?'

I phoned John and said, 'Why didn't you tell them that I didn't want to do it?' He replied, 'Well, I thought you'd change your mind.' So I fell out with LWT. Or they fell out with me.

Then I was asked to replace Barry Norman on the BBC as the presenter of a show that would be called *Floyd on Films*. I'd learned my lesson. I said, 'I can't do it. I don't go to the cinema. I don't have the depth of knowledge that people like Barry have.' And I didn't, though my favourite movie (since you ask) is *Rebel Without a Cause*. 'I can cook and I can talk but I can't do film programmes,' I insisted and that response was regarded as me being difficult once again.

Back to America on Concorde and back to David.

The French had been bemused that we wanted to make programmes about food. The Americans, by contrast, were all desperate to be filmed, whether it was in Santa Fe or way down in Mississippi.

I met a chef – a specialist in cooking black-seared catfish – who was so obese he had to use an electric hoist to place himself in his pick-up truck. In Louisiana a local folk band were brought in to watch me cook a crayfish bake in a big oil drum; the fish was served with red potatoes and oranges, Louisiana style. I asked the band to play 'Jambalaya'. The bandleader said, '"Jambalaya"? We don't know it.'

Incredulous, I said, 'You don't know it?' They were all dressed up like they did.

But, by now, my relationship with David was in a pitiful state. We could continue to create entertainment and hear the stories of the culinary stars of the United States, but the real story was what was going on behind the scenes.

David and I were communicating via notes. On a piece of paper I would scribble, 'Are we still doing the shoot on the beach tomorrow?' Then I'd pass the note to Frances, who, in turn, would hand it to David. Some time later, she'd give me a piece of paper. 'Yes,' it might read, or 'No' perhaps.

I have never heard of anything like this happening in television: director and presenter communicating via notes. It is funny, granted, but at the time it was extremely sad because of what we had achieved together.

When we went to San Francisco and filmed a cooking sketch beside the city's Golden Gate Bridge something within me was desperate to tell viewers that I despised David, even though I could not say it directly to camera. He would have cut it, wouldn't he? Or would he? I had all my ingredients, as usual, prepared and laid out on a table before me and the pot was on the Calor gas flame.

I said, 'Viewers at home, here we are in San Francisco and you can see the Golden Gate Bridge behind me. The director believes that he can do my job. So today he is going to do my job.' At that point I left the counter and the cooker and walked off screen. David then appeared in front of the camera and did my job. And credit where credit is due, he did it pretty well. The brilliance of the programme, as I have mentioned, was its ability to survive without being scripted or rehearsed.

David knew this, too. That is why he didn't cut the segment and it ended up being broadcast. The viewers didn't have a clue what it was all about, but David was well aware and equally he was brilliant enough to acknowledge that it made compelling viewing.

SEVENTEEN

There was another problem, apart from David.

The loneliness of the long-distance cook had really kicked in. Living out of a suitcase, being without friends and family . . . all of it was making me increasingly insular. And I was drinking whisky, quite a bit of it.

I knew I was drinking too much but I didn't know where the exit was. It's hard to leave when you can't find the door.

Even though on television and in my restaurants I was the gregarious, jolly man who had no cares in the world, off screen and when I wasn't front-of-house I was – and still am – a worrier. Call it depression if you like. And you probably wouldn't be wrong. That is not to say that I was a miserable sod when I wasn't standing in front of a camera but gradually I became more insular. When we were travelling around the world and settled into a hotel, I'd sit with a glass of whisky and think. Deep in Johnnie Walker-induced thought, I tried to unravel the wretched aforementioned mystery of my life: that I was a cook who had become a performer and was living a schizophrenic life – there was Floydy and then there was me. Floydy was like a parrot on my shoulder, and one that would never flap his wings and fly away.

Those worries began in a year I cannot pinpoint, but were

certainly there when I became my own boss, running the bistro. Depression and alcohol are not a good marriage but still they can live together.

I have been thinking back on my relationship with alcohol, which began when I was a teenage cub reporter in the sixties. You'll recall that my kind editor, Richard Hawkins, took me for magnificent lunches at the Hole in the Wall.

It was there that I experienced something which, along with food, would change my life for ever. The wine – that first glass of wine – I recall distinctly. It was Gevrey Chambertin, a wonderful burgundy and grown not so very far away from Dijon.

As I grew older, and depending on financial circumstances, I drank as many different varieties of wine as I could, particularly French wine. I didn't see it as a vehicle for getting drunk. I saw it more as an essential accompaniment to fine food.

The more I learned about wine, as well as sherries and cognacs and ports and eau de vies, the more entranced I became. If I had a glass of dry sherry as an aperitif it was partly to enjoy the olives and the cheese biscuits that were offered. In a restaurant and before I tasted the white wine that I had ordered, I'd have a glass of mineral water in order to clear my palate.

I took a great deal of trouble to choose wine that matched the food, even though I have often said on television and in my books that you should drink whatever pleases you. It is not compulsory to drink white wine with fish and red with meat.

I have said that and it's true. Yet for many, many years I took my own wine-drinking experiences very seriously indeed. For example, on a hot summer's day I would not drink a heavy

Châteauneuf-du-Pape or a really robust Rioja. There are seasons for wine. In summer, I had light whites, rosés, often small red burgundies served chilled.

As far as I was concerned, it was just one of those erudite pleasures that are collected, along with food, conviviality and conversation. It was nothing to do with rushing down to the pub and knocking back ten pints of beer to get pissed before the pub shut. (In fact, I rarely drank beer.)

I was a stickler for what was right. For instance, I always had cheese (as the French prefer) after the main course. This enabled me to finish the red wine with the cheese, before moving on to something I have a great fondness for – sweet dessert wines – with my pudding. In fact, I was quite a snob, I am afraid to say, when it came to wine.

Drinking depended on the country I was in. In Italy, with my coffee I liked iced aqua vitae. In France, at the end of the meal I enjoyed a small, smoky Armagnac. Or, in the summer, I'd have an iced eau de vie, probably eau de vie de poire, an exquisite drink; the pears grow into wine bottles on the branches of the trees, and then alcohol is added and remains to absorb the flavour of the pears. It's a bit like a ship in a bottle to look at: how the hell did that get in there?

I didn't drink the wine for the sake of it. I seldom drank it without food and if, for instance, I was having spicy or aromatic food – maybe Indian or Thai – I went along with local light lagers or indeed non-alcoholic drinks like the yoghurt-based drink lassi, or freshly squeezed lime juice with fizzy water, or perhaps freshly prepared mango juice.

Through my experiences in France I found that in the family environment champagne was invariably served with dessert. Or it was taken without ceremony at cellar temperature as an aperitif before lunch. Champagne didn't have any of those British connotations: that it was only to be drunk at birthdays or celebrations, or when racing drivers were looking for something to squirt all over each other. In the Champagne region of France making the time for a glass of champagne was just a normal part of the day.

In Spain, if you were having a few aperitifs before lunch, or at any time of the day, the custom was to have a small snack, tapas. And indeed, if you are not feeling particularly hungry then a meal of tiny portions – ham, little red shrimps, finely chopped octopus in vinaigrette or slivers of aged Manchego (the Spanish equivalent of a mature cheddar, but quite different) – provides an agreeable light lunch.

On occasion I quite enjoyed, as an aperitif at a cocktail party, a whisky. Or in summertime, I liked Pimm's made with lots of gin.

During these years I was eating well, enjoying food, enjoying cooking and enjoying wine. I was in no way dependent upon alcohol, be it for stimulation or escapism.

But I suppose over the latter years, sitting in some hotel room in some exotic foreign country unable to sleep, or being worried about the next day's work – so often being alone – I took to drinking whisky quite a lot. To paraphrase Bob Dylan, who often seems to capture my life in his lyrics, while I started out drinking burgundy I soon hit the harder stuff. (The funny thing is, there's an unusual red wine from the Champagne district called Bouzey Rouge, and down here in Provence there's a Côte du Rhone called Vin Sobre. So you've got a boozy red and a sober Côte du Rhone. I have often had to apologise to publishers, advertising agents and other such exploitative people who have used my name to get them into restaurants they themselves would not be able to enter and then let me order the wine. 'I'm so sorry,' I would say, 'I assumed it was the year, not the price of the wine that I ordered.')

People don't realize that my programmes took five days to make but are edited to thirty minutes. It looks like I am forever drinking. I couldn't go into a pub without people plying me with drink and then whipping out their camera. They wanted to say to their mates, 'I had a glass of wine with Keith Floyd and here's the picture to prove it.' I was fed up with being in a railway station and people saying, 'Where's your wine, Floydy?'

Sure, at the end of the shoot we'd all get pissed when the director said, 'That's a wrap.' But that was nothing more than having a celebration at a game of rugby. But I say again, I am not one for going to pubs, pouring booze down my throat and telling jokes, which is what I am sometimes perceived to be.

But I found it increasingly difficult to maintain the gruelling schedule that I had – non-stop travelling, non-stop performing, non-stop interviews – and whisky became a prop.

Eventually, however, this joyous experience of drinking descended into a desperate kind of survival, as you will see.

In America I was suffering the most appalling migraines night after night after night. I stood under a cold shower for hours at a time, night after night, desperately unhappy, desperately unwell.

As my story progresses few chapters will be complete without a visit to hospital. In this case, it came about after I'd suggested doing a shot of me in a '57 Chevy, driving across the Memphis City Bridge (back in the edit suite we could lay on the music of Chuck Berry, who would be among my heroes, if I had any).

We hired a car and a driver for a few hours and on the day I saw on the front pages of the newspapers that it was the thirtieth anniversary of Buddy Holly's death, I said, 'Wow, we could do a superb piece to camera with this.' It went well. I climbed out of the car and the next thing I knew I woke up in the Memphis Memorial Baptist hospital. I had collapsed though I don't know why. It's true that I was drinking too much at the time, and I was not eating well. 'This is where Elvis died' were the doctor's greeting words as I opened my eyes.

Shortly before we finished filming *American Pie*, I managed to find time to speak to David. I was brief and to the point. Eight words exactly: 'I never want to work with you again.'

Peabody Hotel
Memphis, Tennessee

Dear Reader

Just back from hospital. The Baptist Memorial Hospital. Where after a collapse I was treated by a doctor who said, 'Welcome, you've come through. And this is where Elvis died.' Pritchard hated Presley because he never wrote his own songs. Fair point. But Elvis changed my life and I went round Gracelands on a private visit except for the camera crew, escorted by, I think, Priscilla.

I met his granny, Minnie Presley, who still lived in the house. His grave was unkempt, he never wore blue suede shoes and never had a garage for all his Cadillacs.

I boozed in every bar in town, from Bourbon Street to the gutter, all the black singers and musicians were cooks. I sucked my ribs and drank my Bourbon, they just howled like the wolf singing the blues. In Memphis it's only rock and roll, but I like it. Thank you Mick, or should I say Keith.

Floyd

EIGHTEEN

We should talk about the BBC and its wine-and-dine culture. The heads of the Corporation certainly seemed to wine and dine themselves, but they never wined and dined presenters. David Pritchard's office contained a fridge packed with wine.

Licence payers will be pleased to know that their money was never spent on schmoozing me. Though that is not to say that when executives were filling in their expenses forms, they didn't attach a hefty restaurant receipt and write, 'For entertaining Keith Floyd.'

Lofty and grand, the BBC does not invite you to events. It instructs you to be there. I was told to be here or to be there. One year I was told to turn up to a Christmas party being hosted by the board of governors at Broadcasting House. It was extremely inconvenient because on the same evening I was due to give a speech in Exeter, and would therefore have to do the party and then dash to catch a train to get me to the West Country.

I arrived at the governors' party, and a man came up to me, shook my hand, and started chatting. He was one of the few guests not to be an octogenarian, and I noticed that he was wearing high-heeled cowboy boots with winkle-picker-type toes to them. And on that basis I assumed he was a disc jockey, perhaps one of John Miles's clients.

Disc jockey: 'So what do you think of the BBC then?'

Me: 'Well, since you ask, I think it's absolutely crap.'

A second or two later, he'd scurried away in his cowboy boots and vanished into the crowd. He turned out to be the next controller of the BBC.

Another man, with an accent so posh it had comedic value, came up to me, again without introducing himself, and said, 'Keith. How nice. What are you doing?'

I said, 'Oh, work-wise I am having great fun. I'm cooking all kinds of British food: pigs' trotters, stuffed hearts and offal and things like that.'

He nodded. 'And how are you enjoying it?'

Me: 'It's quite hard really, but I think it's vitally important to get across that it's not just the middle cut of beef or the middle cut of salmon that we should be eating. We should be eating everything. And with a well-butchered pig there is nothing left but the squeal . . .'

No sooner had I finished the word *squeal* than he, too, was gone. He turned out to be the current controller of BBC1 and a raging vegetarian to boot.

There was one guest at the party I was delighted to see. I've always adored Terry Wogan and he was the only person in the room I recognized. At the time Terry was the host of a long-running BBC chat show, entitled simply *Wogan*, which was broadcast every weekday evening.

My mother was a fan, and long before I even met Terry, she used to say to me, "Ere, you're on television. When you see that Terry Wogan, can you ask him to give me his autograph?' So one day I did see him: I was invited on to his show.

It was an hour or so before curtain up – the show was broadcast live – and a band was playing. I wandered up to what I assumed was a production assistant and she was also quite beautiful and had glanced over at me (remember, I was younger, had nice hair and was smartly dressed).

I said to her, 'I've just been watching the band rehearse. They're good. Do you know what they're called?'

She gave me a quizzical look, and replied, 'They're called the Bee Gees.'

An hour or so later the beautiful production assistant was sitting beside me, Herbert Lom and Kiri te Kanawa and being interviewed by Terry Wogan in front of millions of viewers. She wasn't a production assistant at all but the Hollywood star Ali McGraw, one-time wife of Steve McQueen.

The BBC instructed me – via some route or other, some messenger – to leave my home in Devon, get myself to London, book myself into a hotel, and attend the BAFTA awards ceremony at the Grosvenor House Hotel. At the ceremony, the instructions continued, I was to present the award for the Best Foreign Film.

I hired a driver for my Bentley, booked a room in the hotel, and by then I was 700 quid down the line. I unpacked my case, changed into a dinner jacket, well-pressed evening shirt, bow tie, white silk evening scarf, the lot, and duly headed off to the event.

At the entrance of the Grosvenor House was the obligatory red carpet, at the side of which were railings and behind which were some sixty photographers. As I walked along the carpet the flashbulbs exploded, as they say, and sixty photographers shouted, 'Floydy, over here . . . Floydy, a smile over here.' Yell after yell of 'Floydy!' Click, click, click.

I stepped off the carpet and reached the reception desk, where a girl from the BBC said, 'Name?'

I said, 'Where's the bar?'

She tried again. 'Name?'

'Keith Floyd.'

'What are you here for . . .?' And then, after studying her clipboard, 'Oh yeah, I see.'

I said, 'I've not got instructions on what to do. Could you tell me what to do, please?' She told me to go and ask the floor manager.

By now I was feeling pretty cheesed off. I had just split up from a girlfriend, and was feeling heartbroken. It's not enjoyable to be at a glittering event on your own, and my irritation was not about to be relieved by the offer of a drink from the BBC.

I hit the bar and then found the floor manager, who explained which table I'd be at and so I walked over to the table in what was still an empty room, empty of guests but filled with busy staff setting up. When I looked at the names at the table it became clear that my duty for the night was not only to present an award, but also entertain nine executives from the Shell oil company. I was expected to be their puppet celebrity.

I thought, no, I am not doing that. All I need to do is sit in a room at the back and wait until it's time to walk out and present the award. I am not hosting a sponsored table. Why should I? Back in the bar, I was talking to another guest when I found myself saying, 'I am out of here. This stinks.' I didn't want to sit with a dozen executives from Shell and listen to them saying, 'How do you cook frogs' legs?'

So I left. The actor Jeremy Brett, who played Sherlock Holmes, was drafted in to fill my slot and present the award.

The BBC didn't kick up a fuss about my swift departure. The following morning the newspapers were full of photographs of John Hurt wildly laying into a paparazzo. Clearly, John was more than happy to pay for his own drinks, and it looked like he'd bought a few of them.

The *Daily Mirror*, however, found out that I'd scarpered. They phoned my agent, John Miles, who did his best to kill the story by saying I left because 'I didn't feel well', and was duly quoted when the story appeared in the paper.

I was instructed to appear on *Children in Need* in a sketch with the BBC weatherman Michael Fish. Using mirrors and clever editing, I was apparently sitting on Michael's knee – Floyd on Fish, get it? – and on a weather map behind us, Hurricane Floyd was blowing across Britain. (I put in a claim for expenses and then withdrew it because I thought it was wrong.)

And I overheard Stephen Fry say to his comic partner Hugh Laurie, 'Look at that guy. He's a cook. He's not an actor. He delivered a perfect line in one take.' He came up to me later and said, 'Do you want to come to a party?' I said no, but I wish I had said yes.

John Miles phoned me one day in a state of uncontrollable excitement. He said, 'Jimmy Savile really, really wants you go on his show.' John, I am sure, would have known Jimmy of old, as Jimmy had been a disc jockey. Now he was presenting *Jim'll Fix It*, an extraordinarily popular Saturday evening show in which Jimmy made people's dreams come true.

If in the eighties you were aged ten and besotted by Showaddywaddy or some such pop band, he'd introduce you (in front of the cameras) to the band . . . and you'd sing with them on the show.

I said to John, 'What does he want me to do?'

John relayed the details of the chore. 'Travel up to London and cook as Father Christmas for a twelve-year-old girl.' I made my own way there, and I'd make my own way back. I didn't get to meet Jimmy Savile; he would have been busy.

After the show, I walked from the top of Broadcasting House, went to the front desk and said, 'Can you please get me a taxi?' I was told, 'Walk down to the street and get one. We don't do taxis.'

When I finally I arrived home I phoned John and said, 'What did you put me into? It was monstrous.'

Fast-forward a few years to probably the early nineties. I had a new manager, Stan Green. He called and said, 'Great news. Noel Edmonds really, really wants you to turn up on *Noel's House Party*.'

'What is *Noel's House Party*?'

Stan said, 'It's a high-profile show. Can't do you any harm. Everybody does it.' So I said, 'OK.'

He gave the thumbs-up to Noel's team, and then a production assistant was on the phone to thank me very much for agreeing to do the show. I explained that I had never watched it and asked, 'What do I need to do exactly?'

'It's great fun,' she told me. Go on. 'The set is like a house. Noel is downstairs and above him is a balcony. You walk on to the balcony and the audience see you.' Right, what next? 'Then you walk along the balcony and then you get shot down a chute and end up in a bucket of green gunk.'

I could hear myself repeating, 'Green gunk?'

'Yes. You, the chute, the gunk. We do it every week. It's the most popular part of the show.' We ended the conversation with me saying how nice it was of them to think of me, thank you for inviting me on to the show, and that I was very much looking forward to going down the chute and into the green gunk. I don't know why I said that but I did.

I arrived at the studio on the Saturday, as arranged, wearing a linen suit that I had recently bought for £700. And I took along new clothes that I could change into after being shot into the green gunk. I was with Stan and in the green room, rather than the green gunk, we met John Miles, who was there with his client Carol Vorderman. John would have known Noel of old because Noel had been a disc jockey. I made the introductions. 'Stan this is John. John this is Stan.'

A production assistant shook my hand, clocked the expensive linen upon me, and said, 'Don't worry. We'll return your suit, your bow tie and your shoes. All clean and lovely.'

An hour later I was sliding down a chute and then drowning in green gunk. It wasn't the worst experience of my life; a bit like being immersed in warm jelly. I changed and headed home with words of reassurance from one of the team, 'Don't worry about the suit. Leave it with us. I'll be all clean and lovely.'

Two days later a man arrived at the front door of my home. He was holding a black bin bag, sent to me from the BBC. Inside, and you'll know where this is going, were my clothes. But not as I knew them.

Someone had put the lot in a washing machine and then sent them back wet and ruined. The shoes? Destroyed. Bow tie? Shrivelled. As for my linen suit? Shrunk to fit an Action

Man. They sent a letter that was gushing and kind and thanked me for going on to the show to be gunked.

A few years ago, and for some strange reason, I agreed to do a political programme in return for about two quid.

The theme of the piece centred on the story that prior to the general election of 1997, Tony Blair and Gordon Brown had lunch at an Italian restaurant. Over the meal they apparently made a pact: Blair would serve one term and then stand down to make way for Brown.

The producer phoned. She was so young that if she'd been born male her voice wouldn't have broken. She said, 'We'd like to film a sequence of you in a kitchen.' Fine. 'Could you please find a location?' she asked.

In my compliant way I agreed to find a kitchen, and when I put down the phone I thought, why should I have to find a location? I turned to my good friend Richard Shepherd, who said we could shoot in the basement kitchen of his restaurant, Langan's.

It was agreed we'd film just before service at twelve o'clock. I got up at six and made my way from Oxfordshire to London and then on to the restaurant, where I prepared the food and prepared myself. No one came. At noon – the agreed time of the shoot – the producer phoned. She said, 'I am ever so sorry. I'm going to be late. We can't find a cameraman.'

Can't find a cameraman? But you're the BBC for heaven's sake. That's what I thought, but I didn't say it.

Again, I complied. I said, 'Oh, don't worry. I'll have lunch anyhow.' The wonderful thing about lunch is that you can lose yourself, can't you? I was fed up with the producer and the BBC, and by the time she arrived at the restaurant with a recently discovered cameraman I was quite pissed and angry.

I said, 'You can pay for lunch.' I had been up early, the BBC had failed to get a location, failed to find a cameraman and then, I felt, been imposing and demanding about what they wanted to do.

When it was time to film, I was asked, 'Now then, Keith Floyd. How many famous people have you cooked for?'

I don't really like questions like that, so I said, 'None.' And it went downhill from there.

Can we dwell on notoriety for a moment? Can we give some thought to the subject because, after all, famously fame can give and it can snatch away? It can give riches, but it has no respect for reality; it does not appreciate personal lives, family and the home.

When I became famous, I became famous overnight. Suddenly everybody wanted to know Floyd. Everybody. Women, radio stations, publishers, advertising agencies and after-dinner speaker agents. People with whom I didn't want to be friends befriended me without asking my permission.

Going to the supermarket was a nightmare. If I happened to put into my basket Heinz tomato ketchup, Heinz cream of tomato soup and Marmite – and all these funny things that I like – people peered into my supermarket basket. 'Oh, do *you* eat baked beans?' they said. Yes, I do.

It was as if people thought that I got hung up in a cupboard until it was time to release me in front of the cameras again. People are intrusive, by the way. They didn't get it; that I want nothing more than to sit here, in my garden in Montfrin, or go to the rugby or to Ireland. But I don't blame these people.

After all, I am the man who thought Warren Mitchell was really Alf Garnett.

People seemed to think that I led some sort of charmed and magical life. But I was quite cunning. When companies wanted to use me for this or that, and started telling me that I had to go to places, I'd say, 'Have you ever noticed the trucks that these supermarkets use to carry their potatoes in? The potatoes travel in state-of-the-art trucks made by Mercedes. And if you want me going anywhere I am travelling in style too, because I know you just see me as a product, as a potato. So wherever I go, I'm going first class and if you can't afford that, I don't want to do it. Because I know you are going to have me over in the end.'

It was pretty bold of me to say that, but I said it because I didn't actually give a damn. I did give a damn for my audience. I really cared about them. But I didn't give a damn about ever-smiling executives who wanted to milk me for all I was worth.

Then I got completely overwhelmed by fan mail, for requests for a bow tie, for one shoe to nail up in the Old Cobbler's Bar in Rye, or wherever, or to attend the marriage of somebody in Greece just because I happened to mention in an interview that I like Greece. I was bestowed the privilege of being given an entry in *Who's Who*, the Lefty red bible of Britain's influential men and women. And one day I received a call from a man asking how I felt about being in Madame Tussauds. I thought it was a reporter from the *Sun* winding me up. But no, it was Madame Tussauds seeking my approval to be turned into a wax model. They've probably melted me down by now.

In the end . . . actually, not in the end, in the beginning, the notoriety bestowed upon me would drive my friends crazy because *they* just couldn't take it any more, because while we were sitting having a pint, someone would come and push them aside, and say to me, 'What's it like being on television?' Or, 'How do you cook squid?'

My private life became public. I'd go to the pub with my mates and the groupies – and that's an unkind word, but there were thousands of them – didn't pay any respect to my friends. So my friends got cheesed off and didn't want to go out with me, because all I'd be doing was signing autographs with a little squiggle of a glass at the bottom. My friends didn't enjoy that, and I don't suppose your friends would enjoy it, either.

I wish this whole issue of fame didn't make me so grumpy, but I need to confront it so please humour me.

There were times when I'd drive to a pub, park the car and then remain seated in it. I couldn't go in; bizarre though it sounds, I feared walking into the bar because I knew that to do so would involve signing autographs with little squiggles of wine glasses and answering queries about cooking. So I'd sit in the car, thinking, I have now got a fantastic Jaguar, I've got hand-made shoes, I've got things I never had in my life before, and I'm frightened to go into a pub. Frightened to go into a pub because I didn't want to talk about food.

One day I got a letter on House of Lords notepaper, and written by the Earl of something or other, and he was a real belted-ermine, proper hereditary earl, who lived in the West Country.

The letter read: 'Dear Floyd, for some extraordinary reason my wife, who is a total lunatic, is completely taken with your television programmes, and I would esteem it at least courteous of you to come to my house and have dinner so I can get rid of all this nonsense about her infatuation with you.' The letter was signed, with a traditionally confident thick nib and in black ink, without any use of Christian name.

I decided to go. The earl was right out of the pages of P. G. Wodehouse. He was the eccentric aristocrat who had married the showgirl, and there she was, aged about seventy-five, tottering on her patent leather shoes and hidden under an ostrich-feathered shoulder wrap.

I'd approached the evening as if I were being invited to my commanding officer's home for dinner, that is to say very formally. But, as with Warren Mitchell in Sydney, I was unsure what to call my host. Previously, I had asked a few friends how to address an earl – 'Is it my Lord, or Earlship?' – but all of them were as clueless as me; none of them knew.

But I needn't have worried. Shortly after I had crossed the threshold of the stately pile, the earl took me to one side. 'Now listen to me, Floyd,' he said. 'Do you enjoy a whisky?'

I said politely, 'Yes, I do.' It's not a lie.

'Well, thank fuck for that,' he replied. Then he shook my hand with a strong grip and added, 'Now, my name is Bob . . . '

When you are famous, people assume that they know you . . . and that even if they don't, then they can soon become your friend.

It might sound an exaggeration, but a lot of the time I felt hunted.

If I was working at a theatre, I would say to the theatre manager, 'Please, when I go back into the dressing room, don't let anyone in.' Next thing, the theatre manager would be at the dressing room door, saying, 'Oh, there's a mate of yours wants to see you.' It wasn't a mate of mine, but a stranger.

Maybe I'd be on a ferry going to Ireland, and there would

be a bunch of guys on a golf trip, all drunk of course. I'd be with my wife and then one of the guys would come up and say, 'Floydy, do you remember that night we had up in Strathclyde with those two girls?'

And I'd know I'd never met the man and wasn't in Strathclyde, but rather than cause offence, I'd say, 'Oh, it was a great night, wasn't it?' And he'd say come and meet the wife because I've told her we've been out a couple of nights, which we hadn't. Then the wife would say to her husband, 'Have you been cheating on me. Why have you been going to Strathclyde?'

As for relationships, fame ruined nearly all of mine. Then there were huge demands for charitable requests, and I fulfilled as many as I could. There were invitations to cricket or rugby matches, just because people wanted to be seen with me. People would book me to open this, that, the other. I opened an £80 million office block in Reading and said to the organizers, 'What do you want me to do?'

And they said, 'Just do your own thing.'

I said, 'What is my own thing?'

As Charles Dickens wrote, 'It was the best of times; it was the worst of times.' What were the best of times? I can barely remember one.

I can barely remember one, until I give it a little more thought (and even more thought as I progress within these pages). I was able to buy a house. And I bought a Bentley or two; that was good fun.

Also, I feel a terrific sense of achievement. I was and still am extremely proud of what I've been able to do. I was lucky enough to be able to travel the world, at someone else's expense, and to taste magnificent dishes, cook with unusual and interesting ingredients, and share this knowledge with millions upon millions of television viewers and readers of my cookery books; not the British but people all around the globe. (And let's not forget Finland, where I published a book about hangover cures: the Finnish are the biggest boozers of any nation.)

My approach, my attitude? It was: I don't know anything at all. And the way you find out about things is to say, 'Excuse me, what, why, where, when and how did you do that?'

I don't want to know the general manager of the Ritz although I am sure he or she is charming. I want to know the doorman. I don't want to know the managing director. I want to know his driver.

I want to have high friends in low places, because the doorman of some hotel in the Punjab has a mother who is a cook on the street, and just by observing her you will learn more about Indian food than you could learn from reading the entire works of Madhur Jaffrey.

One of the upsides of fame is that you get to meet interesting people. For instance, compare and contrast these two snapshots of my life.

The first is of me, when I was a restaurateur in Bristol. The Rolling Stones were going to be playing in Bristol and I had a friend, a local boy called Mike Goode, who had a strange manufacturing business, making portable lavatories. One of his commissions was to provide the portable lavatories in Wales for the Pope's visit, and he received recognition within the portable loo industry for being the man who provided the toilets for the Stones concert.

Within minutes of the band arriving in Bristol, the city was alive with rumours of them demanding six cases of Jack Daniel's, twenty cases of guava juice, a hundredweight of

Smarties – but no green ones, so somebody had to sift through the sweets and remove the offending green ones. There were stories flying around of how the money was removed from the stadium by helicopter. The usual gossip and probably all true.

This meant that my friend Mike was, in effect, working for the concert promoter, Harvey Goldsmith. Mike and Harvey must have been chatting, my name must have come up, and the next thing, the promoter came round to my restaurant. He was carrying a briefcase stuffed with cash, and he said to me, 'We'll buy the restaurant out for Sunday night. I don't want anybody coming in, because if Mick and the boys want to come, you're on standby.'

He gave me lots of cash and in return I promised to close the restaurant to other customers, and keep it open just for the Stones to have dinner after their performance.

I left my staff in the restaurant and went along to the concert, though I was bitterly disappointed that they felt they were still creative artists instead of performers, and they were singing stupid new songs when everyone wanted to hear '(I Can't Get No) Satisfaction' and 'Get Off Of My Cloud' and stuff like that. Then I went back to my restaurant and waited for Mick and the boys. I waited and waited, but they didn't come. Later I discovered Harvey had done the same in four other restaurants in the town, and the Stones didn't go to any of them anyhow. They weren't hungry.

So I didn't get to meet them then.

But now look at the second snapshot in this compare and contrast experience . . .

I was in Singapore, staying at the Four Seasons, and being paid well to do cookery demonstrations as well as oversee a kitchen brigade of forty chefs who were cooking, to my specifications, a grand dinner for the guests. This was a huge gig, as John Miles would say.

It was two in the morning, like it always is, and I had signed every menu, posed for every photograph, chatted to every person, and there were hundreds of them. I'd kissed every child, hugged every man and flirted with every wife. I'd signed hundreds of books (including books for the people who say, 'Could you sign it to my mum?' and I say, 'What's your mum's name?' and they look to their partner. 'Oh, I don't know. Just sign it to Mum.' And I say, 'She's not my mum . . .').

I'd been at it non-stop and was feeling dead. I went over to the corner of the bar, a long way away, out of anyone's sight, to an area where I could smoke. So I smoked and ordered a large Johnnie Walker on ice. I sat and savoured the moment and thought, thank heavens for that, the endurance test is completed, well done you.

Then someone found me. He was a young man in an immaculate suit and he was from reception. I could see him coming from the gloom, as the staff cleared up the ballroom where the event had been held. When he reached me he said, 'I am sorry to trouble you.'

I said, 'You better be.'

He said, 'Could you do me a favour?'

'Oh my God. I have just spent the last seven hours signing autographs for everybody, holding up a glass while posing for pictures for cameras that don't work, and dealing with people who hand me their mobile phones and ask me to say hello to their mother in Wokingham . . .'

The man from reception said, 'Could you ring room three-zero-nine-four?'

I said, 'What the hell for?'

He said, 'Please just ring room three-zero-nine-four and ask to speak to Mr Smith.'

I told him I didn't know anyone in the hotel called Mr Smith, but he was insistent. 'Please do it. My job's on the line.' I was too tired to ask him any more questions, so I asked him to please bring a phone to me and dial the number.

The phone was answered and I said, 'I am very sorry to trouble you, Mr Smith. I've got a maniac sitting next to me in the bottom bar of the hotel who has begged me to call you. My name is Keith Floyd.'

And Ronnie Wood said, 'Floydy! I'll be down immediately.' The Stones, it transpired, had been trapped in the hotel penthouse. They were due to be playing in Hong Kong but the SARS epidemic meant that flights to Hong Kong had been stopped in order to contain the epidemic. Unable to leave the country and travel to their next gig, they were imprisoned in the luxury of the Four Seasons, squabbling, sulking, playing billiards and doing whatever else Stones do when they cannot roll.

Ronnie came down to the bar and greeted me with the words, 'Floydy, it's been a long time since Punchestown.' (Punchestown is another story, for another time, and irrelevant here.)

The following day, the Stones and their entourage were sitting in the front row, watching me do a cookery demonstration. In fact, Mick didn't come; he was probably sulking. But the rest did.

My point is, at one time in my life I was hovering outside my restaurant in Bristol waiting to see the Stones. At a later stage, and because of fame, they came to see me. And who can grumble? I'm beginning to feel better already.

NINETEEN

There was, in my mind, no doubt that my days on television were coming to an end.

After the chaos of filming *American Pie* in 1988, and having fallen out with David, I was so fed up with him that I couldn't see myself working with him ever again.

Even if I were to work with another director, I believed that the Warhol fifteen minutes of fame had run its course, albeit about five years longer than fifteen minutes. 'That's it,' I said to myself. 'Finished. No more.' Financially, I was comfortable and I had an increasing desire to return to what I saw as 'reality'.

Once I had got into television, in the lulls in between filming, when I didn't know if anything was going to happen next, that is when I used to worry and wonder about what I would do afterwards.

I started to think about life away from the cameras and what I would do with myself. It was 1989 and I was living in a flat in Bristol and madly in love with Zoe, the girlfriend who didn't want me to buy a Bentley. She was blonde, very curvaceous, extremely attractive and she had an IQ of some astronomical figure. If Mensa had a top ten she'd be in it.

Zoe was a property developer and was quite a wow person,

actually. She had a pilot's licence and she also had a friend who owned a pretty cottage in south Devon, on the slopes of Dartmoor and halfway between Plymouth and Exeter.

'What you should do if you've got a few quid is buy the cottage,' said Zoe. 'It would be great for weekends.' I love the countryside so the idea appealed to me, and indeed I bought Stancombe Cottage, renovated it and from time to time to Zoe and I would leave the city to spend weekends in the tranquillity of Devon. It wasn't long before I sold the flat in Bristol and resettled permanently in Stancombe Cottage.

I found a nice local, the Waterman's Arms, which was run by a chap called Terry Wing. He was the son of a successful London publican, and was a forty-ish, English stereotype, always dapper in waistcoat and cufflinks. Terry was neat and proper and he kept his pub neat and clean. He had terrible battles with his head chef – they hated each other – but the pub was good and I'd drink there and became quite friendly with Terry and could see that a pub in this part of Devon could do well.

A couple of miles from Totnes is the village of Tuckenhay, where there was a pub called the Malster's Arms and that is where I found myself one day, though I didn't want to stay too long when I walked through the front door. The pub had a Formica bar, behind which were cheap knotty pine shelves supported by imitation wrought-iron brackets. Get the scene? It had been refurbished in the sixties and was a disgrace.

There was an overpowering stench of chips and the carpet was a pool of beer that squelched as you walked across it. But sitting outside and beside the River Dart, the Malster's was unquestionably set in a beautiful location.

Reckoning that I had nothing to do now that my career in

television was over, and having learned that the Malster's was up for sale, I offered to buy it. Of course, the price increased sharply when I expressed an interest because I was seen as a stinking-rich celebrity.

I employed my two great friends Geoff and Biff to sort the place out. They'd helped me transform Creek Lodge. 'Boys, this place will open on the 14th of July,' I said. 'Go for it.' And they did.

They were patient as well, hardly kicking up too much of a fuss when I inspected their work and insisted that what they had just done was not quite right so would they mind ripping it down and starting all over again? Or the paint was not, I now knew, the right colour so would they mind repainting with this colour instead?

The pub was large. I created the Quiet Room, which had easy chairs, comfy carpets, glass cases full of stuffed fish and fishing reels, and every conceivable newspaper and magazine. Children were banned from the Quiet Room and, as you'd expect from its name, it was free of music too.

Then there was the bar and at the other end of the room was the Barnes Suite, named after Stuart Barnes, the English rugby player. The walls were covered in rugby memorabilia: shirts from Scott Gibbs, pictures autographed by the former Ireland captain, Willie John McBride. The Barnes Suite doubled as a children's play den, with boxes crammed with toys and Lego. Normally kids get sent to a corrugated shed at the back of the pub. Here, kids could play to their hearts' content and parents could keep an eye on them.

We created four guest bedrooms above the pub, and these would boost the income.

I commissioned a man who made film props to make me

two crocodiles. The crocs were then weighted and placed on the river. At high tide they floated and at low tide they sank into the mud. Believe me or believe me not, when the sun was setting and you looked across the water and caught a glimpse of the crocodiles you thought you were on the Amazon. Of course the harbour master ten miles downstream got very upset about it. 'You can't do that with those crocodiles.' But I stood my ground.

The pub housed two restaurants. On the ground floor was the Canteen, which had banquette seating, overlooked the Dart and served dishes like bangers and mash, fish and chips, and later there were Thai dishes that I had learned to cook in Thailand. Downstairs was the posh restaurant, an exquisite place called George's (named after a teddy bear), which had a terrace overlooking the river and my crocs. The food was outstanding, though none of the locals dined there because they considered it too expensive.

Before reopening the pub, I invited representatives from the local authorities to come and carry out inspections. The planning officers came, the fire brigade and the police, too. We were all ready for the 14 July opening when a police officer arrived to carry out a final inspection. 'By the way,' he said, 'you have informed the court haven't you?'

'About what?' I asked. The officer explained that as I had rearranged the bar areas I would need approval from the local magistrates. I didn't know you couldn't move a bar in a pub without permission. And once you have permission to do it, you then have to apply for a new licence.

So I went to court and this was eleventh-hour stuff. In fact, I was effectively summoned before magistrates to be punished. The punishment was that I couldn't open the downstairs restaurant for nine months. By now I had spent fortunes on the pub, and being deprived of serving food meant being deprived of revenue and therefore profits. It messed me up financially and was a real blow. I felt that I had done everything correctly, by the book, and while I know ignorance is not an excuse in the eyes of the law, I genuinely did not know that I had to apply for permission.

We opened on 14 July and the pub's name was changed. It went from the Malster's Arms to become the Floyd's Inn (Sometimes). My friend Widge painted a pub sign which depicted me with a big brown trout leaping in waters behind. On that night and every 14 July after we celebrated in style. An anchored raft was placed in the river and used for a fireworks display. On the balcony of the restaurant we had a brilliant singer, Jamie Marshall, who has a big Joe Cocker kind of voice.

These celebrations were huge events, enjoyed by all except for the grumpy people who'd read about the event in the local paper and they'd turn up with their bags full of crisps and Coca-Cola so they didn't have to buy a drink in my pub. At ten past eight they'd say, 'The fireworks display hasn't started yet. It gave out in the paper that it's going to be eight o'clock.'

The press arrived and asked me to stand on the pavement, beneath the pub sign, to pose for photographs. Looking at those pictures now, there is a twist of irony. While I am beaming away and feeling confident about my new project, the pub sign predicts how it will all end. The Floyd's Inn (Sometimes): those four words could have told me that it would never work. A publican has to be there *always*, rather than sometimes.

As country folk say, the best fertilizer is the sole of the farmer's boot. When the farmer ain't there it goes to pot and to rot. As I have said, I did not expect my television career to continue . . . but it did. It took me away from the pub, away from the business that required my constant attention.

But in the meantime, I moved into a studio flat – it had a kitchenette, a couple of sofas and a bed – above the pub. I'd awake and come downstairs to the pub at ten-ish and have a meeting with the head chef . . . if I had one. Trying to find a decent chef was an almighty challenge. No chef wanted to work in Devon and the ones that did turn up were frequently second rate and would last no more than a week or two.

I don't think it's too unfair to say that the service industry skills at that time in Devon amounted to this: they just about knew how to wrap up a stainless-steel knife and fork very tightly in a cheap red paper napkin. That's all.

Late morning, the tea drinkers would arrive. They were the ones who wanted a pot of tea and biscuits because they were people who never wanted to pay for lunch and then you'd hear them grumble, 'It's so expensive.' Then, if we were in the summer season, the Canteen was busy at lunchtime and the salmon sandwiches and sausages sold well. I used to play jokes in the Canteen, though no one ever got them.

For example, I'd put a fresh Brixham lobster on the blackboard and price it at £4.50 when in fact it should have been fifteen quid. And underneath, I'd write, 'baked beans on toast, £3.50'. People would moan, 'That's outrageous. He's charging £3.50 for baked beans on toast.' It amused me. As it was, I never charged for baked beans on toast.

When I was cooking in the kitchen, and I did when I could, I was very keen on game. One winter, I made some little *barquettes* – boat-shaped pastry shells – and filled them with lead shot before placing them on the bar. It was quite clear

Autograph for a young fan
somewhere in Spain.

In Bosnia in March 1996 to cook for
the troops. I prepared a quick snack for the
local head man, at the time homeless and
being looked after by the British army.

Costumed and ready for my one man show,
Floyd Uncorked.

Nick Patten, director-producer of *Floyd Uncorked* and *Floyd's India*. Surely one of
television's most organized and meticulous directors. It was a joy to work with him.

Eat your heart out Jenson Button! Formula One has got nothing on arctic dogs sledding (*Fjord Fiesta*).

The irrepressible and brilliant Mike Connor somewhere in Greenland while filming *Floyd's Fjord Fiesta*.

If you can't stand the heat, get out of the kitchen. In my case, I went to the Arctic Circle.

A Floyd gig in the ballroom of the Four Seasons, Singapore.

Ronnie and Jo Wood at the Floyd gig in Singapore.

Big Bad Bird, who looked after my every need while filming throughout Thailand and during my visits to Khun Akorn's fabled Tong Sia Bay in Koh Samui. PS There is nothing bad about Bird.

My personal bodyguard during my visit to the North West frontier, Afghanistan.

The beginnings of the garden at Montfrin. Bentley to the right.

La Maison des Églantines 2020

And painted by me.

Celia,

As a capricorn I can be a stubborn.! but its January and I am hoping xx

My own way of apologizing to Celia.

With Poppy at Montfrin.

My son Patrick being cool,
as usual.

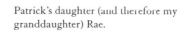

Patrick's daughter (and therefore my
granddaughter) Rae.

With Celia in the garden at Montfrin, 2009.

the pastry was filled with lead shot but of course some presumably short-sighted punter bit into one and broke his tooth. He didn't say a word to me, but a couple of mornings later there was a damning indictment in the local paper: 'Customer nearly dies at Floyd's pub . . .' or some such thing.

Although I was using my name to assist business – the pub, after all, was named after me – it began to dawn on me that while I thought I was leaving the entertainment business, I had actually set myself up on an invisible stage at the bar. Punters would come in and expect to hear funny stories about my travels. I was being Floydy all the time, rather than Keith.

Expectations were high because of my associations with food. Punters would phone up from London saying, 'Have you got a helicopter pad?' If I happened to take the call, I'd say, 'No. This is a pub in Devon.' There was this fantastic misconception and that showed a total ignorance of a large section of Britain's eating-out public. They wanted to come to my pub because they had seen my programmes. And my programmes were raw, filmed in the fresh air, invariably in any kind of dangerous or bizarre situation.

If you think about it, the man who made those programmes is hardly of the character to have a neat Georgian country house restaurant with a long gravel drive leading up to it and a helicopter pad on site. These people, the ones who'd describe themselves as foodies, didn't quite get it.

The working man and his wife – Floydy fans – found it a bit expensive but they still wanted to come and I like to think they enjoyed it.

By now I was well accustomed to receiving specific but familiar questions. So I got a great big blackboard, hung it by the bar and wrote on it, from numbers one to thirty, a list

which went like this: '1. Thailand, actually; 2. Probably Australia; 3. Yes, it was really good . . .' And so on. Then, when
a customer asked me a question – Where did you eat really
well? What's your favourite place in the world? Did you like
Memphis? – I simply pointed at the blackboard and said, 'May
I refer you to number . . .', and there they had the response
that matched the respective question.

One of the privileges of being well known is the invitation
that comes to appear on *Desert Island Discs*. In the sixties this
was one of the programmes that I would listen to, and then,
in the late eighties, I was asked to go on. At the time, Sue
Lawley was its presenter.

You'll know the format of this weekly Radio 4 programme:
the subject talks about his or her life and the influences of
eight pieces of music; music that you would take with you if
you were stranded on a desert island.

Everyone who has featured on the programme says it's so
hard to choose eight records, and I cannot disagree. I didn't
choose records that reminded me of wives or girlfriends or
the birth of Patrick or Poppy. I was told not to do that. I frequently listen to *Desert Island Discs* and hear the interviewee
pick a song that brings back memories of the birth of his child.
But a producer said to me, 'We just want the music.'

This afternoon I listened to a CD of the programme, which
was sent to me by the BBC.

Sue Lawley opened with this introduction, 'Five years ago
he wasn't always sure he could afford the ingredients for his
next meal. Now five television series and nine books later he
can buy all the food and drink he needs. His success lies in
his enthusiasm for his subject and his anarchic approach to its
representation. His television programmes are appreciated as

much for the garrulous charm of their presenter as for their culinary content. A constantly replenished wine glass usually in the hand, he's become known as the drinking man's cook. He is Keith Floyd.'

I told her that my favourite music had to be rock 'n' roll and blues. 'Rock 'n' roll is absolutely vital to me. I have been on desert islands all my life. To imaginary desert islands where I was running a restaurant on my own desert island; and being a child and sitting fishing, stuff like that. Being alone. And when I was very little, I was about twelve, a strange thing happened. The world changed completely, from David Whitfield suddenly there was rock 'n' roll. And so when I first heard "Blue Suede Shoes", I have from that day to this wanted a pair of blue suede shoes.' You'll guess my first track: 'Blue Suede Shoes' by Elvis.

My second choice was Nina Simone's 'To Love Somebody' because: 'I love those sad songs. When you are flying to Australia, or having too much Shiraz poured down you, you wish there was someone there who would know what you were really doing. For that reason I've always been terribly stirred by [this song].'

Sue asked if I felt I had been unlucky in love. 'I wouldn't say unlucky is the word. Catastrophic would be closer to the mark.'

Sue: 'Married twice, divorced twice. How many times has your heart been broken?'

Me: 'Two or three. I'm impossible to live with but I don't think it's my fault. I'm not grumpy. I can go so far and then I get grumpy or I lose my temper. If I do something, I do it to the maximum, I really do. And that sometimes leaves people breathless. And then when I collapse, temperamentally or for a long time or short time, they think, hang on something's wrong with him. Because I've been running too fast and then when I stop it seems like my character changes and I go into being very quiet, reclusive. There is the other side, and it is a quiet introspective, dull, boring person.'

Sue: 'It's a classic tale. You talk of being isolated and probably underneath it you're a bit unhappy.'

Me: 'Yeah, yeah. I shouldn't be because I've got all the toys. But you see when I am working I am so happy. You're grumpy because you think, not another take and all that stuff. But that's so much fun. I am so fortunate to be paid for what I love doing. And I think if I am lucky in that way I can't be lucky right across the board.'

I then made a reference to David and Celia Martin, without mentioning them by name. I said, 'In the sixties, all my chums were wearing kaftans, all getting into Transit vans and driving to Greece on their wife's father's money. I, on the other hand, was always pulling out dustbins at two in the morning and mopping kitchen floors, carving myself a superb and very happy lifestyle in restaurants. And if there was one record that encouraged me and said you can really do it, it was "Hey Jude".'

She asked me about the pub and I told her, 'Like all mistresses, she's terribly expensive and very demanding. It's very hard work but it's also very important to me. Again, I shouldn't be doing it. It's costing me more than I make but that again doesn't matter, because it gives me some sort of reality. If the bass is off they tell me. If the chips aren't right they tell me. It's a real thing.'

Of the eight tracks, I said I'd take 'Hey Jude'. You're allowed to take a book and I picked Meryvn Peake's *Gormenghast*, which David Martin introduced me to. 'It's a fundamental story of good triumphing over evil. I've read it four times.' You're also allowed to take a luxury item. I said, 'On Saturday nights I want to go and do a bit of rock 'n' rolling. I want a really good pair of blue suede shoes. Size nine, please.'

Listening back to the programme, I am struck by the sense of fun that I associated with filming. 'When I am working I am so happy.' I think when I am working it is great. I don't want to be a couch potato. This morning I was painting a table top in the garden, and I was happy doing that. What is happiness? Is it a place, a state of mind? Is it a painting on the wall? What the hell is it? I don't know.

After appearing on *Desert Island Discs* I met a woman in my pub and she said cheerfully, 'Hi, I'm Sue Lawley's sister.' She told me, 'After you did *Desert Island Discs* Sue came away with the impression that you were incredibly lonely.' And I was.

Sydney, 1990

Dear Reader

I'm in the Sebel Townhouse Hotel. Jett Harris
from the Shadows has just asked for my autograph. A moment later Johnny Cash walked by
with Kris Kristofferson and Willie Nelson.
Kristofferson looked at me and said, 'You come
on and join the show tonight.'

I sat in the stadium and listened to them all,
but specially two songs, 'Help Me Make It
Through The Night' and 'Me And Bobby
McGee', the words telling me it was OK to feel
sad when listening to the blues.

Johnny Cash fronted the band called The
Highwaymen. I bought a 78 rpm of his and froze
to death calling, 'I walked the line because you
are mine'. He went on to sing one of the most
important songs ever written, 'San Quentin'. His
wife then sang with him while he strummed his
guitar, oozing the love he held for her. God bless
you both.

Floy

TWENTY

Fan mail arrived at the pub and was kept in the office. I say *fan* mail though a lot of it came from women who were looking – how shall I put this? – for a good time. 'If you ever find yourself in Tunbridge Wells, you can steam up my kitchen any time' was the gist of the letters, postcards and faxes.

One Sunday night there were only about three people in the pub and I was utterly bored. I said to a waiter, 'Please go and get the fan mail letters from my office and we'll ring a few of them up.' I was drunk, of course.

Many of the 'fans' attached photographs of themselves, which made the decision process a hell of a lot easier. Or so you would have thought. One lady had written the steam-up-my-kitchen-anytime sort of letter and attached a photo of herself. She looked sensationally elegant and was standing by a candelabra. I phoned her up and said, 'Hello. You sent me a lovely letter. Would you like to come down and stay at the pub?' She said she'd be there the next day.

The following afternoon a waiter came up to me and said, 'There's a lady here to see you.'

I scanned the bar but couldn't see anyone who resembled the lady in the photograph. 'Where is she?' I asked the waiter and he pointed to a spot at the bar. I followed the line of his pointing finger, which took me to a woman at the bar. She had omitted to tell me in her sweet letter that some twenty years at least had passed since the taking of the photograph. Overly rouged and with a crinkled face caked in foundation, as well as tottering in ludicrously high-heeled shoes, she resembled the whore from hell. I spent the next five hours on a mission to get rid of her.

Women came into the pub in pairs. It's funny that they often hunt in pairs – the pretty one and the not so pretty one. And it is quite true that on the odd occasion I invited one of them to stay in one of the guest rooms, and so forth.

Likewise, I invited women to come and stay with me at Creek Lodge in Ireland. But these sorts of relationships were generally doomed and unsatisfactory for both parties concerned. The women had boyfriends or even husbands back at home, which they'd failed to tell me about and mid-clinch they'd say, 'My God, what am I doing?'

No matter how many people came through the doors and how much money went through the tills, there was always a continual problem with staff.

With hindsight I can see that I was too soft on them. You have to be tough to run a restaurant. Take Richard Shepherd, who has, among other places, Langan's. I am sure he's a wonderful boss and he has staff who have been working for him for years and he is also extremely successful. But he doesn't give anybody an inch: no initiative; no nothing. You've got to be like that. There is a difference between maintaining high standards with fairness, and caving in to the emotions of the staff.

For instance, a really lovely boy came over from Kinsale to work for me and he thought he knew a few things. He put all the silver-plated cutlery into a bucket of bleach overnight and the next morning he had succeed in peeling the silver off £2,000 worth of cutlery. He came to me crying and saying, 'I'm ever so sorry.' And I said, 'Oh, don't worry, we all make mistakes. That's why there are rubbers on the ends of pencils.' Yet he had cost me £2,000 and I should've fired him there and then. Many of the strongest characters in the restaurant business have been fired for far less.

But I gave everybody a chance. I tried to get the staff to wear uniforms. They'd wear them one day, come in the next and I'd say, 'Why aren't you wearing your uniform?' They forgot. But they didn't forget to wear dirty trainers and scruffy clothes. The casual attitude got to me and one day I rounded them up and gave them all a lecture. 'Look,' I said, 'I want you to know that while this place has got to be fun it is not a joke.'

Fat lot of good that did.

Rick Stein had kept in touch. When I was still in Bristol he'd phone for advice, saying things like, 'Some Australian customer has complained there is sediment in the wine.' And I'd say, 'Explain to the Australian that good French wine has sediment.' The Australians are so clever their wine never has sediment. But if you order old Burgundy or Bordeaux in a fine restaurant the sommelier will decant it over a candle flame, so they can see when the sediment rises and stop pouring, leaving it in the bottom of the bottle. Uncouth customers have been known to say, ''Ere, you've pinched a bit of my wine.' When Rick had opened rooms at the Seafood Restaurant in Padstow, he called to say, 'I'd love you to come down as my guest, stay overnight and have dinner with me. I said, 'What a lovely invitation. Can I bring my mother and daughter?' Of course, he said, and the Floyd trio turned up on the agreed date. We went in the Bentley and it was all very grand. It was also a memorable occasion because Poppy was about five and my mother about seventy and they both ate lobster for the first time.

Rick also helped me out with my staffing problems at the pub. I phoned him and said, 'I'm going crazy. I can't find a cook anywhere. They turn up in filthy trainers and haven't got a clue. Can you help me find a cook?'

He said, 'I've got this French guy. Do you want to meet him?' Send him over, I told Rick.

The French guy turned out to be Jean-Christophe Novelli, known as JC, who'd left his hometown of Arras in northern France at the age of twenty-one, bought a one-way ferry ticket and come to Britain to learn English. He stayed in Britain, and today he is an acclaimed chef, Michelin star winner and all the rest of it. And having worked in a few places by the time he reached me, he carried a portfolio of photographs which showed his spun-sugar creations and snaps of palm trees made out of chocolate. I hired him as head chef in the pub's restaurant, George's. It was one of the smartest moves of my life.

JC was quite difficult – stubborn, I suppose – but he was on a mission to heaven. I wanted to serve coq au vin and ratatouille, dishes that were far too basic for him to know how to cook. But he put his heart and soul into the job and was willing to learn. His gift at the stove only boosted the reputation of the restaurant.

JC has become an extremely good friend who is loyal and generous to a fault and, as you will see, he is one of those guys who are there when you most need them.

It was also around about this time, in the late eighties, that I met Marco Pierre White. Marco is the youngest chef ever to win three Michelin stars and a man who has opened some thirty restaurants. When I met him he'd just opened his first, and he was a lanky, wild-haired, pallid cook in his mid-twenties.

The restaurant was Harveys, in Bellevue Road, overlooking Wandsworth Common in south London. It is now Chez Bruce, an acclaimed restaurant run by Bruce Poole. But then it was Harveys and had acquired a reputation as something of a destination dining room, and anyone with an expense account would hurry to Harveys for a slow lunch or dinner. This was in the days when long lunches were the norm in London, yet to be replaced by a sandwich at the desk and in front of the computer.

We were introduced by Sheila Keating, the food writer and wife of Tim White, the sound man on the Floyd series. Sheila (who incidentally helped me with the writing of *Floyd's American Pie* and *Floyd on Africa*) was working for the *Sunday Express* and asked one day if I'd like to come and have lunch with her and Marco. She would interview the pair of us together and it didn't take me long to see the angle.

Marco was the new kid on the block but ruffling feathers within the culinary world because he did things like wear a kitchen apprentice's blue-and-white striped apron and didn't wear a tall white hat, as well as having a reputation for throwing people out of his restaurants; meanwhile, I was regarded as rebellious and forthright. The two mavericks, in other words, were being brought together. Sheila wasn't so obvious when she invited me. 'Would you like to meet the new kid on the block?' And I said yes.

The restaurant was chic, and the cooking sensational, and Marco and I hit it off immediately. We talked about our mothers' cooking and all that nonsense, and Marco told me about his childhood in Leeds and entwined in his conversation were a few Oscar Wilde quotations. I don't think he has ever read any of Wilde's work, but his mind is a mass of quotes.

Whenever I was in London, I often tried to find time for a meal at Harveys, which Marco has previously described as akin to a circus – people went to see what would happen, what this beast might do were he to step from the kitchen and into the dining room. There was a fine pastry chef, by the way, and his name was Gordon Ramsay.

I happened to be at Harveys for two interesting lunchtime encounters.

The first occurred as I was sitting enjoying my meal when the door opened and a film crew trounced through the restaurant. They were there to film Marco for a television series, and they busily went about setting up cameras, lights, sorting out the boom mikes and doing it all in that thoroughly disrespectful manner that so many film crews seem to have mastered. Chairs and tables were pushed aside to make way for tripods.

When Marco emerged from the kitchen he had the look of a proud chef who had just had his dining room completely rearranged haphazardly, and that would be because he *had* just seen his dining room completely rearranged. He was ushered to a chair and told to sit down so that he could be interviewed, but a minute later the clitter-clatter, hustle-bustle of the room was brought to a sudden and most definite halt by a booming voice: 'Get out of my restaurant! And get out now!' His eyes were filled with rage in that way that meant no one – including Marco – would ever know what might happen next. But you wouldn't want to stay and chance it.

Rarely have I seen film crews move as fast as that bunch as they rushed to get their gear and escape from Harveys and the beast within it. Marco returned to the kitchen (his comfort zone, you see) and the crew were outside, rapidly loading their equipment into the back of a van. I left my table and went into the kitchen. 'Marco,' I said, 'you might not like these people – they are, after all, television people – but it's terribly important that you are nice to them because they can help your business.' Then I went outside and had a word with the film crew and ten minutes later Marco and the crew were all filming happily and harmony had been restored. Well, not quite, but almost.

The second interesting lunchtime at Harveys was about a year later when Marco was due to be cooking for the French chef Louis Outhier, who in the fifties created L'Oasis, the famed restaurant in the south of France which had since won him three Michelin stars – while Marco had two stars. Louis was in London and wanted to try out the little restaurant in Wandsworth that everyone was raving about. He was coming with three friends and had booked a table for 1 p.m., but when they were fifteen minutes late Marco was pacing the room, looking out of the window and saying, 'Where the hell is he?' I kept telling him to calm down, but with each passing minute he seemed to become more agitated.

They arrived – heavens above – at 1.45 p.m., and they looked typically French and suave and casually removed their cashmere coats and handed them to the maître d', completely unaware of the tension they had caused.

I left my table and went into the kitchen. Marco was in a rage. 'That's it,' he said. 'I won't serve them. They can't take the piss out of me like this. Let's see how a Michelin three-star chef reacts when a two-star chef tells him to fuck off.' I experienced one of those beam-me-up-Scotty moments. I wasn't beamed anywhere unfortunately, but dashed into the restaurant, ordered drinks for Louis and his ever-smiling entourage and chatted to them. In so doing I discovered that they did not speak English. And Marco did not speak French.

Darting from the table to the kitchen, I explained to the still simmering head chef that he had to calm down. They were here now, all was well, and he must cook for them. 'Cook,' I said, 'and when you are finished cooking get out there and sit and talk to them.'

'Do they speak English?'

'Not very well, no. In fact, not a word of it. But even if you can't talk French and they can't speak English you can still enjoy the experience of their company.'

A couple of hours later, Marco and Louis were at the same table, both nodding along to unintelligible grunts. Not for nothing has Marco (in his own autobiography, *Devil in the Kitchen*) described me as the Kofi Annan of gastronomy, and when he fell out with his mentor, Albert Roux, I acted as an intermediary in an effort to help heal the rift. Alas, their feud was so bitter that any words of wisdom I had to offer were unsuccessful.

But they hadn't fallen out, of course, in August 1992, when Marco married his second wife, the model Lisa Butcher. In fact, Albert was best man. And Marco decided to have his stag night in a private room at Albert's restaurant, Le Gavroche, to which I was invited. There were about ten of us there, and it was very much a boys' night out, rowdy and fun. The guests included Michael Caine, who was Marco's partner in a restaurant at

Chelsea Harbour, as well as Tom and Eugene McCoy, the chefs from Yorkshire, and friends of Marco from way back. There was also a man called Jim.

Although we were in one of the finest French restaurants in Britain, the food was simple – we had fish and chips, and it was great. At some point we managed to stagger out of the restaurant and ended up in a dreadful bar full of hookers and men who looked like sleazy law lords and most certainly were.

Some weeks later, I got a call. 'Keith, hi, it's Jim Croce.' I love Jim Croce. He was an American folk singer and I say *was* because he's dead.

I was mystified. I said, 'You can't be Jim Croce because you're dead. You died in a plane crash in 1973. So who are you really, and what are you putting me on?'

The voice said, 'No, not Jim Croce. Jim Capaldi. Drummer.'

This was the Jim that I'd met at Marco's stag night and I remembered him to be a really nice bloke. Jim said, 'I'm having a party and Marco's coming. I'd love to invite you along.' He was, in fact, a drummer with the sixties band Traffic, and a hugely influential songwriter, having worked with Eric Clapton and Paul Weller.

I drove from Devon to Marlow, the historic town on the Thames in Buckinghamshire, and booked into that upmarket inn the Compleat Angler. Then I went round to Jim's party. I knocked on the door and to my astonishment it was opened by George Harrison.

We'd never met although we'd both been invited to participate in one of those 'An Audience With . . .' TV shows. As usual, I was sitting quietly waiting for the programme to begin, surrounded by famous people I didn't dare talk to, when a few rows away, Ringo Starr turned to George Harrison and said loudly, 'That's Floydy!'

Now George said, 'Floydy,' as if we were old mates, and then whisked me into the house, gave me a drink and began the conversation with, 'Have you tried those new vegetarian stock cubes . . .' Guests who were milling around included Sting and Joe Brown and an entire collection of very rock 'n' roll people. It was unreal and totally unexpected and I didn't know quite what to do. I wanted to ask about *Sgt. Pepper* and all the rest of it, but the crowd just wanted to talk about food.

As a wedding gift I bought Marco and Lisa his and hers fishing rods, at great expense and with considerable thought. I pictured the happy young couple on the sunlit banks of a river, picnic hamper beside them as they reeled in trout for tea. A few months after attending the wedding and still feeling chuffed by the gift I'd given them, I picked up a newspaper and read that they had separated and that divorce was on the cards. Marco was clearly trying to compete with me when it came to duration of relationships.

It really bothered me, that. Not the divorce, but the rods.

I spent years trying to forget about it and had just managed to do so when I went to party and a woman came up to me. She introduced herself as Lisa's mother and said, 'And you gave them those lovely fishing rods. Don't you remember?'

I didn't but I do now.

TWENTY-ONE

When John Miles phoned to say he'd negotiated a three-series television deal I was genuinely shocked. Having convinced myself that my television career was over I was just getting accustomed to life as a landlord.

John and I met and he talked me through the deal. An independent production company, Lifetime TV, would make the trio of series to be broadcast by the BBC: *Floyd on Oz*, *Floyd on Spain* and *Far Flung Floyd*, which were screened respectively in 1991, 1992 and 1993. Despite all my misgivings, I thought the devil I know is better than the one I don't so I insisted that I would only make the three series if David Pritchard could be the director and the producer.

David and I hadn't spoken for some time. My last words to him had been, 'I never want to work with you again.' Now I phoned him and said, 'How do you fancy it? I'm going to try and sort this out for you.' We'd had genuine problems but I believe in the good of people and, say what you like about David (as I have done), he is talented.

It was a lifeline to David because he had taken early retirement from the BBC and was therefore unemployed. When he had left the BBC he'd suggested we set up an independent production company. And I said, 'David, there is no way whatsoever.' This is in stark contrast to what David remembers. In his memoir, *Shooting the Cook*, he writes that I was the one who wanted to set up an independent production company.

Floyd on Oz took us across Australia and one memory stays with me. We had to get up at four o'clock in the morning to begin making our way to an oyster farm that was situated on an island off the east coast. The plan was to see the oysters and cook some fish.

It wasn't an easy place to reach. The journey meant taking a fixed-wing plane to somewhere. Then we transferred to helicopters. Then we drove in four-wheel drives. Finally, a boat took us across the waters to the island, and we arrived at about ten in the morning.

Again, the research was absolutely brilliant. After a six-hour journey we discovered that the island has an oyster farm, but the island is also home to a bomber command base used by the Royal Australian Air Force (RAAF), and all that week they were having bombing practice. There was no way we could turn over because the bombs were going off every two minutes.

David said to an assistant, 'Can we tell them to stop?' I mean, the arrogance of the director. Tell them to stop because we've got to make a film. They tried and the RAAF said, 'Don't be so ridiculous.'

However, we learned that the bombs were going to stop dropping about twenty minutes before sunset so that gave us the window of twenty minutes to do the cooking sketch. Once the sun went it was black and it was finished. We spent the rest of the day enduring the heat and the biting flies; some of us played cards, others slept. I couldn't do either because I was so angry they hadn't researched the location properly. You know I can get angry sometimes. I spent the day thinking, what if we miss it? What if that window isn't twenty minutes, but two minutes? Because you can't make the sun rise again, although David thinks he can. But we got it done in those twenty minutes.

Meanwhile, in the top end of Australia, I was at Fitzroy Crossing with two Aborigine guides who gave me witchetty grubs to eat. No, not very pleasant. The grubs are the larvae of certain moths and so named because they feed on the roots of the witchetty bush.

I asked one of the Aborigines his age, and he pointed to a tree and said, 'Like this tree. It's Dreamtime. I am that old.' He didn't know his age, in other words.

I took the Aborigines to the local motel but when we neared the door they said, 'We can't go in there. We are not allowed.'

Remember, it was not so many years ago that Aborigines and others were imprisoned in that remarkable tree, the baobab: its trunk is hollow and, once a door was fitted, for those poor Australian natives it became a prison. It was the devil's tree: the roots were in the sky and the branches were underground.

I said to the Aborigines, 'My name is Floyd. You come with me.' And although eyebrows were raised as we walked into the bar, I did not give a hoot because I believe in equality. I said to the barman, 'I'll have a large Bundy rum and my two friends here will have whatever they like and make it snappy.'

By the way, if you find yourself up in the top end and if by some rare chance there is a 7-11 store you can buy a tin of witchetty grub soup. It tastes exactly like Campbell's condensed mushroom soup. But that's Oz and as they say in Oz, 'She'll be right.'

If you really want to know about the history of Australia and its effect on the indigenous Aboriginal people read a book called *The Naked Shore* written by Robert Hughes. I recommend it.

We were in Australia for three months, during which time I had to buy clothes – shirts, shoes, trousers, belts – and I bought Australian cookery books. I had about three trunks full of stuff when I landed at Heathrow and as I was going through Nothing to Declare I was stopped.

A customs officer said, 'Have you got anything to declare?' I said no because I didn't see clothes that I had bought as being something to declare. However naive and daft you might think I am, anything to declare is 'Yes, I have 10,000 bottles of whisky and 700 sticks of cigarettes.' I don't think a pair of shoes I bought in Melbourne is something to declare. The officer went through my trunks and then he said, 'Can I see your wallet, please?'

I said, 'Yes, sure, of course, you can.' It was stacked full of receipts. He said, 'What's all this then, sir?'

I said, 'They're receipts for clothes I bought when I was filming.' They arrested me . . . for smuggling. I was taken to a room to be interrogated. The officer said, 'You have a choice. You can pay a fine of £4,000, or go to Marylebone High Court.' He left a pause before adding, 'But surely a man of your position would rather avoid going to court.'

I said, 'Yes.' They wanted £4,000 there and then and I had to get the cash from a bureau de change. I handed over the money and was free to go, but before I left the interrogation room a couple of officers came in. They said, 'Can we have your autograph, please?'

I said, 'That's a bit rich, isn't it?' I gave it to them but I was disgusted.

A couple of years later I was coming through Customs and had bought cookery books and other knick-knacks. I'd kept all the receipts and this time I went through Something to Declare, the red channel. I stopped at a customs officer and said, 'I've been working abroad but bought some things. I've got the receipts.' Before I could finish explaining how I was willing to pay, he said, 'Oh, we're not interested in stuff like that,' and he waved me on.

The pub devoured cash. But I was still making television commercial after television commercial, and doing voice-overs for radio ads. One day I was at Elstree studios making a commercial that was hoping simultaneously to sell both a brand of microwave ovens and the same brand of washing machines.

The commercial went like this: the viewer sees me cooking something in the microwave and then, when I remove the plate from the oven, I clumsily spill the dish's contents over my shirt. The reason for the spillage? Answer: I was assumed to be a completely incompetent drunk. Cut to me, muck all over my shirt, but a Cheshire cat grin on my face because, I said in ecstatic tones, 'It doesn't matter. I've got a washing machine.' Then, still blissful that I have managed to cover myself shirt in piping hot food, I unbutton my shirt and pop the soiled garment straight into the tub of the washing machine . . . turn to camera, big smile.

I could do all this in one take. But the advertising agencies never want you to do that because their aim is to milk as much cash as possible out of the client. Time is money, and when it comes to making commercials, it's always the client's money.

When I think of it, most of the commercials I made could have been done and dusted within a few minutes. In reality, they took days to make because a regiment of advertising executives would be hovering behind the cameras, clipboards in hands, and every so often whispering to the director, 'Shall we try one more?'

Then you have the directors. Often they were big names, talented people, who had created major movies, and they'd wander over in between takes in an effort to excuse themselves, distance themselves, from the degradation of shooting a commercial. They'd grope a lens hanging from a string around their neck and say in a whisper, 'I'm only doing this to pay the mortgage, old boy. I don't normally approve of it.' Too true they approved of it. They got bundles of dough.

When I was at Elstree chucking microwaved food over one shirt after another for take after take, someone had finally seen enough of me pinging microwaves and setting washing machines and a lunch break was called. I went to the studio's restaurant and had lunch with an executive from the company that produced the microwaves and washing machines. Over the meal, he tried to sell me one of his microwaves, telling me how brilliant they were and how they beat all competition. I said, 'Look, I'm advertising the blasted things for you. You don't need to tell me how good they are.'

I did a commercial that involved me standing on the stage wearing a hula skirt and advertising kiwi fruit. But there's nothing amusing to tell you about that, except that I had to stand on a stage in a hula skirt and hold a kiwi fruit.

Then there was the commercial for a dish, a bit like Pyrex but called Vision. I had to hold it up and say, 'It's a Vision.' The advertising executives said, 'Can you try it one more time,

Floydy?' I held up the dish and said, with an entirely different emphasis, 'It is a Vision.'

Twenty takes later I was still standing there, holding up the blasted plate and saying, 'It's a Vision.' How do you say the same few words in twenty different ways? They didn't like it and went into huddles.

So I went down the back of the hangar where we were filming. There was a chippie sitting there, reading the *Sun*. 'How you doing?' he said. 'Bit boring, isn't it?' We got talking and he told me that the previous week he had been working with Sir Donald Sinden, the renowned thespian, film star and Associate Artist, no less, of the Royal Shakespeare Company.

The chippie said, 'It was some commercial for a sherry or wine, and like a Brian Rix thing. A farce. They were all in shorts and that Donald Sinden, he's got to step through some French windows and say, "It's amazing." All he's got to do is step through and say, "It's amazing." That's all. All morning he's walking up and down practising, and saying, "It's amazing." He must have worked out a hundred different ways of saying it.'

The carpenter continued: 'Rehearsing all morning. Two words. Shakespearean actor and all. It was only a TV commercial. Finally, it was time to turn over. He was standing outside with his tennis racket and he came through the French windows and said, "Outstanding."'

The chippie's story had an effect. I'm not quite sure what the moral of the tale was, but I returned to the set and with all my heart boomed out, 'It's a Vision.' The director shouted, 'Cut! That's a wrap.'

TWENTY-TWO

The restaurant manager said, 'What would you like for supper?'

And I said, 'I'd like a cobra, please.' The type of snake rather than the brand of beer.

It was 1992 and I was in a restaurant in Vietnam, one of the strangest restaurants I'd ever set foot in. There in front of me was the writhing cobra, which he then lifted and . . .

Actually, let's not start there. Let's not begin with 1992 and the filming of *Far Flung Floyd*. I want to go right back, if you don't mind, to my introduction to far-flung food. We're in Bristol now, and I was a teenager and former cub reporter working at the Crossfield and Bowdie corn mill. I worked the night shift, unloading sacks of cow cake, and collecting a salary of £1 10s a week. As far as my parents were concerned, being a mill hand was not terribly acceptable, considering they had worked hard to send me to Wellington.

At six every evening I was picked up by one of the other labourers, who had an Austin A40 and was obese and quite horrible and came from Bedminster.

I'd squeeze into the back seat, alongside other labourers on the night shift, and they were all real working-class people who were marvellous and all had nicknames. We were a gang of about eight and the leader was called Old Ted. He was called Old Ted because I suspect he was fifty, which to me and the others was 110.

Old Ted was wiry, spindly, strong and clever, and didn't overexert himself. I mean, he was the sort who knew how to build a pyramid but didn't have to hew the stones. They transported themselves.

Among my co-workers there were thieves, and the currency was half-hundredweight sacks of sugar, sugar being part of the processing of these cow cakes. Some mornings, when the shift finished, I'd get into the car and my head would be touching the ceiling. That's when I knew there was a half-hundredweight of sugar 'hidden' underneath the back seat. At the gate, Old Ted used to have a quiet word with the security guards, tipping them off about a planned sugar theft. He'd say, 'You wanna watch out tomorrow night. Old Mick is going to be nicking some sugar. So search him.'

Obviously, he'd get warm handshakes from the grateful guards, as if he were the defender of the mill, a man who could do no wrong. Then he'd give a quick 'cheerio' to the guards, climb into the car and we'd all drive off, our heads touching the roof, the sweet stuff beneath us. The following night when all cars were searched, ours was completely free of nicked sugar.

It brings to mind the lovely story of the man, let's call him Tom, who left the dockyard in Plymouth every evening with a wheelbarrow covered by a piece of tarpaulin.

Every night the security guards stopped him so that they could look under the tarpaulin. But no, the wheelbarrow was empty; he wasn't stealing anything. When, after forty years in the job, the man retired, George the security guard said, 'All right, Tom, come clean. I know for the past forty years you have been stealing. What is it?'

And Tom said, 'Wheelbarrows.'

My nickname was Quintin Hogg, because I spoke as posh as the Conservative lord, while the youngest member of the gang had two nicknames. Old Ted called him Elvis, simply because he loved rock 'n' roll, had long hair and was tall. He was also known as Jungle because he had done his national service in Malaya during the communist guerrilla war for independence, known as the Malayan Emergency.

I loved my loutish colleagues and one day, after we'd all received a bonus from the bosses who didn't know we were stealing from them, I said to the gang, 'Why don't we all go out for dinner?'

Initially, they were alarmed. Judging from their faces, I might as well have suggested we all perform hara-kiri. You simply didn't go out to dinner in those days unless you were extremely wealthy or had a landmark birthday to celebrate. Or rather, people like Old Ted and Jungle didn't go out for dinner. Back then, most people wolfed down egg and chips at home and then dashed off to the Red Bull to get smashed on Red Barrel and other dreadful drinks.

However, when the gang had overcome the initial shock of my suggestion they warmed to the idea. It was agreed we'd go out to dinner, and do it in style. Old Ted's team, you see, was an adventurous bunch, willing to experiment with new concepts.

Old Ted reckoned we should all dress smartly for the occasion, and we decided that the venue for this inauguration event – and here comes the *Far Flung* connection – would be a Chinese restaurant that occupied the first floor of a building in Silver Street.

I probably wore my worsted blazer, trousers and black Church's brogues, the clothes my father couldn't afford. Old Ted and Co. arrived in ill-fitting suits, red ties and shirts with collars either too tight or too loose.

We met on Silver Street and then went upstairs and stepped into an amazing event. This was a place where they had chop suey, which I would later learn isn't any more Chinese than spaghetti Bolognese is Italian. They are American inventions. Chop suey was a noodle dish created by laundry workers in the San Francisco gold rush of the 1890s.

Anyhow I thought chop suey was the donkey's bollocks, which I mean as a compliment rather than as a description of the ingredients. A great big bowl of noodles, with fried egg and bean sprouts in it. The menu wasn't extensive but it included dishes like chicken and sweet corn soup and fried banana fritters for dessert. I thought it was absolutely fantastic.

Things were going well and Old Ted and the boys were on their best behaviour; not burping, trying not to swear and being very conscious that this was a big evening.

However, we all got terribly drunk, which I think was inevitable because we all liked to drink. The alcohol had a strange effect on Elvis/Jungle and momentarily his mind was propelled back to his days in the Malayan jungle. The Chinese faces reminded him of combat against guerrillas from the Malayan National Liberation Army. He mistook the waiters for the enemy, and as he had been temporarily held captive he really loathed the enemy. He was probably, and understandably, angry and something awful had been triggered in his head.

Jungle started screaming, 'You brought me to a concentration camp! These slant-eyed, yellow-skinned, snot-grovelling . . .'

Then he swore for several minutes and rounded off the curses by announcing, 'I am going to kill them.' He thought he was going to kill the enemy, but we knew he was going to kill our waiters.

He stood up and was about to launch himself on to a waiter. There was a sudden sense that something terrible was about to happen, a rush of adrenalin that swept through diners, waiters, everyone in the restaurant. We were seconds away from having dead waiters. That meant the police and perhaps court. Jail for Jungle? Undoubtedly.

At that moment I felt a wave of strength within me and even though Old Ted was unquestionably the leader, the one who should have stepped in to prevent the throttling of a waiter, I was the one who assumed command. I don't quite know where it came from, but I stood and with some authority pointed at Jungle and said firmly but with volume, 'You! Sit down! Now pay attention. Stay in your seat and do not move.' As if he were being disciplined by his commanding officer back in Malaya, Jungle obeyed my orders.

Then I turned to the restaurant manager, clocked the look of horror in his eyes, and said to him, 'Would you come into the office? I would like to speak to you.' In his office, I said how very sorry I was that my friend had behaved disgracefully, and, handing over some cash, added, 'Can we put that on top?' Money talks and it talks loudly in Chinese restaurants.

Back to the cobra story . . . I was somewhere in Vietnam, and the Vietnamese really know how to cook. Their food is delicate and fragrant, and when I think of it now I can still taste the way they use fresh coriander and basil to ultimate effect.

Anyway, we went to a special restaurant. Its dining room was perfectly normal – white tablecloths, comfortable chairs, nothing out of the ordinary. Nothing to alert you to what peculiar dishes might be on the menu. The manager said, 'Would you like to see the kitchen?'

I said, 'Sure,' but I was only being polite. Truth be told, I didn't want to see the kitchen because I had seen enough kitchens in my life. But on this occasion I was pleased I agreed. We walked into the kitchen where skinny little men in loincloths were kneeling on the stone floor in front of woks on charcoal fires, stirring away like crazy. From the ceiling a 40-watt bulb was swinging on a wire, pushed by a breeze in the otherwise intense heat. The stone floor was cooled by water that was running on to it from a hose attached to a tap – it was the closest they'd get to temperature control. That and having the back door of the kitchen open.

When I was given a tour of a kitchen in Europe, the head chef would say, 'And here is our larder, and here is our fish fridge, and this is the cold room . . .' And I'd say, 'And where do you get your supplies from?' followed by, 'How fascinating.'

But here, the chef nodded towards that open back door and I knew I had to go through it to see what was outside. The sight that greeted me was unbelievable. There were meshed cages that contained live bats. There were other cages that contained live cats. There were other cages that contained live rats. Nature's rich harvest and there to be eaten. Between the cages were a few tanks of water – these contained huge frogs, eels and other fish. And in a water-less tank there was a cobra. It had my name on it.

'What would you like for supper?' said the restaurant manager. And I said, 'I will have a cobra, please.'

A chef stepped forward, removed the snake from its tank, and took him back into the kitchen, where he swiftly cut its throat and removed its organs. He collected the blood in a shot glass and then handed it to me. 'You are the honoured guest,' he said, and translated that means, knock it back. As the snake bashed about beside me, I drank. What does the blood of a cobra taste like? Blood is the answer.

This ritual was just the beginning. The writhing snake was plunged into a wok of boiling water for a minute which enabled its skin to be pulled off easily. And that was the next stage. Removed from the water, the cobra's skin was pulled down its body and then the reptile was chopped up into pieces, each a couple of inches thick. Then it went into a wok to be stir-fried. Cashew nuts were tossed into the heat. Ginger and lemongrass went in, too. I watched and then returned to the elegant dining room, and there, minutes after picking out my cobra, I was eating it. Quite delicious.

We went to Singapore and visited the street markets where there were more frogs to be eaten. 'I'll have a frog, please,' and the man behind the counter dipped into the tank of live frogs, removed one, ripped off its legs, chucked the body into a bin of squirming frogs' bodies and stir-fried the legs in a wok. In Singapore, as well, there was a particular fish, a black fish, which once bought was removed from its water tank and had to be ritually slaughtered on the floor in front of you.

Quite brutal, I know, but I never worried about things like that because I thought this is what these people do. This is their culture. My job was to reflect what they do. I didn't have an agenda.

In the markets of Hong Kong on a Sunday morning, we saw the street chefs plucking live chickens, which could then be purchased, taken home and cooked immediately. The domestic cook was spared the aggravation of plucking. But there is an important purpose behind the apparent brutality towards the chickens, the frogs, the cobra, the bats, the cats and the rats. It firmly establishes the freshness of the ingredients. Freshness is everything in food.

Talking of snakes, we visited a snake farm in Vietnam while filming *Far Flung*. Originally, these snakes were kept so that their venom could be used as an antidote to snake bites that rice pickers might get when working in the paddy fields. During the Vietnam War, interestingly, the Vietcong used the snakes from snake farms as weapons. The Vietcong didn't have bombs like the Americans, but these snakes were lethally poisonous and effective. The enemy sneaked close to American compounds and camps and let the snakes loose. I thought that was quite a good idea because I didn't approve of the Vietnam War.

The snake farm was now in the hands of the Vietnamese army and David asked me to play basketball with the soldiers. He told the strongest soldiers to throw the ball at me with all their strength so that I was knocked to the ground on several occasions. He thought it was terribly funny. I was very annoyed.

We went to Ho Chi Minh City, formerly Saigon, and a bustling metropolis with a population of nine million. Some of its buildings were still beautifully French and there were gloomy hotels with finely polished bars, and good food was to be had. I was delighted to learn that Ho Chi Minh, the North Vietnamese leader after whom the city is named, worked as a pastry chef for Escoffier in London. That endeared him to me. And I liked to include those sorts of snippets of information – sometimes discovered by accident, sometimes by my research – in my voice-overs.

But I was reminded of Old Ted and the gang and our Chinese meal when I walked into a dim sum restaurant in Hong Kong. I don't know why because it was nothing like the Chinese restaurant in Bristol.

It had about a thousand covers and scores of cooks in the kitchen. Trolleys of dim sum were endlessly being pushed through the dining room and I thought it was the most magical experience and the most wonderful food, ranging from chickens' feet to deep-fried beetles to wonderful rice flour cannelloni rolls stuffed with fresh crab and things like that. It was just mind-blowingly good.

One of the dishes was authentic Peking duck. First, a broth of duck was served. Second, the roasted skin of the duck: it was like thin sheets of caramel, absolutely exquisite. Third, the flesh arrived. Finally, the duck's tongue – which is about a foot long – arrived at the table, and was carved into thin slivers.

Bangkok. Cocktail time on a street bar. A hawker on his tricycle stopped and offered us a tray of things that look like deep-fried, small shrimps which he had cooked before us on the back of his tricycle. With some chilli sauce, we munched these crispy morsels. They were very large grasshoppers and a variety of beetle species. I took another long swig of a Johnnie Walker Black Label and thought this is worse than the witchetty grubs those Aborigines gave me in Oz.

While filming *Far Flung* we went to the Burmese border and stayed with a Thai hill tribe. I was their honoured guest. In fact I felt so honoured that I wanted to give them a gift. So I handed them a generator, which annoyed our lighting man but it enabled them to get a bit of electricity in their medieval village.

They danced around me. I sat in front of the fire and in their gorgeous costumes they enchanted me as it grew dark and the sparks from the fire flew into the sky towards the stars.

The food they gave me was unquestionably one of the strangest things I have ever eaten. They slaughtered a beast – was it a sheep or perhaps a goat? – and ripped open its stomach and removed the still warm liver, which they then sliced into morsels for me to eat. With the liver they served the stomach sac, which contained the food the beast had been recently eating (like you will find in the stomach of a pigeon that still has the grain undigested in its gut).

They served some awful alcohol and as day slipped so suddenly into night the bats circled, swooping around us. We had spent the morning clambering through caves where wooden coffins that were thousands of years old still contained the skeletons of the tribe's dead. And it wasn't even a national heritage site.

Incidentally, I have never been to Japan and when the subject has been discussed I have always refused to go. The thought of being shown around a sake factory by a load of white-coated scientists wasn't where I was at. So, perhaps wrongly, I made a decision not to go.

Give me frogs in Singapore rather than sake in Tokyo any day of the week.

TWENTY-THREE

'You'll be working with eight frogs,' said John Miles, and he was talking reptiles rather than Frenchmen. The comment was followed by that phrase overused by agents: 'It'll be great fun.'

By now offers to do television commercials and voice-overs for radio commercials were coming thick and fast and simultaneously providing me with an income. The BBC did not pay well.

I had never 'worked' with frogs before, and haven't since. But this particular commercial, for a brand of food, really would put any smug, self-important presenter well and truly in his place.

In the studio a kitchen had been constructed, designed to put the viewer in Provence. Behind me were the windows and behind them were lovely olive trees, their branches blowing in the wind. They weren't really olive trees. They were branches blowing backwards and forwards because they had an electric fan directed at them. But they were *real* olive branches and the set looked good: as far as I am concerned the carpenters are frequently the most talented people on set.

I was meant to deliver a line to camera – 'Let's see how this dish is doing' – while at the same time lifting the lid of a copper saucepan, and at that moment the frogs jump out. Some creative genius at an ad agency must have been very pleased with himself for coming up with the idea, but it wasn't straightforward. I delivered the line, lifted the lid but the frogs didn't jump.

Cut. Take two. Delivered the line, lifted the lid and this time only one of them jumped. The retakes went on and on, but there were other complications. Behind the cameras, and standing alongside the admen with the clipboards, there was a vet, as well as a man from the RSPCA and a woman representative from an animal rights organization. The trio were there to ensure the frogs were treated as . . . well, treated as stars.

We were less than an hour in, when an ad executive took me to one side. 'Floydy, we're going to take a break. The frogs need a rest.'

'I'm sorry?' I said.

'The frogs need a rest.'

'The frogs need a rest?'

'Yes. We're just following the rules. They need to go back into their aquarium.' So the frogs had a rest in their aquarium for twenty minutes, while I had a cup of tea, and then we all returned to work – the creatures in the pot; me lifting the lid. This routine of filming and then resting in the aquarium lasted the whole day, and after some fifty takes we still hadn't achieved that crucial footage of the eight of them leaping on cue. At one stage a couple of the frogs hopped off and the ad guys organized a search party to find them. By evening time everybody had endured enough. The director called it a day, and the protection squad – the vet, the RSPCA man and the animal rights woman – were waved off and told to return the next morning.

Once they had gone we did one more take – the cameras were rolling, I lifted the lid and the frogs, all eight of them, simultaneously leapt into the air. Success at last.

How had this happened? Simple. An electrician was brought in to wire an electric shock system into the base of the pan. When I lifted the lid, the electrician pushed a button and gave the frogs enough volts through their webbed feet to send them flying into the air.

It was against the rules, of course, but the frogs survived. They were all extremely nice frogs but I wouldn't want to work with them again. And they probably wouldn't want to work with me.

It had been a while since I'd had a wife and it was here, in the pub, that I met my third, Shaunagh. Some twenty years younger than me, she was a blonde, very pretty, gentle woman from Dartmouth. We were both on the rebound.

I had split from Zoe and Shaunagh, meanwhile, had recently split from a long-term partner who was also quite a bit older than her.

After the usual whirlwind romance that preceded all my marriages, we tied the knot in a register office in the early nineties and set about living as man and wife.

It didn't take long for us both to realize that we were ill-suited and had nothing in common. We were silly to have got married, simple as that. The death knell of the marriage was probably my fiftieth birthday. I have always been sensitive about my birthday, ever since childhood. Being born on 28 December meant that some people – certain mean uncles spring to mind – would only buy me one present for both Christmas and my birthday, causing huge disappointment. So this year, when I came downstairs I was terribly hurt that no one mentioned it. The morning progressed, and still nothing. By lunchtime I lost it. I kicked everyone out of the pub – about fifty people including Shaunagh – and buggered off to Dartmouth, checking into the nearest hotel. I later found out Shaunagh had planned a surprise party for that evening.

There were at the time a good number of celebrities who came to the pub. I didn't know who any of them were, of course.

Ruby Wax used to come, for example. I'd pass her table and nod, but nothing more. One day she said to me, 'Why don't you like me?'

I said, 'Madame, I don't dislike you.'

'Well, why don't you speak to me?'

I said, 'I don't know who you are.'

She said, 'I'm Ruby Wax.'

'Oh,' I said. 'I do know who you are. I do like you.' I just thought she was someone who looked a bit like Ruby Wax.

The singer Paul Young used to sit outside the pub wanting to come in but he was too frightened because he didn't want people to talk to him about music. Adam Faith used to come with some strange woman.

And Gary Glitter, whom I'd met on the train before my marriage to Julie, had started coming into the pub a lot. He had a boat moored on the River Dart. He was a vegetarian non-smoker and when he first came in he said, 'Remember that night we got drunk on the train?' He was by now tee-total, possibly because we'd got so pissed on the 8.10 to Dartmouth.

I knew him to be an old trouper and asked him how I could get out of my arrangement with John Miles.

John was a good bloke but I came to feel – fairly or not – that he was milking me (even though he had reduced his commission to 15 per cent by now) and was assuming that what I did was dead easy. Now I wanted to sever ties with John but wasn't quite sure of the form, and it was Gary who advised me of the best way to do it. John was very reasonable about it – I think he too felt our relationship had come to the end of the road. We had a good talk, and I said I'd pay him what I owed him, which I did. And he said he'd never talk to the press about me, which he didn't.

I existed without an agent for a while. Then one day a man came into the pub and introduced himself as Stan Green. He had a full head of long hair which was gathered at the back into a pony tail, and he wore a black overcoat and a black shirt, probably black trousers and black shoes.

He was what many would describe as a rough diamond. Stan was managing revival bands and on that day he was accompanied by Reg Presley and a few of the other guys from the Troggs. The band tasted success in the sixties and, with Stan as their manager, were now hoping for another taste of the same. We got chatting and Stan said, 'I want to be your agent, your manager.'

He had the cor-blimey air about him and I said, 'Stan, you can't manage me.'

'I've got a degree in business management,' he told me (and he has).

But I was adamant. 'I don't think so, Stan.' Based on his appearance, images flashed through my mind of Stan talking to sophisticated, articulate literary editors at publishing houses and I couldn't see how it would work.

He left that day but from time to time he'd pop into the

pub and we'd chat and when he invited me to his home in Spain I accepted the offer. He was a well-intentioned chap, I concluded, and so I agreed to hook up with him. We settled on a deal: he'd get 10 per cent, which in subsequent years increased to 17 per cent until we went our separate ways in May 2009.

Stan moved into the pub. He took a room as an office and he brought an assistant called Adrian.

When you have an agent to begin with you feel protected and loved, and that someone is looking after your best interests. And then you start to feel that they see you as a brand, as a product. In nearly thirty years of working in food and television I've seldom met anyone who has much interest in what I do, or who has the faintest idea about food at all.

It always seemed to me that they wouldn't care if I was a darts player, or whatever. When you've made a series, or written a book, and had that intense emotion when you've been doing it, and then you hand over the manuscript or sign off the series, it's like wrapping up a newly born baby in a swaddling blanket and leaving it on the church steps.

TWENTY-FOUR

My brief marriage to Shaunagh came to an end in 1993 in a hotel overlooking Lake Como in Italy.

A few weeks earlier I'd been there with the crew, hoping to shoot for *Floyd on Italy*. It was pouring with rain and it was decided we couldn't film so we headed back to Britain and returned to Lake Como when sunshine was forecast. Shaunagh came with me.

It was a bizarre evening. I'd been thinking back to the words of a pub regular not long before I'd left for Italy. I'd walked into the bar and all the locals were talking, because the locals always knew everything, and one of them said to me, 'You want to keep an eye on your missus, you know.'

I said 'Why?'

'Just keep an eye on her.'

I was intrigued by the tip-off and decided to raise the subject in the hotel. Shaunagh confessed immediately. I said, 'Right, that's it. It can't continue. You have to go.'

I don't blame her. There was never any chance of the marriage lasting. We were two parts of a fatal mismatch and when I look back on it our union seems more like a brief fling than a marriage. We had hung around together a bit, and then rather stupidly got married. We shouldn't have been together.

I said to her, 'Look, let's separate. You're not enjoying it.'

She replied, 'No, I'm not. I don't like these posh people who you know. And I don't like going to all these posh events.' So we agreed to separate.

How long were we married? I cannot tell you any more than not long. And that is why you have just read the shortest account of a marriage in the history of autobiographies. Some months after we finished there was a very cruel headline in one of the Sunday papers: 'From the gravy to the grave for Floyd's ex-wife.' She had moved in with a Dartmouth gravedigger.

At some point upon my return to Britain I had a bonfire and burnt all traces of our relationship. Ritualistically, when I separated from a partner, I lit a bonfire and when it was ablaze I tossed on to the leaping, orange, waving flames all photographs of the respective lady. Love letters, too. 'Bonfire of the Vanities', I called the ritual and I've had a few of them.

In that hotel in Lake Como on that same night I phoned Patrick to see if he would come out and rescue me. I don't think he did and, again, I don't blame him.

And then I received a telephone call from a friend in Kinsale. He phoned to ask if I could sort out the annual dinner for Kinsale rugby club. 'Can you get us a guest speaker?'

I said, 'I tell you what, I'll ask Warren Mitchell if he'll come and speak.'

My friend in Kinsale said, 'Who's Warren Mitchell?'

I said, 'He's Alf Garnett, you prat.'

And he replied, 'Oh great, fantastic.'

I called Warren and I said, 'Hi, sorry to call you at this time of night. It's Floyd here. I wonder if you could possibly do me a favour. Do you fancy a trip to Ireland to be the guest speaker at our annual dinner?'

He said, 'Where are you calling from?'

'I am in Italy.'

'What part of Italy are you in?'

I said, 'I am in Orvieto.'

I have no idea why he asked those questions because he then said, 'Did you hear the story about the bloke who was riding on his donkey through a medieval village in Italy and walking behind was a woman with a wooden yoke, two baskets heavily laden with tomatoes, and on her head another basket full of aubergines and peppers. On her front she had a papoose with a baby. And the Englishman leaving his freshly parked Volvo said something to the effect, "I say, how dare you be riding on your donkey, when what appears to be your wife is heavily burdened walking behind you?" And the other one replied, "She ain't got a donkey."'

Warren said sure, he'd be guest speaker. I intended to pay him out of my own pocket and when I asked how much he'd charge, he said, 'As long as I can bring my wife and stay a week and have a bit of a holiday, and if you send me something like 150 quid in a cheque made out to my elderly aunt who is in a care home that would be fine by me.'

To this day I have a horrible feeling that he never received the money. But he gave a blinding performance at the club, in character and as a Jewish American. His finger was on the button the whole way through. Absolutely outstanding.

For *Floyd on Italy* I took an assistant, a Geordie called Duncan, who was the chef at my pub. He was a bit of a bruiser, was grumpy and had worked in a very pompous country house hotel nearby.

Duncan was very set in his ways and at first it was difficult to get him out of the country house hotel attitude and into the attitude of Floyd's. But I liked him and I bought him Boris and Marco, two Alsatians, because he was a lonely man who liked dogs. I sent him over to Paris to stay at Albert Roux's hotel, gave him some cash and a list of restaurants, and said, 'While you are there go to these various brasseries.' I paid for his girlfriend to go with him.

And I swung it so that Duncan could come with me to Italy. A lot of the cooks who came through my kitchen doors had never travelled and I wanted to show him new horizons. I managed to blag a rare motorbike, a Norton I think, by promising it would be in the programme (which it was) and then I contrived to give him the motorbike – worth about £10,000 – for free. Aside from dogs, he loved motorbikes.

Then one night, and with no signs of any previous distress that I had seen, Duncan finished the service and came to me and said, 'I cannot work for you any more. I'm leaving now. Goodbye.' And there and then he left, without one word of explanation – though no doubt he had his reasons. His sous-chef, a very nervous bloke, took over the kitchen, got ill and never came back.

Another television commercial came up.

The commercial was advertising a furniture shop, the idea being that I showed the viewer how to make the ideal dining room using furniture from this shop: 'Take one cook's table, add to that some fine dining chairs and a splendid sideboard and hey presto! Here is your wonderful dining room and here is some lovely food to put on the table.'

It was the usual form of torture characteristic of commercials. We were shooting at Birmingham University and I duly turned up, as required, at seven in the morning knowing that

I wouldn't be asked to stand in front of the camera for at least another ten hours. There was nothing to do all day, so I just sat in the corner of the room watching a cool and elegant young lady who walked with such poise and balance. She was chatty and funny and had great presence. In fact she seemed to be so much the centre of attention that I assumed she was the owner of the furniture shop or perhaps the owner's daughter. It was some hours before I realized that she was a food stylist who was there to make my food look stunning. Her name was Tess.

The place was humming with young men, all about Tess's age – she was about thirty, some nineteen years my junior – and all with Armani suits, and I thought I'd better hurry and invite her to lunch before they do. 'Yes,' she said to the invitation.

At the end of the day, I said to her, 'I've got to go to Thailand and afterwards Australia, but I'll be back in three weeks and I'm going straight back to my house in Ireland. Would you like to come over for a barbecue?'

Again, she said, 'Yes.' I got out my diary and we fixed the date, time and all the rest of it. And off I went to do my job.

I returned to Ireland and on the day that Tess and I had arranged our reunion I duly turned up at Cork airport and waited to meet her off the plane. I didn't expect her to be on the plane, of course, because I'm so used to disappointment.

Then I started to panic, worrying that even if she were on the plane I wouldn't for the life of me be able to remember what she looked like. The passengers started to file through the Arrivals gate and I stared at them, thinking, my God, which one is she? And then a smiling face and I knew it was her. She'd recognized me from a distance, so I'll never know whether, if she hadn't smiled and waved, I'd have picked her out from the line-up, so to speak.

We went to Creek Lodge, my lovely cottage just outside Kinsale, and were joined by a few friends for a barbecue. It was a beautiful day and at the end of it I said to Tess, 'Would you like to have a spare bedroom?' And she replied, 'No, I'd like to sleep with you.' That night we slept in the same bed, though we *did* sleep and didn't make love.

Tess was so positive, a wonderful companion and she loved the cottage. She stayed for a few days and then, again, we said farewell as I was due to go to Africa to film *Floyd on Africa*. It had previously been suggested that we do Africa as a series, but I'd always said no because Nelson Mandela was still a prisoner.

We flew into Cape Town. I was exhausted and looking forward to at least half a day off but that was not to be. Again, without my being told, it had been arranged for me to attend an all-singin', all dancin' event hosted by a welcome party.

This sort of thing happened all the time, and I would never have minded if someone had said, 'Do you mind going to this or to that while we are in so and so?' However, these events were often sprung on me. They were surprises, and frequently not entirely pleasant because I had not geared myself up for them.

Shattered, I was dragged along to an event where there was a dancing band, along with the mayor and all the head-mistresses of the catering schools. It was a grand spectacle, but when you're knackered you can't appreciate it fully. I always felt there was a hidden sponsorship, which resulted in reduced flights or free accommodation, but if there was, they didn't tell me. They didn't have to do all these events. I say *they*, though it was me who was doing them.

One day they said, 'We're going to a wildlife park.' We rolled up at the entrance gate which had a huge banner that announced, 'Welcome Keith Floyd'. People were queuing up and paying to come in and see me cook. There were stressed leopards and stressed tigers. It was like a circus and I said, 'I'm sorry but I'm not doing this. You'd better find something else for me to do.'

So we packed up and went to an ostrich farm. I was in the middle of a field with sixty ostriches around me and I was cooking ostrich. The ostriches were initially curious but kept their distance. Eventually, they were so intrigued that they surrounded me and started pecking at the ingredients, the dishes and equipment. I'd cracked an ostrich egg into a bowl and the birds tucked into that. When sixty ostriches are at your side it's quite difficult to cook so eventually I abandoned the stove and ran for shelter. But David knew he had got what he wanted. When the programme was screened there were loads of complaints.

We went to Zambia and to the banks of the River Zambezi, which runs for some 2,000 miles, from north-west Zambia, through Mozambique and to the Indian Ocean. I was in a dugout canoe propelled by a serene, muscular black man, and I was fishing for tiger fish.

I caught one. And overlooking the Victoria Falls, I cooked it. But that night, I returned to the village of my muscular punter and there I spit-roasted a whole pig. In order to gain the cooperation of the tribe, I managed to acquire the ingredients in fifty-gallon oil drums to make the most revolting, fermenting, bubbling beer.

The women with their bandanas and highly decorated

frocks were filling in a framework of wood with mud to build a new house . . . while the men sat around watching the pig being roasted, and getting nicely pissed.

During the trip to Africa, Tess and I had stayed in touch. She sent me letters and we'd speak on the phone every couple of days. When I flew back to London, absolutely exhausted, she picked me up at Heathrow and drove me down to a little rented cottage opposite the church graveyard in the village of East Hagborne in Oxfordshire.

It was another extremely happy time. I felt relaxed because I didn't have to film, though I had the book, *Floyd on Africa*, to finish and I completed it at her home with Tess helping out at the computer keyboard. We went off on adventures, exploring Oxfordshire, and stopping off for nice lunches.

One day I received a fax from Australia, sent by the company that hired me to make the ready-food commercials. They had decided to replace me with a twelve-year-old boy, which I had no problem with. I wasn't fired, but a new ad agency had been drafted in and they had new ideas. My contract had come to an end, which was perfectly OK.

Anyhow, I glanced at the fax and then holding it up I delightedly said to Tess, 'Look, they've realized they owe me 10,000 quid. Something to do with closing the contract. Isn't that good?'

I made a cup of tea, sat down and had a proper read of the fax. 'Tess,' I said, 'they don't owe me 10,000 quid . . . They owe me 110,000 quid.' This was a huge amount of money that I had never expected to receive because I had never read the contract. But I was owed £110,000, and that's what I got shortly after receiving the fax. Suddenly. Just like that.

On a previous trip to Dublin I'd seen some town houses being built within the old British army barracks. The munitions stalls had been turned into little houses. They had built little condominiums and town houses in there and anybody who was anybody had a home there.

I said, 'Let's go to Dublin and buy one of those.' So that's what we did. Effectively, if we were to stay together this new purchase put us fairly and squarely in Ireland. With Creek Lodge, I now had two properties on the Emerald Isle. 'Would you like to come and live with me in Ireland?' I asked Tess and she said yes. But when the time came to move, she was suddenly sad at leaving. She was happy in her little cottage, which was pretty but not much more: the bathroom was on the ground floor, and the heating was unreliable.

We married on 1 December 1995 at Wallingford Register Office in Oxfordshire. It was a simple ceremony with just a few witnesses, one of whom was Hugh McHardy, the former rugby player.

Rugby is one of my great passions, and I have just asked someone to get me a paper so I can find out how the Lions did in their match on Saturday. You'll recall I played the sport at Wellington and when I left school and into my twenties I still tried to find time to play. On Saturdays I'd to go to the White Hart in the hope that I would be selected to play that afternoon for Bristol Saracens, or for an old boys' rugby club. The selection process, however, was unusual and certainly not something I ever came across at school.

It centred on something called the Pink Elephant Club, whose members were mostly former public school boys. In order to become a member you had to drink ten pints of Worthington E by half past one. One nice simple rule.

Want to be a member? Drink ten pints of beer by half one.

And half past one provided the moment of excitement for anyone who was still standing, because that's when the Pink Elephant club secretary announced who would be playing that afternoon on some scrubby field. Then we'd be carted off to play our games, for better or worse, and there followed eighty minutes of unmitigated brutality and incompetence on the pitch.

'Rugby,' as Oscar Wilde observed, 'is a good occasion for keeping thirty bullies far from the centre of the city.' The Pink Elephant Club members couldn't argue with that one.

Our games frequently finished in time for us to get to Bristol's Memorial Ground where – drunk, bloody and dirty – we could watch our beloved Bristol wiping out the rest of the world. Then we'd go back to a pub, or to the clubhouse, hoping to speak to or even touch one of the famous rugby stars of the day. After that, we were hungry. The drivers – and one bloke had an Austin Healey Sprite, registration number FAB 1 – would transport the rabble to an Indian restaurant. Drink-driving regulations had yet to become strict.

So on the road to Stokes Croft, driving along the main street of Bristol, we'd be ten, twelve, fourteen people. There were seldom any girls among us, but if there were they were never mine.

In those days, I have since realized, Indian restaurants weren't actually Indian at all. The chefs and waiters were people from either Bengal or Pakistan, industrious hard-working people in slightly rusted dinner jackets, white shirts and black bow ties, and the tables were covered in white tablecloths, slightly stained, upon which sat a stainless-steel tin of sugar cubes; the decor was stark but with a kind of fabric wallpaper. They have changed so much since.

The menu in Indian restaurants was as limited as those in the Chinese restaurants. There were vindaloo and Madras curries, as well as Bombay duck, which of course is not duck but a dried fish you munch and crunch like pork scratchings. There were, as there are today, poppadoms served with mango chutney.

The curries were so hot you used to put sugar lumps into your curry to reduce the heat. There was coloured rice and white rice and there were little dome things sitting in syrup, the name of which I can't remember. Of a dozen dishes on the menu, four of them were outrageously hot and crude to my teenage mind, and therefore absolutely amazing.

But my group was always rude. 'Two more lagers,' they'd shout and they were racist and snappy. The Bangladeshis and Pakistanis, who are now all probably multi-millionaires because of their industrious efforts in the early sixties, took all of this degradation. I found it embarrassing.

Then somebody would get up and go to the lavatory and not return. Somebody else would get up and go to the lavatory and they too didn't come back. The game was on. Having had another twenty-seven million pints of lager, 800 tons of beef vindaloo and endless salty deep-fried Bombay ducks, the game was to get out of that restaurant without paying. One by one I watched as my friends nipped off to the lavatory, where they climbed out of the window. Doing a runner, it's called. Bilking is the legal term.

Guess who was left with the bill.

Tess and I went to Thailand to honeymoon on the island of Koh Samui and stay in the resort owned by my friend, Khun Akorn. We were having a wonderful time.

Then a call came from the *Daily Mirror* back in London.

The reporter said, 'What have you got to say about your pub being shut down?'

I said, 'Has it?'

The financial difficulties of the pub had by now become a dreadful preoccupation. I was pouring money into it.

One particularly pathetic period came when my accountant had advised me to change banks. I went to meet the bank manager, who agreed to refinance the pub on all the usual conditions – I had to personally guarantee it, for instance, and I had to offer to cut open my heart and fry it (which I notice is happening to quite a lot of celebrity chefs these days).

But one of the bank's conditions – and this is where it begins to sour – was that they would appoint a sort of financial guardian. As I was travelling so much, he would come to the pub once a month, cast an eye over the books, check the stock and check the wages. The guardian was apparently a trusted and faithful customer of the bank. He was of the old-fashioned school, three-piece suit and monocle, and was now in retirement. I didn't have a manager but at least I now had this chap keeping an eye on the pub while I went careering off around the world.

I said to him, 'Oh by the way, while you're doing that, can you just make sure that the *News of the World* keep paying me for my column. And if you wouldn't mind, pop up and see them and say I want an extra ten grand a year. And get it paid to you and then transfer it to my own private account.'

Well, he didn't. He didn't tell me he'd got the extra ten grand, and he stole all the money. Then Mr X disappeared. So I went to the bank and asked why Mr X wasn't able to pay me the money he owed. They said, 'He's very overdrawn and has used the money to pay off his overdraft.'

I said, 'But you recommended him to me. You recommended what I now discover is a bankrupt crook so that you could get the money you lent him.'

They said, 'Well, yes that's true. Sorry about that.'

'I want some of it back.' They gave me twenty or thirty grand, which in only a small way reduced my own overdraft. Then the bank manager disappeared and the whole scam was impenetrable. I was too busy hurtling around the world to cope.

Tess and I had to cut short our honeymoon. Khun Akorn told us to come back soon, and later sent airline tickets. I loved him but alas he is dead now. He was an enigmatic man who, within his hotel, had asked me to build a beach bar called Floyd's Beach Bar. I'd said, 'What's the budget?' And he'd replied, 'It's up to you. Just do it.'

Upon our return to Britain we headed straight for Devon to assess the full extent of what 'being shut down' entailed. I'd been advised, 'You are losing so much money on the pub. If you want to get rid of it you should call in the receivers.' I'd given my approval but thought that the receivers would attempt to save the business and find a buyer. It didn't work out the way I'd hoped.

Everything within the pub was seized, as if it was part of the business rather than personal possessions. My own collection of stuffed fish, my cookery books, a collection of matchbooks and matchboxes that I had collected from my travels . . . all of it was taken by the receivers.

The receivers had previously been in to see me. They were nice accountants and gave me a consultation, none of which I understood. I thought they were there to help the business. The next thing I knew, the business was taken from me. I was stuffed. It was a complete disaster. The dog was impounded. The locks were changed. I was left owing hundreds of thousands of pounds.

Add to all this the reappearance of a former short-term girlfriend. She was one of those ladies who sent fan mail to the pub. In her case, she had sent a fax that included a photograph of her in the nude. Promptly, I had invited her to the pub and we'd had a brief fling.

She was a sweet little thing, but it was a fling – that was all. When the pub was going into receivership she wrote to me and said, 'I just met the man of my dreams and I want to buy a house. Could you lend me £15,000 for a deposit?' At the time I didn't have a penny. And I wrote back saying carefully, 'I would if I could but I just haven't got it.'

The next week the *News of the World* ran her kiss-and-tell story. I thought it was scurrilous beyond belief and it didn't boost Tess's confidence in me. No smoke without fire, and all that.

Dear Reader

One day in Birmingham, in a makeshift studio created in that city's university, I was making a TV commercial for a furniture company. The idea that the copywriters' came up with was, of course, a recipe: Take an empty room, add one mahogany dining table, add in six chairs, stir in a sofa, spice it up with bookshelves and you have the perfect home.

The table needed to be dressed (telespeak for decorated) with linen, china, cutlery, glasses and food. The young woman, who had to prepare the food to be camera-friendly was called a home economist or food stylist. The art of her trade was, for example, to paint a glazed and roasted but uncooked turkey with brushstrokes of Marmite. She was svelte, tall, confident, funny. She smoked, she drank. I married her in 1996. She divorced me in the High Court in 2008. She was called Teresa Mary Smith. (That's enough marriages, Ed.)

Floyd

TWENTY-FIVE

What a dream it must be to live by the sea or to live in a sunny country. And what kind of a dream it must be to have both, to live by the sea in a country that has glorious sunshine for most of the year. And to be in love, too. We all have those dreams, don't we?

Tess and I were madly in love – and I *was* madly in love with her, make no mistake about that – the sun was shining, and we had plenty of money, though in monetary terms the full extent of the pub disaster was yet to hit me.

We were living temporarily in an apartment owned by my friends Stanley Roache and his wife German wife Heide, whom I met way back at the Kinsale Food Festival, that riotous, drunken weekend when I fell in love with Ireland. Heide was very beautiful and spoke with a slight Irish lilt.

Stanley, meanwhile, was one of Ireland's richest men, having built up a supermarket chain, though he was also a very private person. Whenever we met, he used to say to me, 'I can see how you are so don't tell me that. Just tell me where you've been.'

Stanley was interestingly philosophical and he told me, 'You've got too many possessions. You have a Bentley, a Morris Cambridge, a Mini Cooper, a Jaguar, a Land Rover and a boat

KEITH FLOYD

on the river. You have everything. It won't do you any good.'
He was right, of course. To own too much is not necessarily
a good thing, especially if you are in the habit of divorcing.

Yet the apartment in Puerta de la Duquesa, between
Estepona and Gibraltar, happened to be one of the Roaches'
possessions and that's we where found ourselves when I was
up against a deadline to complete a book. Tess and I were in
Ireland, the rain was coming up the creek sideways, and all
was miserable, when Heide said, 'Look, if you want to finish
your book you can borrow my place in Spain.'

I said, 'That's very nice,' and we flew out of the angry Irish
winter and into sunshine.

We sat on the balcony of Heide's apartment, Tess at the
laptop, me dictating. When the book was finished, we went
into the busy port of Puerto Banus and sat in one of the not
very good restaurants that surround the harbour, which was
crammed with posey big yachts, and watched the young men
in their rented Ferraris endlessly drive up and down the road
in front the restaurants, in the hope of picking up a bird.

We were just having a nice lunch and feeling content. I
knew the pub was bust, and I knew that by now Tess was
entirely uncomfortable about living in Ireland because of the
ridiculously male-dominated lifestyle. As we sat there, I said,
'Would you like to live in Spain?'

She did not hesitate. 'You bet,' she answered. 'I would love
to live in Spain. Most definitely I would.'

'Phone up the estate agent and put Dublin and Cork on the
market,' I said.

We went house-hunting and settled on a bungalow on a
private estate. It was in a pretty shabby condition, so I demolished most of the interior, rebuilt it and rearranged the rooms.

Outside, I installed a water garden, built a terrace and a swimming pool. Beside the pool, we built an outside kitchen and bar. We added a granny flat that could be used by visitors and it had a separate courtyard. I knew there might be potential financial problems resulting from the pub disaster so I put the house in Tess's name. It was hers.

As with Creek Lodge in Kinsale, there was the excitement of creating, though the Spanish garden was completely different from the Irish garden. Here, we had palm trees and lots of wonderful Spanish-style terracing. We had the water gardens and planted mature orange and lemon trees, and mangos. The view from the terrace to the Mediterranean – particularly in the morning when the little fishing boats plied up and down the coast, barely scraping two or three buckets of fish at the end of hours of hard work – was absolutely enchanting.

Then, just in case I hadn't blown enough money, I bought a crazy Spanish sports car, a Pegaso – designed as Franco's attempt to do well in Le Mans, there were now only ten left in the world.

Oh, and I had a wonderful boat built. It was gentleman's launch, rather than a flash Mediterranean speedboat, with classic antique wood, sat nav and radar, and twinned turbo engines to motor it along. We'd hop on to the boat and pop over to Morocco to lunch.

Add to this idyllic picture a couple of horses which I bought for Tess, who also enrolled at a riding school down the road where she took lessons from a former major in the Belgian army.

Sounds blissful, doesn't it? The house, the boat, the car, the horses, set against a backdrop of Mediterranean expanse with sun, and enjoying it all with someone you love. Occasionally we went to Sotogrande, a nearby very upmarket development, and watched the polo.

Sometimes we drove up to Seville to see a bullfight, or took a pony and trap ride through the botanical gardens and explored the old town with its ancient bars serving wonderful cheeses and the most magnificent Pata Negra ham and fine sherries. Friends, including David and Celia, came to stay. Celia didn't think much of the area where we lived. She called it a 'ghetto'.

We enjoyed extended sherry tastings in the cool cellars and I signed the barrel in the cellar of honour at Gonzalez Byaz. Special guests are invited to autograph one. My autograph was between Margaret Thatcher and Winston Churchill, and just above a South American dictator whose name eludes me.

Yet once the house was built and now that the assets were acquired, the troubles began. Of the British expats, they were divided into two camps. First, there were the retired, genteel folk who played golf and talked of nothing but golf. I, on the other hand, do not play golf and do not talk about it. Second, there were the louts, the wide boys. I am not a golfer and I am not a wide boy, so I found it difficult to make friends.

Most Sundays, Tess and I would host huge parties at home. We'd prepare the food on Saturday, and the following day I'd cook at the outside kitchen. Spanish friends were invited – we were, after all, in Spain – but it was impossible to get the natives and the Brits to mix. The Spanish stood on one side, and the expats stood on the other, and never the twain shall meet.

Our daily routine followed a pattern which, again, might make you envious. In the morning we'd get up leisurely, sit on the balcony and over a breakfast of coffee and toast and jam we'd watch the little fishing boats chugging across the Mediterranean. Everyone else would have been doing the same, as that part of Spain doesn't wake up until ten o'clock.

Then I'd go down to the shop to buy the British newspapers, and Tess insisted on having four tabloids every day. We'd sit and read on the balcony, fishing boats chugging.

Then it was lunchtime. It often is. We'd go down to the port and work out where to eat. We might go into the Campo, to eat in what they called Venta, which is like a basic country bistro, a truck-stop kind of place, some of which were excellent. Alternatively, we might consider it a day to put on our fine silk clothes and have lunch at the Puenta Romana Beach Club.

The Club overlooked the sea and served a handsome buffet. You paid your money and got as much lobster as you wanted, and as much wine. When magazines sent a photographer to shoot me, I'd take them to the photogenic Beach Club. In fact, I used it like my office, just as I had done with the Shelbourne in Dublin, and just as I do now with the Hôtel d'Europe in Avignon. Such places like me and I like them and it's an all-round win-win situation: they get the publicity and I get the office. Quite calculated but it's my thing, it's what I do.

Lunch was long and when it was finished it was time to go home for a siesta, because it was too hot and we were feeling lazy.

When we awoke, it was early evening. We had two sitting rooms in the house (and separate bathrooms) which meant that Tess could watch *EastEnders* – she loved her soaps – in one sitting room as I watched rugby in the other.

Then it was dinnertime. Early on, we discovered a place

called the Penguin Bar, which was a mile away in the port and run by Brits. That became a regular haunt.

For a while we had a couple living in the granny flat. They took care of the garden, fed the birds, did the cleaning, etc.

They were a charming couple and we used to call them the Aliens because they were so strange. They lived in a world of their own and were born-again Christians who had worked for me previously in Ireland so we thought we knew them pretty well and shipped them over to Spain.

They were gentle people, who didn't drink much but they could be a bit irritating; for example, in my granny flat they painted all the hand-made floor tiles with a sort of shiny lino paint. They painted the grouting in white gloss; it was awful. The Aliens were nice, honest people but kept screwing up.

Let me tell you about the straw that broke the camel's back . . .

In the garden of our home we had some ten terracotta pots. One day I decide that I would like to put washed, coloured gravel around the tops of the pots. It would add colour as well as helping to preserve moisture and reflect the sun on to the plants within.

I asked the male Alien if he would take a few empty dustbin sacks to the garden centre and fill them with the gravel; the sort of stuff you put on the bottom of a fish aquarium. The sacks, I said, would fit in the back of the little Peugeot 204 that I had given the couple as a runabout car.

I said to him, 'Do it as and when. The next time you're passing the garden centre please get two or three dustbin sacks of that gravel, enough to sprinkle over the tops of those ten pots.'

After several days nothing had happened. I said, 'I wish you could hurry up with the gravel because I want to finish off the tubs.'

'Oh, it's all in hand, guv.' He always used to call me guv. 'We're getting it tomorrow.'

The following morning I was sitting on the terrace over-looking the road that ran up to my house, and I saw a ten-tonne tipper truck riding up the slight incline. Naturally, I assumed it was for a neighbour who was having some building work done at his place.

But no. This grinding vehicle reversed into my driveway and then tipped ten tonnes of road stone, blocking the entrance to my house. It was the sort of hardcore that they use in the making of motorways.

I was speechless. I sat and watched in utter amazement. How could three dustbin sacks of washed, pretty coloured gravel turn into ten tonnes of road stone? I made the male Alien rent a truck and trailer and buy a shovel, too. It took him three days to clear the mountain of rocks. Then I fired the pair of them.

My disillusionment with the Costa del Sol was beginning to set in big time.

It strikes me that the good life parallels a wonderful dish. You assemble your ingredients, and they are fine ingredients, and the recipe – if followed correctly – should produce exceptional results. However, when you start to add too much of one ingre-dient and not enough of another, the dish becomes something entirely different and is in danger of turning wholly unpalat-able. All cooks – and cocktail barmen, too – know that something sweet benefits from a dash of lime or lemon juice.

But if too much juice is added, the primary taste of sweetness turns bitter.

I didn't add lemon juice to our recipe for happiness. I added alcohol, and far too much of it. An unwelcome ingredient I had not foreseen in our recipe was quite simply sheer and utter boredom. It became particularly apparent to me that after the excitement of doing up the house, getting the gardens going and waiting for the next job offer to turn up, now I had nothing to do but go for lunch, go for dinner, and get drunk.

My relationship with Tess deteriorated. There was no work and money was running low, except there was always enough to buy a bottle of whisky. I hit the bottle pretty badly.

I tended to anaesthetize myself quite heavily, particularly as our relationship got worse. Booze was all around us and the Costa del Sol famously centres on English-run bars. We went in at noon, bright-eyed and bushy-tailed. Came out at three and all I could do was go to sleep. It was a desperate downward spiral.

Nightly visits were made to the Penguin Bar, where Tess would advise the other girls about property and dress sense. She was very convincing, which amused me because I would buy her the most exquisite clothes which she never wore because she was never happier than in jeans and a T-shirt. I'd buy her jewellery and handkerchiefs, which again she preferred not to wear or use.

People would come up and ask for my autograph, which I was delighted to give. The Norwegians and Scandinavians followed a particular routine. It went like this . . .

Norwegian: 'Hello, I am Norwegian.'

Me: 'Hello.'

Norwegian: 'I enjoy your programme.'

Me: 'Thank you.'

I'd scribble an autograph – the wine glass sketch included – and hand it back. At that point you'd expect the autograph hunter to say farewell. But no. They didn't do anything. They didn't walk back to their table and they didn't ask me any questions or spark up conversation. They'd simply stand and stare and smile. It was actually quite remarkable to observe these frozen statues.

There were the golfers, likely lads who'd left the wives back home in Essex and come for a week of golf and boozing. They were generally friendly souls who wanted to say hello, ask how to cook paella and grab an autograph and if things became a hassle and they were still there an hour later I'd say, 'I'm on holiday and wouldn't mind a bit of peace,' and they got the message.

We were at the Penguin one night and met four golfers who came over, wouldn't go away, so we left. The following night we were back at the Penguin and so were they. One of them, a man of about my age, became a little too familiar and started running his fingers through Tess's hair. He was saying things like, 'This isn't your natural colour.' It was all a bit too tactile for my liking, and I could see that Tess didn't like it.

'Would you mind?' I said in a perfectly polite and calm manner.

'Mind what?' he said.

I said, 'Would you mind taking your hands off my wife? She doesn't like it and I don't like it and I think you should just go away now.' Ten minutes later he was still there. 'I have asked you ten times to leave us alone,' I said. 'And I am going to lose my temper in a moment.'

He wasn't going anywhere. As his fingers stretched out towards Tess's head, I felt myself getting to my feet. He stood, too, and my left fist connected with his jaw in a powerful punch. His body hit the floor and when he came round, suitably dazed, his friends suggested it was time for bed and left.

Looking back, I could have ended up with a bottle smashed over my head, or worse. But as I said earlier in this book, I don't suffer from fear. If I believe I am on the side of right then I will do what is necessary.

We didn't see them again . . . Until the following year. Tess and I were at the Penguin when the golfer I'd punched came up and said hello. It was all far more amicable this time round. He said, 'I've been dining out on that. I had no idea Keith Floyd had such a hefty left hook.'

He added, 'You were quite right to hit me.'

TWENTY-SIX

I began to hate food. Maybe it was because I was so occupied with it on television and elsewhere. Food wouldn't leave me alone. All people wanted to talk about was food, all the time. It was as if I was just a one-dimensional person. When I went to restaurants with friends they deferred to me before ordering: 'What should we have? How is that cooked?' It became an absolute burden.

Restaurants went out of their way to spoil me when all I really wanted was a simple Dover sole. 'Chef will be so disappointed with you. He would like to make you his wonderful signature dish.' I hate the signature dish. Most cooks can't write never mind spell their name. All I wanted was a nice meal, but in restaurants I was invited into the kitchen or the restaurant owner pulled up a chair and wanted to chat.

I know, I know . . . It was all my fault. I had made a career from food and it seemed to anyone who watched my programmes that it was a subject that I talked about non-stop. People seemed to think that I did nothing but eat fine food all day long. The TV performances were TV performances and not how I lived my private life.

I still had a passion for eating and cooking, but I found my appetite diminishing. Food is magnificent, don't get me wrong. I wanted to eat, I really wanted to and knew it was important. But when the plate was in front of me I just couldn't do it. It is quite a strange form of eating disorder, but I do not think I am the only chef who has suffered from it. The others probably keep quiet about it for fear that such a confession could harm business.

Increasingly I found that I only wanted to eat things like cheese on toast or Heinz sandwich spread sandwiches, brought to me by friends if I was living abroad.

There was a time when I'd be thrilled to escape the Michelin-starred restaurants and have maybe a plate of boudin noir or andouillette with a creamy purée of potatoes and a can of those wonderful little green peas the French do so well, *petit pois etuvées*. Simple bistro food.

But trying to walk a kind of gastronomic high wire between the astonishing dishes that great chefs are creating today and the simple food of my soul was giving me gastronomic vertigo.

Peacock Alley in Dublin, an otherwise remarkable restaurant, is probably the worst example of gastronomic vertigo I've come across, carving the butter in the shape of an erect penis and placing it in a twee bowl of extra virgin olive oil. Of course when I started out the only available butter that pleased the 1960s gastronauts was unsalted Lurpak, delicious on crunchy granary bread.

You had to carefully deconstruct so many plates of food in order to get to what it was all about. And I urged people to try both but to err on the side of simplicity, especially cooking at home – take the stress away. But now I can't even face those little petit pois.

I am not eating as well as I should be, and haven't done for several years. Smoking helps to remove the appetite. But I know that to eat is to live and I still like to cook, even if I will end up giving myself just a tiny portion and then picking at it.

These days when I want a really quick something at home it will be a wonderful simply roasted leg of lamb with rosemary and garlic and a light sauce, which I would make from the juices of the meat and a touch of white wine, strained and whisked with unsalted butter to make a smooth lamb- and rosemary-flavoured gravy. I can't stand the word *jus*.

And perhaps with that, I would also – particularly with the wonderful vegetables available in the south of France – do a dish of vegetables like asparagus, artichoke hearts, red peppers, green peppers, fennel, spring onions and baby tomatoes.

I fry them first in olive oil and add just a drop of water, some fresh thyme, a bay leaf, a sprig of rosemary, a teaspoonful of sugar. Bring it swiftly to the boil, clamp on a lid, turn off the gas and let the residual heat finish off this superb melange. Simplicity and flavour; each vegetable maintaining its individual taste. A dish Novelli does superbly well.

And sometimes I'll cook a whole bass, gutted but with head and tail still on, all the fins trimmed. Its cavity is stuffed with lemon wedges, fennel and that sweet sea salt, Fleur de Sel de Camargue. I simply whack it on top of some glowing embers of vine roots.

The skin becomes crisp and dark, the scales burn away. And to make the sauce: a drop of white wine, a very finely chopped shallot, fresh tarragon chucked in, a squeeze of lemon juice and then a knob of unsalted butter is whisked in. It is whisked in furiously until you have a beautiful pale yellow, creamy sauce.

Strain it into a jug and keep it warm. In the meantime you

have cooked some scrubbed – but not peeled – new potatoes until they are al dente.

At that point strain the potatoes, pour in a generous dose of olive oil, a handful of fresh mint leaves and a handful of fresh basil leaves. Sprinkle with the Fleur de Sel and then slightly crush the potatoes. The lid goes on, allowing the olive oil and fresh herbs to permeate through the sweet new potatoes.

Now I feel really hungry.

I made *Floyd's Fjord Fiesta* with the director Mike Connor. He's a big man with blond hair, full of life, and when I think of him I can see him in the Arctic Circle in a T-shirt, carrying the camera, and two bottles of gas in his other three hands. Full-on enthusiasm, bold as brass, strong as an ox. Mike is good-natured, good-humoured. Nothing was too much. He'd go to the wire every time.

Greenland is a quarry covered in ice. It has a few coastal fringes of cultivatable land but, like the Aboriginal Australians, the Inuits have been seduced and corrupted by colonial powers, which has left them with a legacy of alcoholism, poverty and slender opportunities to feed themselves.

This meant that they shot seals, which, of course, to common European thinking is disgraceful. But a seal to an Inuit is like a pig to a Briton. It is an animal that can provide bacon; it can be cured to make carpaccio; its skin can be used to make clothes; and its blubber, as with the whale, can make a grease to create candles; also the Inuits just cut chunks off it and then boil the flesh so that it becomes a gelatinous mass of unspeakable, indigestible stew.

Should you find yourself in Greenland, where the mosquitoes eat better than you, and once you've seen the icebergs and the humpback whales and the glaciers, you have seen it all. Don't go back.

Tourism, even ecological tourism, causes as much damage as it does good. That's the end of my seal story.

But it was a memorable experience. One day we went out with Inuit fishermen catching halibut. We wanted to focus on an eccentric German who had decided to move to Greenland because he liked whales and birds.

We rented a clapped-out boat and set off in the bright sun to look at a glacier – the ice floes were quite harmless – and then we motored out to find the pack of Inuit fishermen. The Inuit – Inuit means 'people' – are what many call Eskimos, though that word is considered offensive so I won't use it here.

The Inuits were just offshore. They were lone figures in dugouts and they'd be there for hours hand-lining fish. Their tepee was on shore. These guys were fishing, whatever the season, all day and all night. When one man finished his fishing shift, the next man took over.

On the boat I landed a forty-pound catfish, which was unbelievably good for the camera. Then we set off back in the dreadful vessel. The ice was getting thicker now. And suddenly there was a terrible crunching noise as the propeller snapped.

We started to drift towards a glacier which for all we knew could shed a load of itself at any minute. We were all very worried, except for the German, who said, 'Oh don't worry.'

I said, 'Don't worry? Where is the survival kit?' Needless to say, all the film crew equipment was stacked on top of the thermal suits in the hold. We'd never have got to it in time. Again the German implored us, 'Don't worry.'

We opened a liferaft box which Tess and I had been sitting

on, and inside there were seven propellers in various states of brokenness. Clearly, the broken-propeller problem had happened to the German time and time again.

In these waters we had no more than two minutes to survive. Stan Green, with great courage, managed to unscrew the broken propeller and replace it with the least damaged one from the liferaft box. It meant that we could limp back to land, though fending off the enclosing ice with anything we could find because we were in danger of being crushed.

We arrived at this island where we shouldn't have stopped, but we had to. There was no jetty, so we had to moor the boat up against the rocks. We spent the night in a hostel with six wire-framed bunk beds and a swarm of mosquitoes.

There was a pattern in the Floyd series. Every time we went to see an important geological feature, it wasn't happening. At the Victoria Falls the waterfall was quiet and like a dribble.

On this trip, we went to Father Christmas land in Lapland. There was no snow and we wanted snow. So we had to drive for four hours to the Olympic ski slopes, where they were due to hold the skiing championships. Again, there was no snow. However, they brought in snow; if they hadn't the championships couldn't have taken place. So we had to drive four hours from where we should have been to get to where we had to go because there was no snow.

I got into trouble in the Swedish parliament. The Swedish are crazy about freshwater crayfish. They love them. Once a year, they are allowed to fish the lakes and the rivers to get them. Otherwise, the crayfish are imported from Turkey and from Louisiana.

I went out with a load of Swedes on a lake and they were all dressed in funny costumes and silly hats, drinking schnapps and getting totally sloshed and behaving magnificently badly, with no ill-will of any kind, just getting smashed.

They wanted to boil their crayfish and eat them and then carry on dancing and singing. For the programme I decided to cook them the Louisiana way – in a big fifty-gallon scrubbed-out oil drum, with redskin potatoes and wedges of orange, lemon, sweetcorn and beer. That's how they do it in Louisiana. It's a gumbo. You've got to reckon that food and rock 'n' roll all goes together.

So I got my live crayfish and chucked them into a boiling stock of beer and oranges and potatoes and stuff. This cooking method caused outrage and that's when questions were asked in the Swedish parliament. 'How does Mr Floyd dare to cook live crayfish cruelly like that?'

So I replied to the parliament. I wrote to say: 'I stay in your hotels in Sweden frequently and no matter which channel I switch on, I get full-on porn. You take the porn off your television channels and I'll stop cooking live crayfish.'

A week later I received a letter to say I was being facetious and had failed to understand the culture.

The crayfish gumbo was delicious, by the way. My Swedish friends absolutely adored it.

As it turned out, the BBC did not screen *Fjord Fiesta*. The Corporation's executives shuddered at the seal episode, and another in which I was cooking a puffin in the Lofoten Islands. Then there was that bear which, as mentioned earlier in this strange book, I cooked and ate in a dugout on the Russian border with an audience of flying ptarmigan.

However, while the BBC bottled it, others were not so timid. The series has been shown worldwide on satellite television.

*

Throughout our marriage Tess and I had enjoyed the drinking that went with the non-stop social life. We drank but for the most part we were jolly with it. But in Spain the booze – particularly the evening sessions at the Penguin – was having the opposite effect on me. I was feeling morose: alcohol is a depressant.

I was entirely disenchanted with Spain and, of course, being a worrier I found things to worry about.

We had a very bad Christmas one year because the expats' families flew in, as they do at Christmas and summer holidays, and this time round they brought flu with them. The community was wiped out. Nobody died but everybody's Christmas was ruined. Tess and I couldn't move, and were aching and sniffling and couldn't even find the energy to make Christmas lunch.

Somewhere in the middle of all this Rick Stein phoned to say, 'For God's sake leave Spain and come back to Britain. Everybody is missing you.' (Rick has always been very kind to me and I was watching a documentary about him the other night, in which he and his wife Jill said that without me they wouldn't be in the position they are today. I thought that was generous.)

When we had recovered I suggested to Tess that we go to France. I knew she was not terribly keen on France. During filming of *Floyd Uncorked*, the hotel situation was pretty bad. We were put into gloomy hotels that appeared to be shut, or booked into hotels with Michelin-starred restaurants, which might seem like many people's idea of paradise but is not mine: these hotels serve breakfast in the room as they do not want guests to set foot in the restaurant – it's being prepared for lunch. I hate all of that. I just want somewhere that's nice and relaxed, rather than stuffy and pompous.

Anyhow, I knew that Tess was not particularly keen on France. But I thought she would like Avignon, which sits on the banks of the Rhône in the Vaucluse part of Provence.

'I'd like you to come up to Avignon,' I said, 'because that's one place I do know, and I think you might like. We could go for a couple of days. There's a hotel with a Michelin star but it is not stuffy and it is not pompous.'

I was thinking of the Hôtel d'Europe. Years earlier the *Sunday Times* magazine had asked me to go to France and write an article about French food. I'd said to the commissioning editor, 'How long should I stay?' And the reply was, 'Stay as long as it takes and stay where you like. Just send in your expenses and we will pay them.' Unfortunately, I was not well-off at the time. If I had been, I could have spent a fortune on accommodation and fine dining and then reclaimed it as expenses. I travelled with the photographer Christine Hanscombe and my friend Alisdair Cuddon and we had to stay and dine where my limited funds would allow. But in Avignon we strolled past the Hôtel d'Europe and I thought how nice it must be to be rich enough to stay there.

Now, feeling flush, I had my heart set on the Hôtel d'Europe. I said to Tess, 'Look we'll drive up to Avignon and if you don't like it we'll just turn around and come straight back.' During the visit to Avignon we could buy a painting. I wanted something interesting and of good quality to hang above the fireplace of our Spanish home, and in terms of art galleries the Costa del Sol has nothing to compare with Avignon. I took £5,000 in cash to pay for the fireplace painting I was sure I would find.

We arrived at the hotel, and when I offered my credit card at reception they said, 'No, we don't do that here.' They gave us a wonderful room and the following morning in the court-yard of the hotel we had a beautiful breakfast of boiled eggs and soldiers and fresh fruit juices.

We strolled through this ancient city, taking in the sights. These included Le Palais des Papes (the Palace of the Popes): in the fourteenth century the city was chosen by Pope Clement V as his residence, thereby causing ructions within the Catholic Church. There is the cathedral, Notre-Dame-des-Doms, and the bridge that is commemorated in a favourite children's song, 'Sur le pont d'Avignon'. We went to the food markets and antiques markets.

Tess loved it. She was looking in estate agents' windows because she is always keen on comparing property prices and when we stopped for lunch somewhere she said, 'This is a great place.' Over the next four days we came up with a plan and implemented the plan. We put a £5,000 deposit on an apartment that was 200 yards down the road from the Hôtel d'Europe. And we came away with a painting that Tess liked very much and which I think is now sitting in storage in Oxfordshire.

We made regular trips from Spain to Avignon and back again, interrupted by a trip to Sweden, where I made a tele-vision commercial and returned with £50,000 in cash.

We were in Avignon, and I had fifty grand on me, when I said to Tess, 'You know, we have the apartment in Avignon but I would really like to sell that and buy a house in the area. The Spanish house is yours, and you can keep it or you can sell it. And if you sold you could buy a little house near your parents so if we wanted to pop over and see them we'd have somewhere to stay.' This was all discussed rationally and sens-ibly.

An estate agent supplied us with details of a property in Montfrin, a small town some ten miles away which I had never been to. We drove to Montfrin to see the house. It was drab and run-down. Now, when Tess and I were viewing properties we had a signal to show one another if we liked the place . . . without the estate agent knowing. The signal was an emphasized scratch of the head.

Tess vigorously scratched her head. I said to the agent, 'I will give the owner fifty thousand pounds cash today, as long as we can move in tomorrow. We will let the paperwork take its time.' He phoned the vendor and the vendor agreed.

I bought the house and spent a fortune on improvements, repairs and building work on our new home. We moved in with no furniture, except for the bed and bits and pieces that we could take from the bungalow. The electricity was shot: we had one power point in the kitchen and an electric wok, so meals were cooked in that. I drafted in a team of builders and work began. Meantime, Tess set her heart on owning a racehorse so we popped over to Berkshire and she thought about buying a forty-grand share in the beast, but didn't.

When we returned to Montfrin I was really happy. I had a project to complete, i.e. a house to build. I assumed that Tess, too, was happy. But she was not.

The rows were terrible, really dreadful.

The work coming in included a new series, *Floyd's India*, and off we went. Nick Patten, for whom I have the greatest admiration, was directing and one of the cooking sketches took us to a dilapidated white palace with a dying, shallow, man-made lake in front of it.

I made friends with a Sikh chef who wore a turban and worked in the hotel in which I was staying. Jaipoor is known as the pink city, because in the early 1900s it was painted for the visit of the Prince of Wales. It was also ringed by a fortress wall, with fortresses on the peaks of the surrounding hills.

And of course Sikhs don't drink, and Indians don't eat beef, and my wonderful Sikh friend very kindly got me whisky and beef and pork.

One night we drove up into the small hills surrounding Jaipoor and broke into a fort. We climbed over the gates and looked back at the city, which was sprinkled with street lights as if it were a diamond necklace. We sat there and we talked about the world, about our different religions, different cultures, different aspirations, but most of all we talked. Food unites people.

And my friend cooked. He taught me how to make thalis, which are little tiny pots of Indian food. We ate and I drank whisky and we looked at the necklace around the city, and looked across the hills, and at one point saw a huge wild cat run in front of us. It might have been a tiger.

Then it was back to the hotel, where, intriguingly, two septuagenarian Australian homosexuals stayed every year and one of them, a theatre producer, worked in the laundry every morning, while the other one used to dress himself up as a chef with a white starched toque and then bake cakes. They were paying guests. At night they would come down dressed like maharajas, with flowing silks, and pantaloons, coloured in vermilion, ochre and purple. They did wonderful things for the local community, paying for the kids to have a good education and that sort of thing.

The day after breaking into the fort, I was due to make a

cooking sketch, showing viewers how to cook a biryani. I had my trestle table and my new Sikh friend had found me about thirteen different spices that I needed for the dish.

I was working a kri – which is an Indian wok – and with the most dangerous gas cylinder in the world, and it didn't have a regulator – only 'on' and 'off'. It would blow me to the moon or blow out because it was so windy. Anyhow, it was all set up, the temperature was 45°C, and the wind was howling. Behind us was the maharaja's fading palace and the dying lake. And in the dying lake there were four elephants.

Once I started to cook there could be no stopping. It's like having an orgasm. You can't. And you specifically can't with Indian food: when you throw in your mustard seeds and cumin seeds, and start to crackle them in a dry pan, there's no going back. There was the usual messing about. Lining up the camera, getting the sound right and saying to me, 'Your hair's messy.'

'Yes, because it's blowing a gale.'

'Keith, your bow tie is crooked.'

'Yeah. So?'

Then it's time. 'Stand by . . . Sound ready . . . Camera speed . . . Turn over . . . Action.' I went for it. The ghee went into the pan, and I said, 'Now I put in my goat – every time they say lamb in India, they mean goat. And to make the perfect biryani you have to have these spices which I am now going to add . . .'

I start to add the spices one by one: 'And the essential thing about this is you crackle, you burst out the flavour of these dried herbs. May I remind you that in Thai and Malaysian curries herbs and spices are wet, whereas in India they are dried and you have to explode the oils and explode the senses . . .'

The director shouted, 'Cut!'

I said, 'What?'

He said, 'The elephants have moved.' I turned and looked behind me. Yes, the elephants had moved out of shot. I said, 'Excuse me, this is a cookery programme. I am not David Attenborough. And I'm sure they will all be writing to *Points of View* to say, "It's outrageous. Do you know that Keith Floyd was cooking away and suddenly the elephants moved!"'

But, no, the elephants had to be brought back because Nick, whom I admire very much, felt that he was proceeding with his trade without particularly understanding mine. If he wanted to make a programme about elephants he should have buggered off and done it.

Meanwhile, I was being pursued by creditors dating back to my days as a landlord. The bank, the brewery and others wanted money. Mysterious people would phone me in Spain and tell me they had a deal to offer. I'd say, 'Go through Stan.' None of them did because they were sort of high-level bailiffs trying to reach me so they could serve me with writs and heaven knows what.

In the autumn of 2001, I returned to Britain to promote *Floyd's India*, the book that tied in with the television series. I was in a large shopping centre just outside Bristol, seated at a trestle table and signing copies of the book. Men and women handed me their copies and I autographed them 'Best dishes' and then the squiggle of a wine glass. Book after book and then an envelope was placed in front of me. I had been autographing mechanically and was about to sign the envelope. Then I picked it up and looked up at the man who had placed it before me. He was a rat-faced midget with dandruff. I said, 'What's that?'

He said, 'You've touched it. It's yours.'

I said, 'What is it?' But he scarpered. It was a writ that would determine my personal bankruptcy. I was fucked.

I was forced to go to London to employ a firm of trustees in bankruptcy. They would administer my affairs for the benefit of the creditors, though in particular to the benefit of their huge fees taken off the top.

I would remain bankrupt for three years. I couldn't work because whatever I earned would be handed on to someone else. I'd hardly see a penny of it. I managed to get a few jobs overseas so the money never hit the country, and I was able to keep going, but essentially I was utterly stuffed.

In 2005 I wrote a book, *Floyd's China*, which took me to Beijing. In the backstreets the little houses were painted in battleship grey but it didn't matter what colour they were because they were being destroyed to prepare for the 2008 Olympics.

I wandered into a still-standing, tiny restaurant with a few Formica tables and took a seat. 'I'd like some food with rice,' I said. And within moments little brown morsels of meat had been quickly stir-fried.

They were like little pieces of, say, quail's leg. The meat was slightly spicy, and was accompanied by some rice and there were some greens. I was curious about the meat. What was I eating?

It was a rat.

Not in any way repugnant, I have to say. It tasted similar to duck.

TWENTY-SEVEN

On a hot July day we were at the house in Montfrin when Tess decided she'd had enough. She desperately wanted to leave, to go back to England.

Bitterness and resentment had combined to make our marriage a pathetic and sad series of extreme episodes. We were in an intolerable situation.

There was no question that Tess wanted to go straight away so I phoned Stan Green and said, 'Can you book a flight for Tess to come back to England tomorrow? It's essential.'

I put her on the plane at Montpellier and off she went, to live with her mother.

Two weeks later I got a summons for divorce. I couldn't believe the next seven months. She'd send me the most unbearable faxes via Stan and, meanwhile, I was here in Montfrin on my own, drinking myself stupid. Here on my own.

Eventually, I couldn't stand it any more.

It was Valentine's Day. I went down to the florist, close to the town square, and sent Tess one hundred red roses. I attached a card, upon which I wrote, 'It's never too late.'

One hundred roses sent with a message from a broken heart did the trick.

After months of communication only by fax, Tess phoned

me in France. Friendly, chatty and with no mention of the summons for divorce, she said, 'I've bought a house. Come over to England.' So I went.

We met as if we had never parted. She took me to her little house in the little town of Faringdon, in Oxfordshire, and I thought, oh God, she's been stitched up here. As with the home she had when she first me, the bathroom was on the ground floor next to the sitting room. When you flicked on the light switch it sparked.

But property aside, it was quite clear we were back together again. So I threw my heart and soul into restoring her house, putting bathrooms upstairs and turning the scrapyard in the back into a proper garden.

Then, alas, I had nothing to do. Déjà vu? I had no work and knew that whatever I earned would be paid to creditors. Therefore I couldn't contribute much towards the mortgage repayments. I did not want to appear on television saying everything was fantastic because that was not so.

My heavy drinking had not subsided. Tess and I had made a stab at reconciliation. We wanted things to work out, but in truth the marriage was broken and we couldn't mend it. Nevertheless, we remained together. We would sit in Tess's small home, at the dining room table, staring at each other . . . all day long.

Then I got a call from my great friend James Whitaker, who had been the royal correspondent of the *Daily Mirror*. He suggested I do a theatre tour, a one-man show. It was to be called *Floyd Uncorked*, and after the first show – in which I stood on stage and recounted anecdotes for a couple of hours – was a great success; it kept Tess and me going, and she would drive me from one provincial theatre to another.

*

I was listening to music today. Music is a big part of my life, and one of my favourite songs is Billy Joel's 'Piano Man'.

It's a song about this guy who just wanted to write songs and entertain but he's sitting in this nasty bar with a bunch of drunks, desperate losers and lonely people. He is trying to give them a good time and is paying the price of his own outrageous artistic generosity. He's got to sit and listen to all these people, even if there is a consolation: his friend John at the bar gets him his drinks for free.

The song, of course, is an observation of what it is like to be an entertainer. You see, there is a difference between creating an entertainment and performing it. He plays the piano and the song seems pertinent to my life, not least because I am a cook and, curiously, in French slang the stove is called a piano, at which a master creates his magic.

It reminded me of *Floyd Uncorked*. The audience would move from the theatre's bar to their seats, a frizzle of tension before curtain-up, and I'd be at the side of the stage – invisible to the audience – standing by the aluminium scaffolding, adrenalin pumping.

Nerves colluded with the rush, and I'd vomit on to my dinner jacket. Not a pleasant image; I offer no apologies for that. A quick dab of handkerchief on dinner jacket, and then I'd walk on to the stage, a bottle in one hand, a glass in the other. 'My name is Keith Floyd.' And they were screaming, which is strange because I am not a pop star. I'm just a cook. But I never lost it, even though I thought, Christ, I'm onstage. There's not a script. There's nothing on the clock but the maker's name.

I'd tell lots of funny stories about eating, cooking, filming and being . . . just being Floydy. And I used to go off at half-time, feeling absolutely wrecked. And I'd held people for an hour and a half, two hours. I'd held them: there was a feeling of an enormous power that I'd had over them; actors must experience it all the time.

It is a feeling that comes from being onstage, and not one I ever felt in front of the cameras over the couple of decades I spent making some twenty-three television series.

If I tripped or slipped, or if I insulted, or abused or under-estimated the audience, then I would lose them. I had to entertain. And I did. I did.

I'd wind up the show saying, 'Well, as you see, I have had three divorces, and I have been bankrupt, lost a fortune. So if you need any advice on your marital affairs or your finances, don't hesitate to contact me.'

If I did the show today, I could add another divorce. Divorce from Tess, the woman who was driving me to the shows.

One of these one-man shows took me up to the Lake District and to a town that I think was Kendal. I headed for the hotel and to my initial horror realized that the organizers had booked me into a prestigious country house hotel called Linthwaite House.

I am not a great fan of country house hotels. To me, they have overblown menus and a well-meaning but sometimes absurd obsession with local produce. And, in particular, one thing really gets me: they insist on making their own bread – olive bread, walnut bread, sesame seed bread. Invariably the bread tastes like undercooked lumps of dough. (As far as I am concerned, the only bread to eat with a meal is the classic French baguette, especially when you want to mop up the gravy and the sauce and you don't want it to taste of walnuts and whatnot.)

Such hotels can be pretentious and a bit stuffy and even before the no-smoking ban was introduced they were all so desperate to be politically correct that they forbade lighting up.

However, Linthwaite House proved to be a wonderful exception to my prejudiced rules.

It is set in gorgeous grounds overlooking Lake Windermere, scores of wild flowers abound and red squirrels cavort among the huge variety of deciduous and evergreen trees. The hotel is run by Mike Bevan, one of the most professional and skilful hoteliers that I have ever met. I didn't know he was a member of the theatre committee and I didn't know that he was a Floyd fan.

We met for the first time at breakfast, the morning after the show. He personally took my order for breakfast, which was simple scrambled eggs on toast, fresh fruit juice, toast and home-made damson jam. What was in fact delivered to the table was a plate of golden, creamy scrambled eggs liberally speckled with generous slices of black truffles. I decided to have vodka in my freshly squeezed orange juice as it seemed only appropriate.

A few weeks later circumstances found me staying there again. I had been hired by a very wealthy and prominent Harrogate businessman to cook dinner in his luxurious and sumptuous home as a birthday present for his wife.

They had offered to fly me up in a private plane, but I preferred to go by car and decided to spend the night at Linthwaite before proceeding to the event the following day.

At the hotel I enjoyed the same first-class reception, service and food. 'Would you like a drink?' said Mike and we chewed the professional cud over several glasses of fine whisky. I was very flattered when he told me he had stayed at Floyd's Inn (Sometimes) in Devon and its style, decor and attitude towards food had influenced him considerably when he came to create Linthwaite House.

Anyhow, I did the birthday gig and Tess and I drove back to Oxfordshire. By this time my only income was from the intermittent theatre gigs. But I had often thought that now television work was drying up and I was genuinely getting past my sell-by date perhaps I should start something like a cookery school.

I noticed that many of the current crop of popular chefs like Rick Stein and Jean-Christophe Novelli operated cookery schools with some degree of success. However, I had no money to start my own venture.

On a whim, I decided to call Mike Bevan to see if we could run such a scheme at his hotel. He was most enthusiastic, positive and supportive. 'Let's get together,' he said, so we did, and we thrashed out a deal. It would be called Floyd's Cookery Theatre: cookery demonstrations, tastings and me telling my culinary war stories and exploits as a television chef.

The deal was simple: Mike put up all the money to buy the equipment and we became unofficial partners. In order to repay his capital expenditure the Cookery Theatre paid a kind of rent, bought and paid for its own food, its own staff and its share of electricity. Mike and I split the profits, fifty-fifty.

It had a slow start but it became very popular, cultish, and although we made no money in the first year we were confident that we would be able to see some generous returns if we continued into the second and third years.

Those who came along were largely Floyd fans, usually extremely well heeled. Often the car park was filled with Bentleys and Ferraris. There were men who said, 'Oh, I'm just a builder,' or 'I'm just a scrap metal merchant.' But in fact they were big boys in big business.

There were lots of women, some of whom had an embarrassing obsession with Floyd. When they were leaving they'd hand me a little folded note. When I opened it, there was a scribbled telephone number. Some of the pupils came from overseas and certainly from other parts of Britain.

Of course, it was a double whammy for Mike because the Cookery Theatre students had to stay at the hotel, which increased his occupancy percentage.

For me, and for Tess, it was a win-win situation. Even if we made little money from the project at least we were able to have something to do, enjoy the beautiful Lake District, and be together at no cost to ourselves, rather than sitting at home at the dining table staring at each other and worrying about the non-existent future.

During this time, a great friend of mine phoned to say he was renting a house in Phuket in Thailand for three months, from November to January. His idea was to invite his mates out to stay in the large house and we could all chip in to share the costs and have a cheap good time in what I considered to be paradise.

The friend in question, Paul Hickling, has a restaurant called the Roman Oasis near Sabinillas in Andalucia. Quite by chance I am sitting in the late-afternoon sun in the courtyard known as the inner sanctum, at the Roman Oasis, and my ghost James Steen and I are sipping the occasional pastis as we hammer out this amazing tale.

When Paul started the restaurant twenty-five years ago he called it the Roman Oasis because just a kilometre up the track are some perfectly preserved Roman baths, a relic of the Roman occupation of centuries ago.

The Roman Oasis has to be the most weird but most fascinating restaurant on the Costa del Sol. If you ever happen to be passing Paul's place be sure to pop in for a meal. Mention my name and he'll charge you double.

How Tess and I got together the money to go to Thailand with Paul I have no idea. But off we set and Tess too fell in love with the place.

We all have fanciful and absurdly romantic ideas and conversations on holiday, and I had one with Tess which went like this: 'Thailand is cheap and my career is going nowhere so perhaps there's the possibility that I could rent premises and open a Floyd's restaurant here.' Tess didn't disapprove. 'It could cater,' I continued, 'for the multinational community of expats and tourists,' all of whom were well aware of Floyd thanks to the programmes being shown (as to this day) worldwide on satellite television.

It was only whisky talk and after a happy holiday we returned to the grim winter of England.

But one thing did come from the trip. As with Linthwaite, Paul and I decided to do Floyd's Cookery Theatre twice a year, in June and September, at the Roman Oasis on exactly the same business arrangement that I had with Mike Bevan. So now Tess and I had two projects to keep us from going mad, and even more than a faint possibility of making a few quid.

Then at some ungodly hour of the night the phone rang. The phone only rings at that time when someone has died or had an accident, or it's a wrong number. Given that Tess's father was a very sick man my first thoughts were of him. So I answered the phone.

The call, over a faint and echoing line, was from Thailand, from Phuket. The caller was Mike Inman, the general manager of a hotel called the Burasari, and he had somehow overheard my fantasy conversation about opening a restaurant in Phuket.

In short he called to say, 'Would you be interested in opening a restaurant in the hotel that I manage?' Within two days he had wired me a ticket and I was on my way to Thailand for a meeting to set up the deal.

Mike Inman was at the airport in Phuket to greet me, along with an air-conditioned chauffeur-driven car, chilled towels, and crystal cut-glass tinkling with ice cubes and Johnnie Walker Black Label.

The hotel is a couple of hundred metres back from Patong beach, an area of Phuket immensely popular with backpackers and hippies; there is the ugly world of sex tourism; there are streets of teeming people, open-fronted bazaars, fish restaurants and Thai restaurants serving food of all kinds; there are hawkers, hustlers, beggars and thieves, and serene Buddhist monks glide through the flotsam and jetsam of humanity. I decided to look at it rather strangely through the eyes of perhaps Somerset Maugham and put the whole place into a 1930s context.

Mike is the classic expat. Brought up in Africa, where his father was a high-flying diplomat, and then educated at an English public school, Mike apprenticed at the Savoy Hotel in London, before spreading his wings and finally becoming the general manager of the Burasari.

Amid the chaos of Patong, you stepped into the calm, cool, quiet hotel with its waterways, its prolific vines, creeping plants and flowers. It was an absolute heaven, indeed an oasis of genteel relaxation run by smiling Thai staff.

Mike and I talked late into the night about the deal and at breakfast I was to meet the owner of the hotel and his boss, the beautiful and enigmatic Lilly.

She was an exquisitely dressed young woman of maybe thirty whose father had given her this hotel – mainly, I think, to lure her back to Thailand from America, where she worked in the influential and, to me, highly mysterious world of Wall Street banking and the stock exchange.

We ate breakfast and we hit it off immediately. A deal was struck and I returned to England, waiting for the lawyers to draw up the contract for Floyd's Brasserie in Phuket.

The deal: Tess and I would go to Thailand twice a year, all expenses paid. As with the Linthwaite and Spain deals, even if we couldn't make any money it wouldn't cost us anything and we'd still have a good holiday; if we made money it would be a bonus.

So now we had four projects going: the one-man shows, the cookery schools at Linthwaite and in Spain; and the brasserie in Thailand. For the next couple of years, we flitted from one place to another, returning to Montfrin for the occasional visit.

After the humiliation of the receivership followed by my personal bankruptcy, as well as the slowdown of my television career, the future was wide open.

TWENTY-EIGHT

I've said that not much happens in Montfrin. Not much except the flood, the drug raids . . . and then there was the nightmare I had while I slept in bed alone; Tess was back in Oxfordshire.

I started off sleeping on the sofa in the sitting room. Before crashing out I had locked the French windows but not the shutters and I always slept downstairs when Tess wasn't there because I preferred not to sleep alone upstairs and also because I like to listen to the radio – Radio 4 followed by the World Service – and the radio is in the sitting room. I awoke at about four in the morning, feeling tired and fed up, and wanting to go and lie on a proper bed. So I went upstairs, stripped off completely, lay in bed and fell asleep.

That's when I had the nightmare. I dreamed I was being pulled from my bed by two strong men.

But it wasn't a dream. There were two men in balaclavas, tracksuits and gloves, grabbing hold of my arms and dragging me out of bed. They shouted in French and in thick Provençal accents, 'Where are the keys to the safe? Where are the keys to the safe?'

Quickly, they dragged me down the marble staircase and into the kitchen. There in the kitchen were two more men, both in tracksuits and balaclavas. Each held a pistol. 'Open the safe,' they yelled.

Still naked, I crouched on the floor and opened the safe. They bent down beside me, pulled out the contents of the safe and rummaged through it. There were documents but no cash. They said, 'Where's the money?'

Reader, you have come this far. You know I had no money. They did not.

I said, 'There is no money.'

They yelled, 'No pounds? No dinero? No dollars?'

'No,' I told them. 'There is no money.'

I thought, my God, there is no money. What are they going to do? Are they going to shoot me? Will they beat me up? Will they spare me but trash the house?

As it was they just ran off with a small, but very expensive leather bag, which contained a few hundred euros in cash, some sterling, a couple of Dupont lighters and my passport. I shouted out, 'Please give me my passport back.' The man who was holding the bag turned and looked back. Naked and broken, I must have looked a sorry sight. 'Please give me my passport back,' I repeated. He took the passport from the bag and threw it at me.

I didn't phone the police, don't ask me why. I was paralysed with shock and fear. I sat on my sofa in the sitting room, trembling. When I could manage it, I put on a dressing gown, went to the kitchen, opened the cupboard that contains the bottles and poured myself a very large Scotch.

The next day, I boarded up the place – locked the doors, the windows and shutters – took a taxi to Avignon and checked into the Hôtel d'Europe. I couldn't spend another night in my wonderful house. I was scared they would come back.

It was the second burglary at my French home. The other burglary happened after I invited someone to come and stay with me. He was a really nice chap, who had found himself in L'Isle-sur-la-Sorgue, where he hooked up with mutual friends. We got on well, and I said, 'Look, why don't you come and stay at my house? You could do a bit of handiwork and painting and things for me. In return I won't charge you rent.'

I was going away, and told him: 'At all times maintain the security . . . and don't forget to lock the shutters.' You can see what's coming. He fell in love with a French woman – he was utterly obsessed with her – and she phoned him one night to say she was throwing a party and would he like to come? You bet! He dashed out; didn't shut the doors, let alone lock the shutters.

The burglars came in and wiped out the place. They took the television and stereo but more importantly they stole items of immense sentimental value. They swiped a collection of Dinky toys that I'd spent most of a lifetime amassing. They pinched my collection of pocket watches. Then they must have gone into the room where I keep the suitcases – about thirty of them – which have been with me when I filmed around the world.

Two of the suitcases were locked, so the burglars must have assumed the contents were valuable. In fact, they were suitcases that my sister Brenda had given to me following the death of my mother. I hadn't got round to opening them yet. They contained, as I mentioned earlier, just press cuttings: features and articles that had been written about me and of which Mum was proud.

They made off with expensive oil paintings, none of which I could claim against insurance because I hadn't kept the receipts. Before fleeing they knocked the globe of the world on to the floor, though luckily it didn't break.

*

The public perception of Floydy was of a rogueish guzzler, though as I have said I was never drunk when I appeared before the cameras to make my television series.

In private, however, I was drinking heavily and on 9 November 2004 my private life and the public perception were brought together.

It had all started with a phone call from a property developer I'd known from the old days in Bristol.

He told me that he had contacts who were launching a restaurant in a hotel in Highworth, not far from Faringdon. 'Would you like to front it?' he asked. The hotel was one of those Agatha Christie types of place, stylish, charming and endearing. And I liked Highworth. This is great, I thought. I talked it through with Tess and she agreed I should have a pop at it.

My contact told me that a banker was coming from London to Highworth to look at the property with a view to investing in the business, and it would be good if the three of us could meet on a particular day at the agreed time of noon.

Ordinarily, Tess would drive me. She is a good driver and throughout our marriage was invariably the one behind the wheel. But Tess didn't want to come. So I set off, in our Peugeot 806, a left-hand drive that we'd bought in Spain. I arrived at the hotel half an hour early and ordered a drink – a large Scotch.

The banker and the contact arrived but our meeting was not productive. I didn't like the banker, and he didn't like me so we didn't hit it off and I never heard from him again. I had drunk just the one large whisky but what I hadn't taken into account was the previous night, when I had got absolutely smashed. Basically, I was still full of whisky from last night. I got into the Peugeot and headed home.

I wasn't aware that I was drunk until . . . Until on a very narrow humped-back bridge in the village of Coleshill I smashed straight into the front of an oncoming Land Rover. I climbed out of the car. The driver of the Land Rover was not hurt (she suffered minor injuries but didn't need hospital treatment is how it was later described). A crowd gathered. They knew who I was, and there were shouts of 'Your car was wobbling all over the road, you madman.'

The police arrived. Was I the driver, they asked. Yes, I replied. I was breathalysed and found to be more than three times over the legal limit. My reading showed 120 micrograms of alcohol per 100 millilitres of breath. The limit is 35.

A policeman waved a hand towards his car and I said, 'Are you arresting me?'

He said, 'Yes.'

'Oh, I'm sorry,' I said. 'I'm really sorry.' And boy, I was sorry.

At the station I was asked to empty my pockets, and I had to sign some documents. They allowed me to keep my cigarettes and my cigarette lighter and then I was taken to a cell, which contained a bog with a lid and a wooden pallet on the floor, upon which to sit.

Nobody was in any way impolite. Quite the contrary. Periodically, a policeman would come down to see me and, although I didn't realize it at the time, they were waiting for me to sober up before releasing me.

Then a senior officer appeared, and he was a gentle man, almost like a counsellor. He said, 'Are you being looked after OK? Have you got any complaints? Have you had anything to eat?' I said I'd run out of cigarettes, and he produced a packet and said, 'Here we are. Have some of mine.'

I am a fatalist.

It stems from my experience in the army and my experience of filming – hurry up and wait. When I am required to wait I have an ability to switch off completely. I can put myself into a state of suspended animation, when I don't think about anything. When I was making shoots for commercials – when you have to sit and wait for hours – it really used to frighten people on set because I was sitting in the corner, waiting until it was time. I was like a lizard that will not move until the sun swings round to him.

In the cell – while the police hurried up and waited for me to sober up – I did my lizard act. In fact, I did think about something: I was worried about Tess worrying about me. I asked if an officer would phone on my behalf to let her know what had happened and reassure her that I was all right. He did.

At eleven o'clock at night I was deemed sober. I was charged, fingerprinted and all the rest of it, and then released. As I was leaving a load of Asians, all barefoot and in calf-length trousers and T-shirts, were marched in, all of them handcuffed together. They must have been illegal immigrants, and I thought, poor sods.

Before I left the station, a solicitor spoke to me and offered to represent me (free of charge) in court. 'I don't need that,' I said. 'Oh yes you do,' he replied. What I assumed was a ban and a fine was in fact far more serious. As I had hit another car I was potentially facing a custodial sentence – a stretch behind bars.

Tess didn't collect me from the police station, but when I got home – to find three photographers camped on the doorstep – she was sympathetic and kind. 'I knew I shouldn't have let you drive,' she said, and she was right. By the following morning a swarm of photographers and hacks had arrived and Tess and

Stan were furious with me. How could I have done it, they wanted to know.

A fortnight later I was before Swindon Magistrates' Court to face the charges, to which I pleaded guilty, of course.

In forty-one years of driving I had never had so much as a speeding ticket. It was a dreadful experience, though I am not looking for sympathy. The prosecuting lawyer told the court that after my arrest I told police, 'I had a few the night before with my wife and I suppose it topped me up. But I'm making no excuses. It's not good enough. I'm totally ashamed. I'm mortified. Being incarcerated is no joke.'

My solicitor was keen to tell the magistrates that I did a lot of charity work, and I didn't approve of him saying that because it seemed irrelevant. It's lucky I was able to speak myself. I explained how ashamed I was.

The chairman of the magistrates, Eileen Charles, told me that I had committed 'an extremely serious offence because your reading was very high and a collision has occurred'. However, she said, 'In your favour you have pleaded guilty at the first opportunity and cooperated with the police and shown a great deal of remorse.' And it is true. I was utterly full of remorse.

I was banned from driving for thirty-two months and fined £1,500.

I emerged from court into the press scrum and told reporters, 'I was guilty as charged. This is the first time in forty-one years that I have ever had any kind of driving offence. Although I feel ashamed I also feel very relieved. Throughout the whole proceedings the police and the court have treated me courteously, fairly and well. I'm not a drink-driver; it just happened to be a one-off. Normally my wife does the driving or I'm chauffeured.

I would urge everybody not to go through the agony that my wife and I have gone through over the last couple of weeks.'

And I had a message for other drivers: 'It's coming up to Christmas-time. Enjoy yourselves, get pissed at home and don't drive.'

A few months earlier I had done a deal to do a commercial for supermarket champagne. They'd wanted me for obvious reasons – the big-drinking bon viveur. Alas, now I was the big-drinking bon viveur who drove while over the limit. I was promptly ditched from the campaign. They couldn't have a drunk driver as a frontman.

But the ugly episode landed me with another campaign. A few weeks after the court case, I was there on posters telling drivers not to drink and drive. The police had asked if I'd do it, and I was happy to help out.

I'd seriously gone off Faringdon. Come to think of it, I don't know if I was ever on it. The town is – and I'm sorry about this Faringdon – a bit of common. I had a couple of jolly nice friends, who were builders and plasterers, and good blokes. I liked them a lot.

And while I'm not a snob by any means, Faringdon lacked a decent pub and a good restaurant. Instead it was crammed with really nasty takeaways and gangs of kids who stood on the pavement and wouldn't let you pass. It was horrible, although, granted, it was a pretty place.

My home in Montfrin was now the bone of contention in arguments, and they were pretty fierce arguments. Tess wanted me to sell it, but the house belonged to me.

'I won't sell it,' I said. I was stubborn about it. I really love this place. It is not the finest house in the world, but I like it. And I looked at what I'd had and what I'd lost. The pub? Gone. The houses in Kinsale and Dublin? Gone. This house, where I am now sitting, was the last thing I owned. 'I've earned millions,' I told Tess, 'but now I am broke. It's the one thing I have left and I'm not giving it up.'

Her parents were unwell and she wanted to look after them, while I missed life in Montfrin terribly.

On and on the rows went. Likewise, my drinking. Apart from the house, the drink-driving incident became another subject of our fights.

As far as booze is concerned, I thought I could knock it on the head quite easily. But on the other hand, I felt under pressure with Tess and I couldn't help myself. Sometimes, rather than argue, I wouldn't say anything. And then I'd get up and walk out of the house and down to the pub. That did nothing. Tess merely followed me down to the pub and we gave the other regulars some evening entertainment.

Our relationship was deteriorating rapidly, and our life was one long round of screaming matches interspersed with my complete alcoholic blackouts, and romance had long gone. The fairy tale we'd once lived turned into the grim reality that I can now talk about, but it still pains me to do so. The fact is I kept a bottle of Scotch in my bedside table. In the mornings, when I awoke I had to have – I didn't have to but I felt that I did – a few large glasses of whisky before I could get downstairs.

It was terrible. And I don't know how it got like that.

Yes I do. It got like that because I wasn't working any more. I wasn't making any money.

And as they say down in Devon, 'When money don't come through the door, love flies out the window.' Our love had flown and by now was a million miles away.

With Tess it seemed as if we had tried again and again and again to patch it up. This was unlike my previous marriages when I just walked away without trying to resolve things. Finally, in the autumn of 2007, and into our eleventh year of marriage, I moved out, walked away.

How peculiar. There was a time when I would have put myself on a railway track for Tess.

In spring of the same year I'd received some very sad news. Celia Martin phoned to tell me that David had died. He had been diagnosed with a brain tumour and a couple of months after his seventy-third birthday he lost the battle.

I remember David telling me a story about books. John Betjeman was at the Hay-on-Wye literary festival and was asked to judge the most important work of the year. Betjeman's final choice came down to two books. In front of an audience, he lifted both books, one in each hand, and felt the weight of them.

'This is heavier,' he said of the one in his right hand. 'So this is the winner.'

TWENTY-NINE

My own death, meanwhile, was lurking just around the corner. I'd dodge it, but only just.

Before I continue, I should say that very soon the mood of this book will lift dramatically and we shall all be beneath a Van Gogh sky, looking out over fields of sunflowers and cornflowers.

But for now I'd like you to come with me into the spiralling pit of despair, depression and alcoholism that was my life a couple of years ago.

I'd moved out of Tess's home in Faringdon and I was about to enter an even gloomier period. A friend, Glenn Geldard, who owned the Bell in Faringdon, offered to help out. He put me into a garage which had been turned into a bedsit. It was kind of Glenn, but the set-up was grotesque. There was nothing to cook on, and there was an electric meter that I couldn't reach to put a pound coin in. It was terrible. My programmes continued to be broadcast all around the world, but I was like a tramp.

I was still doing the one-man shows in theatres across the country, but now I couldn't drive as I'd lost my licence and Tess wasn't around to transport me. Glenn offered to play the role of chauffeur.

One of the gigs was in Yorkshire in October, and it was while up north that I was hit with the divorce summons from Tess. I was just leaving the hotel to go to the theatre and was in my dinner jacket and preparing myself to be upbeat and jolly for a few hours on stage. There, in the hotel foyer, I was handed the writ.

I read it there and then. It demanded that in three days' time I would have to attend a hearing at the High Court in London. My failure to turn up would result in contempt of court, which meant I could be arrested. The hearing was due to take place on the same day I was booked to do a one-man show in Milton Keynes.

I managed to get to the court, where I learned that my assets had been frozen – worldwide. In other words, I could not withdraw any money from my bank account. Of course, it made no difference to me as I had no money in any bank accounts – worldwide. But I think it was assumed that I had money stashed in Singapore and in Spain and probably France, too.

The hearing was adjourned for three months, until the following year.

Glenn had bought another pub, Chesters, in Newcastle-under-Lyme. He suggested I move out of the Bell and go to Chesters, which has a flat above the pub, and that's where I could live. Again, it might be good for business if punters thought Floyd was connected to the pub.

I spent Christmas in Thailand, returned to Britain in the New Year and in the latter part of January 2008 we headed off to Chesters.

The flat was terrible and contained a rubber inflatable bed, which I couldn't get in and out of. Glenn, meanwhile, set about organizing a grand opening for Chesters. Thousands would flock to the new pub, he thought, and I would be the guest of honour, cutting the ribbon or doing whatever one does to open a pub. Get photographed by the local press pulling the first pint, I suppose.

Anyhow, I knew the opening of the pub was today. That's the last I knew.

My next recollection is of appearing in the television series *Casualty*. It was a weird episode. There were cameras filming, and around me there were Second World War fighter pilots with horrific disabilities and limbs missing. And we, the patients, were all raising money for charity. Anthea Turner, the former GMTV presenter, was standing beside my bed.

After that, I was asleep in a rubber dinghy.

Of course, I wasn't asleep in a rubber dinghy and I hadn't appeared in *Casualty*. None of that was true. It was me being absolutely demented, unconscious and probably having delirium tremens. In truth, I was in the intensive care unit at the University Hospital of North Staffordshire. The hallucinations and dreams though were absolutely terrifying.

Eventually, when I had made a slight improvement, I was moved into a private room. My first memory of coming round is when a doctor spoke to me, as I said back in Chapter One. And perhaps I should remind myself of his words.

'Mr Floyd,' he said, 'you have been hallucinating. The medication we had to give you to keep you alive together with the effects of – how can we say it? – an overindulgence of alcohol . . . The night nurses recorded your cries and your conversations with yourself.

'You were suffering a nasty case of delirium tremens,' continued the doctor. 'DTs, Mr Floyd. We have played our part. Now it is for you to play yours. Drink again as you have before and you will die.'

I might as well tell you that I have since had a drink. Quite a few. But I have tried not to drink as I had before. I never want to go back to that desperate situation I had got into a couple of years ago, when I kept a bottle of Scotch in my bed-side table to blank out the inevitable argument with Tess that was going to take place.

Now I have stabilized myself, though I have gone through all kinds of emotional disappointments as well as my own inability to live with Floyd, the public figure.

Then the shock of the episode began to sink in. Glenn explained how I had collapsed while sitting in the pub. I was vomiting and a real mess, an ambulance was called and I was rushed to hospital. This was it. Alcoholism and malnutrition were finally taking their toll – my body's organs had had enough.

As friends and family started to gather, I was still uncon-scious and they were told that I was unlikely to make it. Patrick arrived first, and spent two nights sleeping on the floor beside the bed – the supposed deathbed – in which I was lying. Poppy flew over from France. She held my hand and helped the nurses out with gruesome chores that amounted to caring for me.

This was not the first, but perhaps the third time that alco-holism and malnutrition had put me in hospital. On the other occasions I'd also collapsed, and the press had said I'd suffered a stroke when, in fact, I had not and never have done. Doc-tors had told me to stop drinking, which I'd done for brief periods but clearly not for long enough. But nothing so far had been this serious.

While I had been in the intensive care unit (ICU) there was a little blue book at my bedside. It was a Critical Care Patient's Diary; what started out as a blank notebook was then filled in by hospital staff and visitors. The diary was not unique to me; nurses have one for every patient in the intensive care unit. Not all patients are lucky enough to survive so obviously will never get around to seeing what was written about them when they were in a coma-like state.

When I was well enough to read the diary, I found it a strange but poignant experience. It opened with an entry from staff nurse Paul Joynson. 'Hi Keith, you have been admitted to the ICU in Stoke. You are currently sedated and on a ventilator. You are receiving drugs to help with your blood pressure and septic. Tess has visited and has had to go back to Oxford now. You are stable at the moment but very critical.'

The next entry was from Patrick. 'All right, Dad, it's first of February and I'm just really glad I'm with you. Apparently you are sedated and in no particular discomfort. Poppy is coming over on Sunday (the earliest flight she can get). Love you, Patrick xxx.'

Another nurse, Benjie, wrote on 2 February: 'It's your third day in ICU. You are still sedated and still poorly but stable. You looked very settled, perhaps you feel good because your son Patrick is beside you all the time.'

A few entries later, Vicki Lawton writes on 2 February: 'Today I am glad to say that you have been taken off the ventilator and are able to converse with us. You are still groggy and have a sore throat but it's been nice to be able to talk to you . . . I hope to meet you again in different circumstances.'

And later that day Patrick wrote: 'Hey Dad, it's now 9.35 p.m. Saturday evening. You are awake and aware but still not sure what's going on. You said earlier you thought you were on a film set. You're not but Poppy and I might make a film of your life yet!! You just smiled at me for the first time.'

At 3.20 on the morning of 3 February clinical support worker Ray wrote: 'It's nice to see you without the tube in your mouth any more and it's nice to hear your voice. You've done really well. Although tonight you felt sick a few times, we needed to freshen you up a few times which you don't like because you feel sick. But we are trying our best to help you relieve what you are feeling. You can't go to sleep too, and you said you feel really weak.'

And then three hours later Ray wrote again: 'Keith, you haven't slept a wink tonight. I know you are trying your best to sleep but it doesn't help. But it's nice to look after you because you are very polite. Bless you!'

On 4 February, Sister Carolyn Emery wrote: 'Bear with it. You'll have good and bad days, with the good ones soon taking over. I'm sure you'll be fighting fit in no time.'

The tone lightened when Nick Rouholumin wrote: 'Hi Keith. It's Nick. I'm one of the doctors looking after you. You called me because you had some chest discomfort. Having examined you, I think you should be OK! Well, I'm off skiing today so probably won't see you again but before I go I wanted to tell you how much of a legend you are in the cookery world. I also didn't make it into lectures during med school as me and my flat-mates watched re-runs of your shows, as well as having loads of your books. I have occasionally tried to emulate your talents in the kitchen. This almost always resulted in take-aways!'

Nick started off a craze. The next entry comes from Vicki Lawton: 'I know it sounds crazy but I am going to say it anyway . . . I am your number one fan and have all your books. Bet you have never had that that said before. Much!!! Anyway, you've been a pleasure to look after and I wish you a speedy recovery.'

The final entry is written by Benjie, who said that I'd be moved from ICU to a ward: 'It's nice to talk and chat with you,' wrote Benjie, 'while you were eating yoghurt and drinking milkshake.'

And then when I flick through the book again, there's an entry I missed. It reads: 'I love you very much and am proud to be a Floyd.' It's from Patrick.

Patrick's own life has not been without difficulties. For many years he seemed unable to decide what he wanted, and drifted from job to job. He was lost.

I find it very hard to work out how guilty I am, and how much of it is down to circumstance. In fact, I agonize about it. We've had that conversation a lot, but never reach conclusions.

When television reared its ugly head, off I went like a race-horse out of that unbolted stable gate. There were long periods when I didn't see Patrick but I remember on his eighteenth birthday taking him for a special celebratory lunch. I hired a chauffeur and a Rolls-Royce, and we went to London, stayed in Duke's Hotel in St James's and had lunch at Le Gavroche.

There he met Albert Roux, who quickly assessed that Patrick was a bright and clever young man who was toying with the idea of becoming a chef. 'If you like you could come and work here. I could make you an apprentice.' It was an amazing offer: Marco Pierre White and Gordon Ramsay are among those who worked under Albert.

However, Patrick made up his mind quickly. He politely declined the offer. I was really disappointed by his decision but didn't let him know I thought he had made an error of judgement. Then I got him a job at the Castle Hotel at Taunton and he seemed to be doing well, but that didn't last.

He moved from job to job, unable to hold on to a position long enough. When I bought the pub, I asked him to come down to work in the kitchens. I rented a farmhouse, where he stayed with his girlfriend and their baby daughter, Rae.

He was not the most reliable employee, which is saying something considering the general standard of my staff in Tuckenhay. In fact, he was totally unreliable and when he did turn up his first task was to cook himself a jolly nice English breakfast. Yet he was, and is, an extraordinarily personable and social character, and wherever he goes he is popular. Other members of staff and the regular punters adored him. Patrick is a very kind person and extremely generous. He hasn't got anything to give but himself and he gives it in spades.

We didn't get on well in those pub days. I felt that people were sponging off him and would tell him so. I told him so too often. One night we were in the bar and I was telling him to get rid of the spongers – 'the freeloaders' – in his life. A few seconds later, we were in the middle of a father-and-son punch-up. I mean, physical stuff with blows being exchanged. Luckily, Patrick gave me an easy ride. He's much bigger than me and could have killed me if he'd wanted.

The fight embarrassed everyone in the pub and once again

I felt a disgrace and was ashamed. I don't know how we smoothed things over after that, but we did.

It occurred to us that Patrick had actually been working at the pub for one whole year – the longest period of time he'd ever served in a job. Sure, he had disappeared a couple of times, but he'd still been a member of staff for an entire twelve months. This was amazing.

As I was marvelling at Patrick's ability to stay in work for a year, I got a call saying that Richard Branson was having a party in a grotesque nightclub in London and personally wanted me to attend. The event was to promote a Virgin business. I didn't know Richard Branson but I was told, 'There will be other celebrities there, but Richard has particularly requested that you be there.'

I turned up and spotted Richard Branson, who didn't seem to know who the hell I was and didn't speak to me.

There was a fee for attending the party. It was not money, but a first-class ticket to any destination in America to which Virgin Airlines flew, as well as a month-long stay – free of charge – in any one of the Virgin-affiliated hotels. I didn't want to go back to America: my memories of the horrendous experiences while filming *American Pie* were still too fresh and raw. But I thought of Patrick. 'Here you are, Patrick, I've got a first-class ticket to America and a month in a nice hotel. Do you want it?'

'Yes,' he said, without hesitation. 'Absolutely.' I sorted him out with an American Express card – 'this is to get you out of any mess' – and gave him several hundred dollars. 'Off you go and have a good time' were my parting words.

Patrick didn't come back for a year and a half. I didn't have a clue where he was so had no way of getting in touch with him.

He returned to Britain, though I didn't know it. When I learned that he was back in the country, he was in the process of being used by people because his surname was Floyd.

He was taken on to manage a restaurant in Bristol. It was not your average restaurant. Waitresses dressed up in school uniforms, complete with fishnet stockings and micro-skirts, and errant diners were spanked in the dining room. No, it's not my idea of a good night out, either. Yet there were a few of the school-dinner restaurants around in the late eighties and early nineties, but eventually they all took a caning, so to speak, and thankfully shut down.

Of course, the one that Patrick managed used his surname to maximize publicity and then they held a launch party. The first I knew about it was when I saw a headline in the *Daily Mail*: 'Floyd snubs son's spanking new restaurant', or something like that. Makes me look terrific, doesn't it?

Time went by. He came over to Spain, when I found him a job in a restaurant. The two most popular restaurants were pretty awful and on Sundays served a roast lunch of horrible beef and horrible pork and overcooked Brussels sprouts. It was not nice food, but all the geriatric expats and holiday-makers seemed to love it. Patrick would stay in the guest apartment beside our villa, and he'd work at one of the two popular restaurants. Again, he was much liked – he is particularly sweet to elderly people and to children. It didn't last though, and neither did the job I found him in L'Isle-sur-la-Sorgue, when Tess and I moved to France.

He just needed to find his own way, and he did, getting a job in Bristol, helping to run a rehab clinic. He told me, 'I drive a minibus and take them out and do counselling and teach them cookery lessons.'

Through his own strength of character he has turned his life around and he is doing really well. He's contemplating getting back into cooking and yearns to achieve something in the world of music, another passion of his. He seems to have focus and he is very sensitive. I mean, I was really down the other day and he spoke to me with sincere tenderness and incredible maturity and wisdom. He, too, suffers from depression from time to time.

'Perhaps the Floyds are their own worst enemies,' he said to me.

The doctors saved my life. Or did they? If Patrick and Poppy had not been at my bedside I am convinced I wouldn't be here today.

Peter Winterbottom, the former England rugby player, super bloke and a dear friend, finally discovered where I was and he and wife, Trish, rescued me and invited me to stay at their home.

I couldn't walk and was on serious medication, and Glenn took me to collect my belongings and then Trish came to pick me up and drive me to the Winterbottoms' house in Surrey. Trish runs her own business, but she took two weeks off so that she could look after me and, true enough, she made sure I ate breakfast, lunch and dinner every day for that fortnight.

By this time Jean-Christophe Novelli, who had been in the States when I was rushed into hospital, was on the case and keen to help out. 'I think you've done enough,' he said to Trish. 'You must get back to business and Keith can come to me now.'

Next stop, JC's place in Luton, where he has an ancient farmhouse that is not only his home but also a cookery school for swooning women who pretend they want to learn to cook well just so they can be in the presence of the man hailed as the World's Sexiest Chef by the *New York Times*.

In fact, I stayed with JC's chauffeur, Tony, who is a lovely man, and some days I'd go to JC's place and sit in on the cookery classes.

JC gave me money, lots of money, and treated me with what I can only describe as extraordinary kindness. One day he said to me, 'As soon as you are feeling better we'll put you on the website and you can do classes in the cookery school.' Sounded great. However, when Stan found out he soon killed the idea. It hadn't occurred to me he'd have a problem but perhaps it should have done. Our relationship was not great by now. This is what he was reported as saying in the press, 'Keith has an exclusive agreement with me. I've been turning down TV offers for him because he's ill and then I find out he's doing this. He hasn't had the guts or decency to get in touch with his own manager. He had better do so pretty sharpish, as I'll be taking legal action.'

Stan didn't but JC backed away, quite rightly. He didn't need that.

While I was staying with Tony, another of my great friends, Bill Padley – a fantastic musician and producer who's written hits and won an Ivor Novello award whom I had met at the Burasari a year earlier – was with a legal friend of his coming down once or twice a week to JC's farm to help me with the reams of terrifying legal papers I was receiving from Tess's lawyers. The stress of dealing with them was horrendous.

When I first met Bill and discovered he was a musician I asked him if he'd play in my bar at the Burasari. This resulted in him doing a show every night for about three or four months and he became an integral part of the Floyd south-east Asia plans.

While things were going quite well, Lilly had said she also intended to open a stand-alone restaurant in Singapore. I was particularly anxious that Bill would be the musical director of the restaurant, which would involve hiring bands – be it rock 'n' roll or jazz. To my amazement, Lilly came to visit at JC's place. Being Lilly, she missed the plane she'd booked (she never turns up in time). We all had dinner in JC's restaurant in Harpenden.

'I've got fantastic news,' said Lilly as we sat at the table. 'I've found the backers, I've got the money, to open a Floyd's restaurant in Singapore. There's a choice of six sites.' The deal, in other words, was done. The money was in place, everything was in place.

'How quickly can you come to Singapore?' She wanted to open the restaurant in time for the first ever Singapore Grand Prix in September of that year.

Three weeks later I was in Singapore. Curiously, Lilly didn't really know who Floyd is. If it hadn't been for Mike Inman, we'd have never done the Burasari job. She had seen how successful that venture was, and it eventually dawned on her that Floyd was internationally famous.

Lilly even had the support of her father, who was not particularly fond of what the Thais call 'farangs' – foreigners. He was a man who, from the humblest and meanest of beginnings, had amassed a fortune, so his faith in me was something of a grand endorsement.

Even in Singapore, where part of the plan was to visit every top restaurant in this bustling fantastic city state to see what the competition would be, she was gobsmacked when people left their tables in restaurants and walked over to shake my hand, or sent over a bottle of wine.

Late one night we were sitting in the back of a taxi when the Chinese driver heard me talking, turned round, and said, 'Hey, that's Floyd in the back.' Lilly said, 'How does he know you?'

Eight hectic days of visiting the best bars and the best restaurants, and looking at the available sites, I selected one on an extravagant new development on the waterfront. I was exhausted and wasn't drinking at the time. Having to go to three restaurants a day, and having to taste food and not drink was very difficult. I still wasn't very fit.

I returned to JC's to find a ticket waiting for me to fly out to Dubai to visit my friend, Ian Fairservice.

Also, there was a postcard from Celia Martin, inviting me to visit her.

Ian, who had gone to Dubai thirty years ago as the first Western manager of one of Dubai's finest hotels, is now the biggest publisher of magazines and books in the Middle East. But his love is still food. I had been out to see him on several occasions and we'd often idle-talked of opening a restaurant in Dubai with JC. It would be called Novelli and Floyd (the Mad Frog and the Englishman) and given that Marco had successfully opened with Frankie Dettori, and Gary Rhodes and Gordon Ramsay had done the same in Dubai, we thought there was a little battle to be had.

So I spent another ten days of meals and dinners with ambassadors. I had a spectacular evening with Hussein bin Laden, cousin of the famous terrorist. He truly was a playboy of the Western world. Hussein carries no money; we were driven around in Rolls-Royces supplied by the hotel, with somebody slicing off the tops of champagne bottles with a scimitar, the most extravagant women coming and going . . . it was a whirlwind of the most extraordinary glitz and glamour.

Hussein was a gentle, fabulous character and had been educated in Switzerland and spoke perfect French and English. You felt that if you shook his hand it was a gesture of honour exchanged.

Anyway, the thought of a Floyd's in Dubai is a work in progress; it's a possibility. I had one hell of a good time but that trip, combined with the one in Singapore, meant that I was a shadow of my former self when I returned to Luton.

I immediately booked a ticket to fly to Faro, to meet Celia. But in the meantime I had to return to France, to my home in Montfrin, because Lilly was flying over and bringing the architect and the designer for the restaurant. Bill was coming too, to talk about the music side of things. It was June 2008.

My next court appearance was in a few days' time and on that day in France, as I talked it through with Lilly, it seemed that everything was ready to rock 'n' roll. 'As long as you approve these designs the building can start straight away,' said Lilly.

I knew the money was coming and a possible share of the profits. On the basis of this, Bill and his friends had negotiated a loan that would enable me to pay off Tess and still keep my house in Montfrin. I just needed the restaurant to happen.

I went to court in London and the case was adjourned again. I left Britain, and have not set foot on British soil since that day.

I flew to Portugal, looking forward to telling Celia about my exciting plans.

THIRTY

I am sick of constantly thinking, if . . .

If I had not had all these marriages then I would be a multi-millionaire. Yet I don't want to be a multi-millionaire. If I had not had fame then I would have long ago found the woman of my dreams. When I was on television, earning big money and extremely well known I could not find her, could not seem to find the woman who was just right for me.

But 'if' is a nonsense.

I say I could not find that woman but she was there, coming in and out of my life. She was a presence, she made me laugh, she was a companion and a friend. She gave advice.

Her name was Celia and she was beautiful, and she dreamed that one day she would be an actress.

I wanted to see Celia. We were good friends and I felt guilty about not attending David's funeral. I had written something to be read at his funeral, but it was considered not quite right. As it happened, a poem that David had written was read aloud: it was a poem about my father and his final days, sitting in his oxygen mask in the garden of my parents' home in Bristol.

I intended to stay with Celia for about ten days. I flew to Faro, in the Algarve, and she met me at the airport. She was living with a friend, staying in a little garden house, paying rent and doing most of the household chores to boot. Celia is a selfless individual. I filled her in on the Tess saga and the looming divorce and we talked happily about old times, and sadly about David's death. 'How are you coping?' I asked, though she is a strong woman and could cope with anything life wants to throw at her. She had run away from Britain, its memories, and she sought a new life. She has always been a big giver, and now she wanted to give something to herself.

One night we went for dinner, nothing grand but a nice little place where we could take a table on the terrace and enjoy the warmth of the sinking sun. I told her about my business plans – there was a new restaurant in Singapore to open, which promised huge sums of money. I told her about my house in Montfrin and said, 'If you like, you could come and stay.' I added, 'What can I do for you, Celia? What do you want out of me?'

'I think I want you,' she said.

There's a story I should tell you about Celia. Way back when I had the bistro and was married to Jesmond, I invited David and Celia for dinner at home one night and cooked a feast. They brought a friend, a television producer.

The producer was about to make a historical film about Berkeley Castle. David was involved in some way and Celia was roped in to help with the wardrobe department and look after the extras – the bods who were paid a fiver a day to dress up in historical costumes.

I explained to the producer what I did for a living, enthused about food, and the next thing I knew I was hired to do the location catering.

This would be a breeze, and a good earner. I had to feed about seventy-five people, namely the artistes and film crew, and so I did the maths and came up with a figure, which was agreed by the production company.

I worked out that I needed two vans for the job, and already had one. David and Celia owned a Transit van and when I mentioned to David that I needed a second vehicle he said kindly, 'Why don't you buy ours?'

'It's very good of you,' I told him. 'But I can't afford it.'

'Don't worry about that,' he said reassuringly. 'Pay me whenever you like.'

The first day was disastrous. Just like the next thirteen days. I had gas burners, microwave generators and Christ knows what, but I didn't have a clue what I was doing.

This was my first experience of film crews, and boy did I learn about their dietary requirements.

The technicians wanted egg, bacon, and sausages all day long. The wardrobe and make-up people were mostly vegetarians, who'd study the bacon and sausages and say, 'What else is there?' The artistes refused to touch the bacon and sausages, wouldn't eat the vegetarian dishes, but insisted on coq au vin and beef stroganoff. All of them wanted a mid-morning snack, lunch, afternoon tea and then an evening meal, including the technicians who were eating eggs, bacon and sausages all day long. These people didn't stop eating.

I had agreed a fee and couldn't up it. I lost every penny I could have possibly made. Feeling obliged to honour the deal, I continued to turn up and cook, even though I knew to do so was actually costing *me* money.

Then there was the matter of the Martins' Transit van. I'd had an innocent conversation with David about buying it, and now that I had ruined it during the location catering exercise, they wouldn't want it back. But the van did not belong to David. He hadn't told me it was Celia's.

Celia considered me villainous and untrustworthy and there was a big row in the Bistro one night when she went potty and demanded I pay her for the van, there and then. Yet I suppose she was the one who introduced me to television.

'I think I want you,' said Celia. For a few moments I was utterly gobsmacked. Then I was elated, euphoric.

I had always loved Celia but she was in my view unattainable and married to one of my best friends. She was loyal to David, and I was loyal to David, but yes, I have to admit that I was enchanted by her.

I believed she had not felt the same way about me. I had always thought she was slightly critical of me. I thought she saw me as a rogue and untrustworthy, but when we spent the next few hours – and subsequent days – discussing our feelings for one another, it became clear that if we had not been in love before, then we were certainly in love now. Celia says, 'I don't think there's destiny. I don't believe we're put on this planet to do anything, succeed in anything. Just to have a good time. That's why I believe in luck.'

When I had gone to Faro, I had done so expecting to hear from Lilly. She'd emailed to say she would send me a ticket to fly to Singapore to supervise the building project. Days went by, no ticket arrived.

Despite frequent emails from me, there was silence. Finally, Bill phoned one day and said that Lilly had contacted him to say that the Singapore deal was off. I was absolutely gutted. Everything I had hoped for, planned for, was in total ruins. It must have sounded to Celia as if I had just been telling lies, fantasizing.

But she decided to return to France with me. She hired a car, loaded up our stuff, and drove to Montfrin, where we tried to put our thinking caps on. I couldn't bring myself to phone Lilly because I was so hurt, so disappointed.

A few more weeks went by and she called me in France to say, 'Singapore is on again. Different building, but definitely on. We won't open until the spring of 2009 so if you could come out in October we could do the Christmas season at Burasari, shoot over to Singapore, get the building work started, and everything will be great.'

Celia and I were happy. We still are. Is it possible to be a teenager in love when you are sixty-five? I reckon it is. Why will this work when my other relationships have failed? For many reasons. We already have a friendship that has lasted forty years – we know each other well.

We know each other's irritating foibles – I can be grumpy and Celia talks to herself and is quite clumsy. She cannot cook and cannot sew and cannot make the flowers grow . . . but she does.

She looks after our chickens and our ducks and she looks after me. At the moment, I am looking after her because she has a nasty throat infection, though she's still got out of bed to go outside and water the plants.

To sit in the garden, under a Provençal sunset, chatting and laughing and loving each other, is my idea of heaven.

I will not mess up this one.

I try not to believe in hindsight, though it seems perfectly normal that Celia and I are together. I don't understand why or how. I am so frightened of relationships and betrayal and my own mess-ups, I just live by the day.

In previous relationships, I have been accused of sleeping

around – which I never did – and staying too long in the bar, which I probably did. But Celia has a kind of tolerance, or a kind of understanding that I have never experienced before. She's not suspicious of me; doesn't demand of me.

I think she loves me, and I think in a bizarre kind of way she respects me. I won't, and I can't, try to step into the shoes of David.

If someone had said to me forty years ago that one day we'd be together, I would have thought it out of the question. 'I couldn't be with a woman of Celia's calibre,' I'd have said. And I recall a conversation with David. I said to him, 'It's OK for you. You only write fiction. I have to live it.' Could David, the master of imagination, have dreamed up this ending?

A few months after she had moved in, it was 14 September, Celia's birthday, and I planned a special meal to celebrate what I hoped would be a wonderful day. Dinnertime was approaching and I felt very weak. I said to Celia, 'I'm just going to lie down for half an hour and then I'll be with you.'

Apparently, I slept and then climbed out of bed, fell over and concussed myself. It was a collapse, not dissimilar to the one in Stoke-on-Trent, when I was at Glenn Geldard's pub, Chesters. The paramedics came and spent three hours resuscitating me before getting me into intensive care in Nîmes hospital, where I spent the next four days.

Celia was there. She brought me clothes and cakes and she listened to my accounts of hallucinations. I was convinced, for example, that I was in a sort of Hellfire club, surrounded by gentlemen in long leather boots and eighteenth-century clothes, and these gentlemen sat and debated and whored as I observed. If I shook someone's hand they disappeared.

I believed that the man in the bed beside me was Richard

Hawkins, my editor from my days as a cub reporter. Celia would ask how I was feeling and I'd say, 'Much better but you won't believe it – the man in the bed next door to me is Richard.' He was, in fact, a lovely old French bloke who used to give us cakes.

On the night Celia and I arrived in Phuket, Lilly phoned to say, 'Singapore is off.' I said, 'Why the hell did you drag me over here to tell me that?' She flew down the next day and told me the credit crunch had hit Singapore, the investors had pulled out and it couldn't be done.

At the same time there was a military revolution in Thailand, the airport was barricaded and tourists could get neither in nor out. Not that they'd have wanted to. Our tourist bookings were cancelled and there were no customers in the Burasari restaurant.

I interviewed a head chef for the restaurant but the next morning Lilly explained she couldn't afford a new head chef. Instead, she installed a local Thai lad to do the cooking. I said, 'I'm not having my name associated with this. Sod it. I'm not hanging around here.'

Celia and I spent ten days in a hellish apartment waiting for the blockade to lift before we could fly out. I was finished with the Burasari, and I was heartbroken.

The apartment was meant to have been my permanent base while I was in Phuket, but it was something of a shambles. The air conditioning didn't work, the hot water was intermittent, and although it was in a relatively modern and allegedly luxurious block of apartments it was all together unsatisfactory.

Indeed, so much so that Celia, who was already stressed by

the situation that had confronted us, and had taken an instant dislike to Patong and the sleazy aspects, was so upset and angry that she left the hot apartment and checked into a hotel across the road. I think she also thought that I was either a fool or a liar after things which I had assured her were going to happen evaporated into thin air.

An emotional crisis was avoided because we now had a firm date for our departure from Phuket, albeit via Kuwait, and onwards to Paris Charles de Gaulle airport. By the way, I don't recommend a twelve-hour stopover in Kuwait airport. Apart from anything else the bloody place is dry.

The weird hotel across the road from the apartment seemed to be run by French people and was full of French people, and it was really rather good fun. Although I was sleeping in the apartment and Celia in the hotel we made it our head-quarters until it was time to leave. Life was distinctly better than hanging around in the now ailing Burasari.

Before we had left for Thailand, David Pritchard's office had contacted me to say he'd love to meet up. A bit strange, I thought, after nearly fifteen or sixteen years. I said, 'Well, that will be difficult because I shall be in Phuket.'

'Ah, no problem,' his assistant said. 'David is in Asia anyway doing a series with Rick [Stein] and on his way home he could divert and meet you in Phuket.' So I thought, what the hell? Let bygones be bygones.

Finally, I spoke to him on the phone in person. He said, 'How wonderful to hear your voice. I've missed you so much.'

I said, 'Don't give me that shit, David. You took the easy option and more or less recreated the Floyd programmes with Rick Stein and Antonio Carluccio. You're a lazy fucker.'

He said, 'Yeah, I know. But you know me. I only ever worked with you before Rick and Antonio. I didn't know anything about cookery programmes.' He was, of course, his usual utterly charming self.

I said, 'David, I am happy to meet you but you are not going to get a comfortable ride from me. As far as I am concerned you were completely out of order.' I didn't go into details on the phone, and I won't go into details now.

In the weird hotel in Phuket I sat and quite anxiously awaited his arrival. Although I felt that many times he had let me down, I also think on his day he is a superb director.

I wondered whether our meeting was going to be rather like Moriarty and Holmes at the Reichenbach Falls. One of us was going to die, maybe. Eventually he came bouncing in, munching on a kebab, flushed and red-faced, overweight, clearly already quite pissed. He hugged me. He is a big man. And he kissed me on the head. He said, 'Dear boy, it's wonderful to see you.'

I said, 'Yeah, what do you want, David?'

He said, 'I know. I know, you are going to have a go at me. And I deserve it, I know. I am sorry. But you know what I am like. I can't help myself.'

We started to swap stories. He said, 'You were bloody difficult to work with.' I said, 'But you were hopeless. You never turned up on time.' We exchanged insults for ten minutes or so, but found ourselves laughing more and more. And it was a truly wonderful and emotional reunion.

He said, 'I wanted to speak to you particularly because I have spent the past two and a half years writing a book. It's called *Shooting the Cooks*. It's just my memoirs of filming you, Rick Stein and Carluccio. And my childhood and my love of food. I just wanted to talk to you to tell you about it and see how you felt.'

I said, 'That's wonderful, David.'

He said, 'More importantly I now realize that if I hadn't met you I wouldn't have achieved what I did. I want to say thank you very much. And even more importantly, Denham Productions want to make a ninety-minute documentary to celebrate your career. And the BBC are absolutely up for it.'

I said, 'David, don't give me any shit. The BBC can't stand me.'

'No,' he said, 'we've had meetings with them and they really want to do it. It's going to be so funny and so good. We can shoot it in Provence in July with the old crew – Clive, Steve, Tim, Frances. Chris Denham will produce it. It will just be fantastic.'

We continued to get pissed and talk about the best of the old times rather than the worst of the old times. We shook hands. He said, 'I must go. I've got a terribly bad tummy upset. Can't stand the food in Thailand.'

Celia and I sat in the hotel every evening and over the next three evenings David turned up, moaning about his stomach upset; not that he hadn't drunk probably seventeen pints of lager and guzzled great helpings of Thai green curry.

Of course not. He's on a diet these days. When wasn't he?

We re-established and cemented a relationship which, in retrospect, had a profound effect on television and cookery.

Anyway, what goes around comes around, as they say. I read *Shooting the Cook* – not the *Cooks*, as he'd said. The illustration on the jacket was clearly an image of me and if I had been Rick Stein I would have been a bit pissed off that about two-thirds of the book was devoted to Floyd and only ten pages or so to Stein.

I read the lines on his version of our meeting in Phuket. There was Floyd, he wrote, looking old, frail, completely sloshed, out of work and miserable. Not my version, David, I can assure you. And by the way I do not buy my blazers from Aquascutum.

In fact, *Shooting the Cook* is quite a good book and I enjoyed it. We parted on the best of terms, with David ensuring me that within just a few weeks he'd have the deal done with the BBC, 'So set aside about two weeks in July.'

Celia and I returned to France in early November but I slumped into depression. Celia went 'home' to Britain for Christmas, and 2008 was the most miserable Christmas I have spent in my life. I closed the shutters and sat in the sitting room, drinking, and when I ate, which was rare, it was all tinned soups. Nobody visited, and I didn't answer the phone. I just wished I would die.

When Celia returned in time for my birthday on 28 December my mood lifted. I can't remember a thing about it. It was an absolutely wonderful day.

However, the depression was getting to me. I couldn't deal with the financial burden and the thought of losing my house. So I was just getting into a worse and worse state. Not sleeping and up all night, though not drinking too much, happily. I managed to really curb the drinking. You see, the trouble with me is me.

Stan Green had received an offer from Victor Lewis-Smith to make a one-hour documentary about me.

Stan advised me not to do it because he said they would just stitch me up. I said I was happy to do it. As far as I can tell Stan was doing his best to make sure it didn't happen.

Victor somehow managed to contact me direct to talk about

the documentary and I said, 'Well, I'd be delighted to do it. I'm really up for it. We can do it at the end of May or early June.'

He and his crew and Keith Allen, the actor and a great guy, turned up and we spent three wonderful days making what I hope and believe will be a terrific documentary. I told Keith, 'I hate the name Keith,' and Keith told me he loved it.

The acrimony of divorce from Tess coincided with the demise of my relationship with Stan Green. I was embarrassed by his behaviour sometimes and I'm sure he had problems with me, too.

When Stan came to visit me in Montfrin in the summer of 2008 we sat down for dinner and had an argument about the role he had played in the making of the *Floyd* series. Eventually, I kicked him out. Asked him to leave the table and to leave my house.

He was upset that I had kicked him out, knowing that his return flight to Britain was not for three days and things did not improve. The following December an article appeared in the *Independent*'s gossip column, 'Pandora', reporting that I had been ordered to pay Tess a lump sum, plus costs. Stan was reported as saying: 'If that is what the judge has awarded Tess, then she has got what she deserves after everything she has put into the business.'

By now I was counting down the months until our contract ended.

By the way, if any agents or managers of mine feel that I've been unkind to them, may I please quote the following story told to me by one of British jazz's icons, George Melly. The story, true or not, he recounted to me was as follows. Two agents were having lunch in The Ivy in London when the latest Oscar-winning actor entered the restaurant with his new girlfriend. Agent A turned to Agent B and said, 'Look at that shit. He takes twenty-five per cent of everything I earn.'

I'd heard nothing from David or Denham Productions when suddenly Celia and I got an email saying the deal was done with the BBC and could he and Chris come over and sort everything out? I booked them a hotel overlooking the village square and a suitably short stroll of fifty yards to Café du Commerce.

When friends visit I always ask them to bring some food, though a lot of food doesn't travel very well; a bit like wine. Pastis doesn't travel well. You can't drink it in Britain. Britain is beer and whisky and sherry and Pimm's; wonderful drinks and they shouldn't be cross-fertilized.

When you are a full-time expat like me, it's best to follow the rules of the country in which you live. When I go into the local supermarket I assume it to be a French supermarket, which it is. I don't believe I am in Waitrose or Sainsbury's. But when my British friends come and visit they want everything to be as it is at home. They just don't get it.

When I'm in Portugal, I will survive on the endless fried pork chops, which are brilliant, and endless plates of fried fish, until I get bored to death with it. My excursions to restaurants are when I am being taken by either a publisher, a producer or an executive from an ad agency. They want to try out the restaurant, and I am the excuse for them to do so. I do go to Michelin-starred restaurants but mostly I love the ordinary restaurants where the same people come each day.

But every now and again, I have an absolute craving for something really ordinary – naff, possibly – and that is where David and Chris would be able to help me out. Something like a Fray Bentos steak and kidney pie which can be baked in its tin. Or a tin of Heinz cream of tomato soup.

Or I crave a jar of Shipham's shrimp paste or crab paste – to take me back to my rugby-playing school days. Or I fancy a jar of Heinz sandwich spread. Or what about a tin of Fray Bentos corned beef with creamy mashed potatoes, pickled walnuts and pickled onions. The French can't do pickled onions, because they make them with white wine vinegar, rather than malt. They're horrible.

Every now and again, I want a great big slab of mature English Cheddar, and I'll cut off slices, lay them on toast and grill it so the cheese is golden and running over the edge.

Rose's lime marmalade is not going to make it in the gastronomic hierarchy of *confitures* that are available in France. The French do make beautiful jams packed with fruit – plums, redcurrants, raspberries, strawberries, or rhubarb. But every now and again, what I really want is Rose's lime marmalade. And while I'm at it, Rose's lime cordial is always welcome in my larder.

Then my mate Marmite. I have travelled all over the world with Marmite. You can have it as a drink and you can spread it on bread and toast.

Every now and again, I have to have these things. If there is one British food I miss above all others it is really good fish and chips, particularly from the North Country or Scotland. It is the ultimate fast food, a world beater. Haddock is my favourite, followed by cod. Curiously enough, if my instincts are right, fish used to be fried in big vats all over London and other big cities and was served always with mushy peas. It wasn't until the cursed French taught us how to make French fries that we then started serving chips with our fish.

The French didn't always know how to cook, though they like to think they did. The Italians were the original masters. The Medicis filtered out their chefs through the royal households of France. It was Italians who invented *petits pois*, for instance, which the French take for granted as their own (hence the French name).

Here in France, you cannot even begin to have roast rib of beef because the butchers have a terrible custom of skimming the fat off the meat. Pork, which you and I love for its crackling, is also crackling-free because the butchers remove most of the fat. My only solution is to buy a whole pig's head, which I do every now and again. I score it and then roast it in the oven. I have the brains and the crackling on the cheek; a good dollop of apple sauce, of course, and roast potatoes.

But then there are joys here. Like the Montfrin potato, which arrives every May, and it knocks Jersey Royals and other British potatoes into a cocked hat.

This talk of food has reminded me of the importance of fridge training for the women in our lives. I have been infuriated by a succession of girlfriends, wives and lovers who insist on putting things like marmalade, jam and pickled onions in the fridge. Haven't they heard of a larder? Since they invariably all shop in supermarkets, I would like them to learn this rule: that which comes from the refrigerated shelves should be unwrapped at home and placed in the fridge, that which is not on the refrigerated shelves should not go in the fridge. My next grounds for divorce are going to be that she put a package of twelve yoghurts, vacuum packed in cellophane, straight into the fridge so when I wanted to eat one, I had to first find the scissors and cut off all the packaging.

One more thing – I'd like to bring up the subject of

pre-heating. Before grilling your steak or basting your leg of lamb, pre-heat the oven or grill. And make sure you've taken the chilled food out of the fridge and allowed it to reach room temperature before you try to cook it.

We had a riotous two-day reunion. David already had an editor taking the best clips from all the *Floyd* series. They came with the contract, which I signed. It was for a very large sum of money.

I told them, 'I have also made a documentary for Channel 4 but I don't think it will clash with what you're doing.' They agreed. 'That shouldn't be a problem,' they said.

It was a great couple of days during which we discussed the programme inside and outside, and it was going to be fun. David would direct and Chris would conduct the interview. Not only that, but we would all get back together again and make some more *Floyd* programmes; these would focus on food as it is, rather than the way it was, casting a cynical eye over today's cookery on television.

I made them a farewell meal – huge paella – washed down with buckets of Provençal rosé.

This, after the disasters of Thailand, was yet another wonderful opportunity. Four days later there was a message on the answerphone from David Pritchard: 'I felt honour-bound to tell the BBC that you made a documentary for Channel 4. So they've dumped ours. They don't want it. Sorry about that.'

Oh well, I thought, there you go. That's the BBC. I felt betrayed, angry and of course foolish for being so gullible once again. But I did receive an email from Chris Denham, saying how gutted he was and that he, too, felt the BBC had made the wrong decision. He reaffirmed: 'Come hell or high water we will all work together again.'

THIRTY-ONE

Poppy has been to stay. She travelled from Toulouse and was with me for the weekend. There is not a day in my life when I don't think of my life's effect upon my children's lives. I feel guilt, remorse or anger, even.

As I have mentioned, she came to live in France with Julie and Jean-Jacques when she was ten years old. I didn't see very much of her, though I sent postcards from all over the world. When I was filming in Australia I wrote to Julie and said, 'Can I take Poppy to Australia with a fully qualified person to look after her?' Julie didn't think that was possible, and I had no problem with that.

Then Poppy, who is amazingly intelligent, through sheer determination submitted herself to the French educational system. She went to a very high-powered school in Toulouse, and I used to go and see her. On one occasion she booked me into a hotel that she knew I would like and she arranged dinner for the two of us. She picked just the right kind of brasserie, one that served a good tarte Tatin, she knew I'd like it. She knew I didn't want to go to a Michelin-starred restaurant. We had a great time, and during the evening she produced a piece of paper and said, 'Dad, can you just sign that, please?' It was a note excusing her from returning to school for the evening. I signed and then she dashed off. It was fine. That's initiative.

She came to London and I took her to Langan's. When we met she looked like a million dollars, all dolled up in clothes she had designed herself. Poppy is unobtrusively sophisticated, and she is as hard as nails as well, by the way. If she gives you a bollocking, you get it. And she's given me a couple.

She came to Montfrin before we both returned to Britain for my mother's funeral. At Nîmes airport we were chatting in the bar and missed the flight. We went out for dinner, and started again the next day. Yes, we made the funeral in time. It was a desperately sad day and I sobbed throughout. My mother was a very special woman.

When Tess and I were in Ireland Poppy came over, and likewise she joined us in Spain. Poppy and Tess got on extremely well and people used to think they looked so similar that they were sisters or even mother and daughter.

Poppy is the ultimate companion.

She said to me one day, 'When I went to France I was ten years old. I had a choice to make. I either had to get myself into the French education system and get on with my life or I could whimper and moan about losing my dad or him abandoning me. Now I've got a degree. I am an architect. And I am free. I have achieved my goal, but now I can see you again.'

She's twenty-six as I write this chronicle and about to start her own company to create housing for disadvantaged people. What a girl.

I am finishing off this book in Spain. There are three reasons for doing so.

I wanted to come and see my friend Jean-Christophe and

his new enterprise at Puerto Banus. I wanted to catch up with Paul at the remarkable Roman Oasis. And perhaps most importantly I wanted to visit my friend, Dr Ernest Guillem, who I have known and trusted for many years. Indeed, I have known Ernest since the time when I lived in Spain.

I had a small growth protruding in my anal passage and I knew that if he was equipped with local anaesthetic and a couple of sharp knives he could swiftly remove it and alleviate the discomfort it had been causing for the last year or two.

I trust Ernest and I think it's important to trust your doctor. He knows what I'm like and he knows everything about me so it's no good pretending I don't drink and I don't smoke. He sees the overall picture.

On a June day of this year Celia and I packed a couple of cases – not much – and began the drive from Montfrin to the Costa del Sol. The next day we finished the journey, arriving at the Roman Oasis, which is in the hills of Manilva, a mile or two back from the coastline. It was nice to see Paul and he's always upbeat and full of energy. In the gents' loos of his restaurant he's pinned up jokes about women. In the ladies' loos, Celia told me, there are jokes about men. I said to Paul, 'Tell me your favourite joke and I'll put it in the book. It'll cheer up the reader because I've been so gloomy at times.'

Paul said, 'Two cannibals are eating a clown. One says, does this taste funny to you?'

Paul says he never tells the same joke twice. You can see why.

Beside his restaurant is the square courtyard, two towering palms and a fountain in the middle, where Celia and I sit during the day, moving occasionally to escape the intense sun and to find a shady spot.

Paul has three parrots, all of which have boys' names because when Paul got them many years ago he believed they were male. He later discovered he was wrong, times three. Two of the parrots like to stay perched on trees in the restaurant. One of the parrots, Bosun, the eldest and most superior, prefers to be in the courtyard with us. When Celia laughs – which she does a lot and loudly, too – Bosun bellows out a mimicking laugh. All three birds say 'hello' to customers and 'thank you' when Paul gives them a treat of that chocolate-coated nut, an M&M.

A couple of days after arriving here we went to see JC at Hotel Lorcrimar, where he has opened a restaurant, and by the pool he and his chefs barbecued fish and meat for about a hundred people. Among the crowd were a dozen or so celebrities, but I didn't recognize any of them. And why should I? I don't watch much television.

And, of course, we went to see Ernest, my doctor. He carried out the operation in his surgery and the growth that was removed was then despatched for a biopsy. The tests showed the growth was a malignant tumour. I had scans and I had tests.

When I sat with Eric and he told me that I had bowel cancer I felt, strange though it might seem, a sense of relief. I felt relief because he said, 'If you had left this much longer then you would have died. But I am confident that we have caught it in time. We can deal with it.'

Celia and I had expected to return to Montfrin by now. The whole thing should have taken about a week, and that included visiting my chums. But over the last three I have been visiting Ernest daily, having the initial operations redressed.

But before they could proceed further with the suspected internal problems, two huge hernias had to be removed.

Now I have to wait ten days before the stitches from my hernia operation can be taken out. When ten days is up I will begin four weeks of either chemotherapy or radiotherapy, and after that I will be given an absolutely clean bill of health.

In the past few weeks I have had five operations and I am writing now, one day after the fifth of them.

So all in all it would have been about two months by the time this episode is completed, some of that time walking around with a bag attached to my leg and connected to my penis so I can pee.

After yesterday's operation it would have been usual to stay in hospital for a few days, but I insisted on leaving so that I could finish this tome in which every word has been hammered on the anvil of truth.

What I have been through in recent weeks is the price you pay, my dear gastronauts, for the kind of life I have led. But I have had such support and such kindness that despite the discomfort I find myself in, I am truly happy for the first time in three or four years. And I am looking forward to getting back to work and enjoying my food once again.

After the tests, Ernest said the most extraordinary thing to me. 'I just cannot believe how your liver is in such condition. It is perfect.' I was as surprised as he was though I didn't bloody well tell him. He added, 'Would you kindly sign this donor's card and make me the beneficiary.'

Without a second's hesitation I signed on the dotted line.

Once I wrote a poem:

> *You climbed on to my roundabout.*
> *You never paid your fare.*
> *But now it's stopped turning*
> *You say, 'I don't care.'*

It's about all the people who've freeloaded on my life.

The roundabout doesn't stop turning. People climb on and people climb off and then maybe – just maybe – one of them climbs back on again.

Celia and I like to listen to Radio 4 and we like to watch British television. She enjoys *Strictly Come Dancing* and as the finalists are about to be announced her eyelids flicker and within a few seconds she is snoozing on the sofa. How ridiculous: to get so excited about a television programme and then fail to watch the most important part of it.

I love Celia.

Before we left for Spain we sat together in the sitting room of our home in Montfrin and watched a programme I had never seen before but apparently it's meant to be really good. Millions have watched it, not just in Britain but all over the world. They love it and they watch the repeats and the reruns. It's been the talk of the town, the city, the continent, the world. Not much happens in Montfrin and Celia and I are a bit behind. But we had to watch it, so we bought a DVD of the programme.

We'd got a pizza from the very good pizza delivery van that pulls up in the town square most evenings. I was on the sofa, surrounded by the memorabilia that I collected during two decades of making television programmes.

I lit a cigarette. Celia put on the DVD. No she didn't. She played with the DVD controls. 'Don't press the red button, Celia, you'll turn the whole system off.' Neither of us has a clue how to work the remote controls. We're completely useless.

Eventually we had lift-off. The programme started.

It was a pretty good programme. I had definitely heard of

it before last night. Though I had never seen one single entire episode of it, only clips.

It was a programme – a cookery programme – about a madman who travels around the world, cooking and eating and drinking. He has no scripts, no nothing. He was a bloke called Keith Floyd. He was Floydy. I didn't recognize him at all. It was like watching a stranger on the screen.

When it was over, when the credits rolled, Celia, who was lying on another sofa, turned her head to me and said, 'I thought you were rather good.'

Boy, I believed her.

It was a line delivered with all the conviction and passion of a theatrical dame. Dame Celia.

And she'd dreamed that one day she would be an actress . . .

EPILOGUE

By James Steen

Mornings and Keith did not get on. Usually he'd step into the kitchen at ten-ish, sit down at the table, light a fag, and say, 'Don't talk to me yet. I'm here, but I'm not awake ... Who's moved the ashtray?'

How reassuringly different he was, however, on the morning of 14 September 2009. He greeted Celia with a jolly, 'Good morning,' and then a hearty, 'Happy birthday, darling.' The two of them planned to celebrate her birthday with a special lunch at a restaurant, but aside from the outing there were other reasons to explain Keith's positive frame of mind.

There was, for instance, this autobiography, which was less than a month away from publication. He had signed off the manuscript in August, was proud of the accomplishment and had earned himself a pastis. Already there were signs that *Stirred But Not Shaken* would be received well. The *Daily Mail* had begun serialization of the book which had served to remind Britain's cooks that the master – last seen heading into the wilderness after divorce and ill-health – was, in fact, still alive.

There was more Floyd coverage due that night because Channel 4 would broadcast *Keith on Keith*, a documentary in which the actor Keith Allen spent a couple of days with his culinary hero. The opening shots of the documentary showed Keith asleep on a sofa; there were sequences of Keith staggering from one table to another. Compelling stuff. Our Keith had already watched a preview DVD of the programme. 'It shows me in a bad light but I like its honesty. Warts and all,' Keith told me.

On that Monday he was also preparing to deal with criticism that would follow the programme. As it turned out, his concern was justified. Many viewers were horrified by the state of Keith and by his rudeness but, as he conceded that day, 'It's a lesson: Why Painkillers and Alcohol Don't Mix.' It is crucial for the viewers of that programme – and the readers of this book – to know that for many months cancer lurked within Keith, but he did not know it. He was in physical pain (hence the medication) and he suffered the anger and anguish engendered by cancer. However, the illness had not yet been diagnosed.

Keith and I had spent recent days talking about the party to celebrate the book's launch, and he was relishing the prospect of renewed recognition; not so much a coming out party, but more a coming back. He was so optimistic that he wanted to have business cards printed, and they'd be embossed with his squiggle of a wine glass – half full, of course, rather than pessimistically half empty. Keith had even gone out and bought himself a pair of red socks: the sartorial evidence of a man's self-confidence.

Keith was happy to be busy and – after the initial letdowns referred to in chapter thirty – he was due to work again with Chris Denham and David Pritchard, two men who played such influential roles in the success of Floydy. They were to make a programme for Good Food Channel, in which Keith, with all his silky eloquence, would cast an eye over today's food fads, things that irritated him and made him swear a lot. His notes reveal a list of subjects that were due a splash of Floydian spleen-venting: 'country house hotels, gastro (enteritis) pubs, farmers' markets, shopping trolleys, the smoking ban . . .'

Working on this book had encouraged him to consider such issues and the list, you will be unsurprised to learn, goes on and on. The original celebrity chef even scribbled a reminder to discuss 'celebrity chefs [. . .] I would rather watch a good chef cooking than watching him swear at a bunch of losers'. The trio – Floyd, Pritch and Denham – were due to fly to France and begin filming before the book launch.

I say fly to France because by now Keith and Celia were living at Celia's home in Bridport, Dorset. After nursing, supporting and caring for Keith, she'd earned a break. Keith was an impatient patient – and he knew it. It was a merely a blip in the relationship but she needed some space and had returned to England. They were only apart for about a week before Keith saw sense: one night he journeyed from Montfrin to Calais and then on to Bridport.

By 14 September Keith had spent a fortnight or so living with Celia and her new puppy, Pansy, in the Dorset market town. Meanwhile, he was becoming uncertain about his health. In Spain, as he has recounted, he was diagnosed with bowel cancer and underwent several operations. When he returned to France he expected to undergo chemotherapy and radiotherapy and when his French doctor did not agree that such treatment was necessary Keith was confused. After crossing the Channel, he was accepted into Celia's home on this one condition: 'That you get the cancer sorted out once for all. We've done Spain and France. I'm not doing Italy and Germany next, you know.'

His to-do list for 14 September includes 'doctor's appointment', a meeting with Mr Watson, the cancer specialist who would have the results of recent tests Keith had undergone.

And so the day was planned: Mr Watson, followed by Celia's birthday lunch (with Keith commenting wryly how 'the news from Mr Watson will set the mood for the lunch table'). Afterwards, the couple would return home, have dinner and then Keith would watch himself on Channel 4.

Mark Hix is an accomplished chef whose London successes have included The Ivy, J Sheekey and Le Caprice, and the West Country lad owns Hix's Oyster and Fish House in Lyme Regis. Hixy, as he is known, is also a Floydy fan and has written that when Keith came on the scene 'it changed the way we thought about cooking and, essentially, made food fun'.

It was here, at Hix's fish restaurant, that Keith had his final lunch. He had come from the appointment with Mr Watson, who said that the test results were promising but that he wanted to conduct a further exploratory examination and enquired whether it would it be possible make a date. Keith flicked through his diary and explained that he had a busy filming schedule coming up. Filming was the priority, of course. Mr Watson wondered if Keith had any allergies. 'Yes, broccoli,' replied Keith. Mr Watson meant medication, rather than food, of course. 'Though I love purple sprouting,' added Keith.

Skip back a few pages and Keith says, 'I am looking

forward to getting back to work and enjoying my food once again.' Those words were said in July 2009. He knew that he had to eat, and he wanted to enjoy food. At Hix's restaurant he ate what he would have considered a considerable amount: two oysters and a spoonful of potted shrimps on toast; for a main course he and Celia ordered grouse and Keith was irritated that he was instead served partridge (the restaurant did not charge for its mistake). Celia later said, 'Keith had a cocktail, a glass of white wine and a glass of red – we took the bottle as we couldn't finish it. He most certainly wasn't drunk.'

I last spoke to Keith at about seven o'clock that evening. He was the happiest I had known him, thrilled by the positive news from Mr Watson, excited about the launch of this book and relishing the prospect of a fight with the critics of *Keith on Keith*. When I asked if he'd liked the restaurant he replied, 'Not really, no. The oysters were too small and the staff didn't know the difference between grouse and partridge.'

Later on he complained of feeling nauseous. He went to lie down on the sofa in the sitting room, *University Challenge* providing the background noise, and it was soon afterwards that he suffered a heart attack. I like to think he died in his sleep, dreaming of a field of Provençal lavender under a Van Gogh sky.

Earlier that day he had spoken to Marco Pierre White. They had talked about food Keith had eaten as a child, with Keith remarking in his notepad, 'licking out the Christmas pudding bowls or the fruit cake mix . . . runner beans and grated cheese and butter.' Of his own children, Patrick and Poppy, he remained full of remorse that he had not 'created a home'. He was always too childlike for such responsibility but through his wonderful programmes he's had a warm welcome in every home in Britain.

He was aware that aspects of his story were shocking – his selfishness, his addictions – but such is the sacrifice of many a chef, restaurateur and entertainer. One day I overheard him on the phone to his friend, Giles Benson. 'Doing this book has made me realize that I have done some terrible things in my life,' he said to Giles. 'But it's also made me realize that I've done some really good things, too.' For confirmation, just think of the millions of people who, after watching Keith, were inspired to cook, eat, drink; to become a gastronaut and savour – truly relish – every morsel, every drop, every bloody bit of it!

'It's his voice I miss,' Celia has said to me. I agree, though often I can hear him saying something like, 'The trouble with me is *me*.' The many gifts he gave to me – Camargue salt, bottles of olive oil, a painting he'd done – are reminders of his extraordinary generosity and the hugely enriching times we spent together. Everything everyone ever said about Keith was probably true, but do not underestimate his generosity.

Although Keith spent his first eight years in Southampton, he often told his story as if life for him had begun in Wiveliscombe, the Somerset town where he discovered a passion for food. And it was at Wellington School where he felt he started to develop his distinctive style. In his to-do notepad, is the page headed 'Next week' and underneath this heading are the words: 'Trip to Wivey and Wellington.' Next week never came.

'That would have been nice,' I can hear him saying. 'Anyhow . . .'

Montfrin, 6 August 2009

Dear Reader

'Just another shitty day in paradise.' And, I wonder, as a friend once said, 'what the poor people are doing today'.

Sometimes I worry about what I've left out. And sometimes I worry about what I've put in. But for now, as this book fades to black, I'll have another pastis.

Thank you and au revoir.

Floyd